"*PARALLEL TIME* IS SUPERB...
The story of who Staples is at heart and
how he got to be that way is written in clear, vivid prose.
It is funny and sad and deeply moving."
Lorene Cary, author of *Black Ice*

"A PAINFULLY HONEST ACCOUNT
of the conflicts and choices caused by growing up and away
from one's roots. Staples's book is less an autobiography
than a meditation on a universal question:
what makes us who we are?"
Entertainment Weekly

"REFRESHING...IRONIC...AFFECTING...
a superbly crafted memoir."
Chicago Sun-Times

"A STUNNINGLY HONEST AND
PAINFULLY REVEALING BOOK
about becoming and being a black man in the United States...
Staples tells his life in a meticulous, stark,
and often poetic way, ultimately challenging readers
to come up with their own answers."
Hartford Courant

"RICHLY DRAWN, BRILLIANTLY WRITTEN,
PARALLEL TIME is bound to become a classic
of American and African-American autobiography."
Paula Giddings, author of *In Search of Sisterhood*

"FUNNY AND TERRIFYING AND HEARTBREAKING...
Brent Staples has written one of the best memoirs
I've ever read about growing up in America."
Russell Baker, author of *The Good Times*

PARALLEL TIME
Growing Up in Black and White

BRENT STAPLES

AVON BOOKS  NEW YORK

AVON BOOKS
A division of
The Hearst Corporation
1350 Avenue of the Americas
New York, New York 10019

Copyright © 1994 by Brent Staples
Front cover photograph by James White Photography
Published by arrangement with Pantheon Books
Library of Congress Catalog Card Number: 93-24258
ISBN: 0-380-72475-8

The Pantheon Books edition contains the following Library of Congress Cataloging in Publication Data:

Staples, Brent A., 1951-
   Parallel Time / Brent Staples.
      p.   cm.
1. Staples, Brent, 1951- 2. Journalists—United States—Biography.   3. Newspaper editors—United States—Biography. 4. Afro-Americans—Biography.   I. Title.
PN4874.S67S73   1994
070.4'1'092—dc20
[B]   93-24258

First Avon Books Trade Printing: May 1995

AVON TRADEMARK REG. U.S. PAT. OFF. AND IN OTHER COUNTRIES, MARCA REGISTRADA, HECHO EN U.S.A.

Printed in the U.S.A.

OPM 10 9 8 7 6 5 4 3 2 1

For Eugene Sparrow (1921–1978):

Amazing Grace

Acknowledgments

With gratitude to:

My mother, whose voice made me a writer.

The Staples family, for the stories I tell.

The women of The Hill, who helped raise and love me.

Linda Healey and Amanda Urban, for honesty and support.

John Darnton, for understanding that books take time.

Sue Kirby, for reading and rereading the manuscript.

Peggy Chance, librarian of the *Delaware County Daily and Sunday Times*, for constant access to the past.

Judith Hirsch, for keeping things straight.

And Frank Conroy, for writing *Stop-Time*.

Contents

Contents

PARALLEL TIME

‖ The Coroner's Photographs

My brother's body lies dead and naked on a stainless steel slab. At his head stands a tall arched spigot that, with tap handles mimicking wings, easily suggests a swan in mourning. His head is squarish and overlarge. (This, when he was a toddler, made him seem top-heavy and unsteady on his feet.) His widow's peak is common among the men in my family, though this one is more dramatic than most. An inverted pyramid, it begins high above the temples and falls steeply to an apex in the boxy forehead, over the heart-shaped face. A triangle into a box over a heart. His eyes (closed here) were big and dark and glittery; they drew you into his sadness when he cried. The lips are ajar as always, but the picture is taken from such an angle that it misses a crucial detail: the left front tooth tucked partly beyond the right one. I need this detail to see my brother full. I paint it in from memory.

A horrendous wound runs the length of the abdomen, from the sternum all the way to the pubic mound. The wound resembles a mouth whose lips are pouting and bloody. Massive staplelike clamps are gouged into these lips at regular intervals along the abdomen. This is a surgeon's incision. The surgeon was presented with a patient shot six times with a large-caliber handgun. Sensing the carnage that lay within, he achieved the largest possible opening and worked frantically trying to save my brother's life. He tied off shattered vessels, resectioned the small intestine, repaired a bullet track on the liver, then backed out. The closing would have required two pairs of hands. An assistant would have gripped the two sides of the wound and drawn them together while a second person cut in the clamps. The pulling together has made my brother's skin into a corset that crushes in on the abdomen from all sides. The pelvic bones jut up through the skin. The back is abnormally arched from the tension. The wound strains at the clamps, threatening to rip itself open. The surgeon worked all night and emerged from surgery gaunt, his greens darkened with sweat. "I tied off everything I could," he said, and then he wept at the savagery and the waste.

This is the body of Blake Melvin Staples, the seventh of my family's nine children, the third of my four brothers, born ten years after me. I know his contours well. I bathed and diapered him when he was a baby and studied his features as he grew. He is the smallest of the brothers, but is built in the same manner: short torso but long arms and legs; a more than ample behind set high on the back; knocking knees; big feet that tend to flat. The second toe is also a signature. It curls softly in an extended arc and rises above the others in a way that's unique to us. His feelings are mine as well. Cold: The sensation moves from my eyes to my shoulder blades to my bare ass as I feel him naked on the steel. I envision the reflex that would run through his body, hear the sharp breath he would draw when the steel met his skin. Below the familiar feet a drain awaits the blood that will flow from this autopsy.

The medical examiner took this picture and several others on February 13, 1984, at 9:45 A.M. The camera's flash is visible everywhere: on the pale-green tiles of the surrounding walls, on the gleaming neck of the spigot, on the stainless steel of the slab, on the bloody lips of the wound.

The coroner's report begins with a terse narrative summary: "The deceased, twenty-two-year-old Negro male, was allegedly shot by another person on the premises of a night club as a result of a 'long standing quarrel.' He sustained multiple gunshot wounds of the abdomen and legs and expired during surgery."

Blake was a drug dealer; he was known for carrying guns and for using them. His killer, Mark McGeorge, was a former customer and cocaine addict. At the trial Mark's lawyer described the shooting as a gunfight in which Blake was beaten to the draw. This was doubtful. Blake was shot six times: three times in the back. No weapon was found on or near his body. Blake's gunbearer testified that my brother was unarmed when Mark ambushed and gunned him down. But a gunbearer is not a plausible witness. A drug dealer known for shooting a rival in plain public view gets no sympathy from a jury. The jury turned back the prosecution's request for a conviction of murder in the first degree. Mark was found guilty of second-degree murder and sentenced to seven years in jail. Five years for the murder. Two years for using the gun.

Blake is said to have cried out for his life as he lay on the ground. "Please don't shoot me no more. I don't want to die." *"Please don't shoot me no more. I don't want to die."* His voice had a touch of that dullness one hears from the deaf, a result of ear infections he suffered as a child. The ear openings had narrowed to the size of pinholes. He tilted his head woefully from side to side trying to pour out the pain. His vowels were locked high in his

throat, behind his nose. This voice kept him a baby to me. This is
the voice in which he would have pleaded for his life.

The coroner dissects the body, organ by organ:

HEART: 300 grams. No valve or chamber lesions. Coronary
arteries show no pathologic changes.

LUNGS: 900 grams combined. Moderate congestion. Tra-
cheobronchial and arterial systems are not remarkable.

LIVER: 1950 grams. There is a sutured bullet track at the
interlobar sulcus and anterior portion of the right hepatic
lobe. There has been moderate subcapsular and intraparen-
chymal hemorrhage.

SPLEEN: 150 grams. No pathologic changes.

KIDNEYS: 300 grams combined. No pathologic changes.

ADRENALS: No pathologic changes.

PANCREAS: No pathologic changes.

GI TRACT: The stomach is empty. Portions of the small bowel
have been resected, along with portions of the omentum.
The bowel surface is dusky reddish-brown, but does not
appear gangrenous.

URINARY BLADDER: Empty.

NECK ORGANS: Intact. No airway obstructions.

BRAIN: 1490 grams. Sagittal and serial coronal sections show
no discrete lesions or evidence of injury.

SKULL: Intact.

VERTEBRAE: Intact.

RIBS: Intact.

PELVIS: There is a chip fracture of the left pubic ramus, and there is also fracturing of the right pubic ramus. There is extensive fracturing of the left femur, and there is a through-and-through bullet wound of the right femur just below the hip joint.

The coroner describes the wounds in detail. The surgical incision and its grisly clamps are dismissed in a single sentence. The six bullet holes receive one full paragraph each. The coroner records the angle that each bullet traveled through the body, the organs it passed through along the way, and where it finally came to rest. With all this to occupy him, the coroner fails to note the scar on Blake's left hand. The scar lies in the webbing between the thumb and index finger and is the result of a gun accident. A shotgun recoiled when Blake fired it and drove the hammer deep into the web, opening a wound that took several stitches to close.

I saw the wound when it was fresh, six weeks before Blake was murdered. I was visiting Roanoke from Chicago, where I then lived. I sought Blake out to tell him that it was time to get out of the business and leave Roanoke. The signs of death were everywhere; his name was hot in the street. Blake and I were making small talk when we slapped each other five. Blake clutched his hand at the wrist and cried out in pain. Then he showed me the stitches. This ended the small talk. I told him that he was in danger of being killed if he didn't leave town.

Staples men have been monolinguists for generations. We love our own voices too much. Blake responded to my alarm by telling me stories. He told me about the awesome power of the shotgun that had injured him. He told me about making asses of the police when they raided his apartment looking for drugs. The door of his apartment was steel, he said; they'd sent for a tow truck to pull it from its frame. Inside they found him twiddling his thumbs in the bathroom. He'd flushed the cocaine down the toilet. The night he told me these stories was the last time I saw him alive.

Six weeks later my brother Bruce called me with the news. "Brent, Blake is dead," he said. "Some guy pulled up in a car and emptied out on him with a magnum. Blake is dead." I told myself to feel nothing. I had already mourned Blake and buried him and was determined not to suffer his death a second time. I skipped the funeral and avoided Roanoke for the next three years. The next time I visited my family I went to see the Roanoke Commonwealth Attorney and questioned him about the case. He was polite but impatient. For him, everything about the killing had been said. This, after all, had been an ordinary death.

I asked to see the files. A secretary brought a manila pouch and handed it to the Commonwealth Attorney, who handed it to me and excused himself from the room. The pouch contained a summary of the trial, the medical examiner's report, and a separate inner pouch wrapped in twine and shaped like photographs. I opened the pouch; there was Blake dead and on the slab, photographed from several angles. The floor gave way, and I fell down and down for miles.

‖ Living in
Motion

As a child I was never where I was. Part of me raced ahead looking for a foothold in the future. Part of me was somewhere behind rushing to catch up. At thirteen I was obsessed with the idea that moments I'd lived were slipping away and becoming lost to me one by one. I would seize onto something I'd just seen or thought and ask myself if I'd remember that thing five minutes, five hours, or five days from now. The answer was always no.

Things weren't hanging together. Even dramatic things floated briefly in memory, then drifted away. Perhaps I had lost a whole lifetime this way. Perhaps my family wasn't my family at all but a counterfeit group with whom I'd fallen in after forgetting who I was. Thoughts like this overran my obsessions with flying and fire and knives.

The fear of losing memories struck keenly when I was happy. An example of this was the day I discovered a trail of crumpled dollar bills on the sidewalk in front of my house. The first bill was a few feet from the front step; the second a few feet behind that one; the third—a five!—lay in the gutter at the corner. There was no one to contest me for the money. It was Sunday morning and the streets were blessedly vacant. The bills had doubtless been dropped by a drunk who'd come reeling out of the speakeasy a few doors away. The money meant games and games of pinball and endless Coca-Colas. It was at rapturous heights like these that I asked myself how long I'd remember this. Not the money itself, but the joy of finding it. The answer was: not long. Giddiness faded. Even a fist full of dollars couldn't sustain it.

Writers have said that children live in an endless present with little thought for what has passed or what will be. Mine was a different childhood. I paid endless dues for sorrows that were yet to come. I was also morbidly vigilant about the past. Not the past of a year ago or even the previous day, but the past of the last few seconds. I handled memories over and over again, hoping to give them permanence.

This vigilance came on me in seizures that could strike me anywhere: while I lay in the grass making out figures in the clouds, as I pushed a shopping cart down the supermarket aisles, and especially while I stood at the crosswalk waiting for the light to change. I clung to every detail of the hot rod that had just roared by: the glint of the sun flowing over its body, the thunder of the engine, the twin puffs of smoke from its dual exhausts. I included the backdrop, too: the steepled church across the street, the sign out front that described the sermon and gave the minister's name; the wrought-iron fence around them. This took concentration; it excluded everything except drawing breath. The sign changed from DON'T WALK to WALK to DON'T WALK again. Someone called out "Hey, you, wake up!" and I did. To them I was a silly boy asleep at the crosswalk. For me this was serious business: I had saved a part of my life that would otherwise have been lost.

*   *   *

I suspected mental illness. My eighth-grade science teacher relieved me of this burden with a movie about the physics of time. The movie was a cartoon. It began with a rocket sitting on the launch pad, ready for takeoff. At the launch site were a perky set of twins, Bill and Bob, accompanied by cheerleaders and a roaring crowd. The twins were fresh from high school, sporting identical pompadours and identical varsity sweaters. Bill climbed into the rocket and blasted off into space at the speed of light. Bob stayed behind with the crowd and waved. What the narrator said next made me sit up and take notice. He said that time passed more slowly for the traveling twin than for the one who stayed at home. Light speed slowed the clock and the beating of the heart. Bill returned from space as perky and erect as the day he left. His brother, Bob, was old and withered and confined to a wheelchair.

The movie was a saving bolt from the blue. I wasn't mentally ill. In fact, I'd gotten it exactly right: Time was sneaky and elastic, not at all what it was cracked up to be. That science had studied the problem brought me an enormous sense of relief.

This fixation had come from the way my family lived. We moved all the time. We went on and on like bedouins with couches, tables, and mattresses jumbled in the backs of pickup trucks. We moved as the family grew. We moved when my parents were separated and again when they reconciled. We moved when we fell behind in the rent. We moved when the sheriffs put our furniture on the sidewalk. We moved after the family had pounded a house to pieces. We'd had seven different addresses by the time I reached the eighth grade. That's why I was never where I was. The move was out there lurking, just off the mental shore. Best to be ready when it came.

My mother went house hunting when we were about to be

evicted. The places were chosen swiftly, and we moved without preparation. The household dissolved into a river of stuff and children that flowed through the door in spasms, keyed to the coming and going of the truck.

The chaos of these nights exhausted even the deepest goodwill. The friends and relatives who helped us drove up in their trucks to find us dashing through the house, hurling things into boxes. First they grumbled under their breaths. Then they withdrew into sullen reveries. We raced to move the heavy things before these helpers quit. This meant triage with the furniture, abandoning bedsteads and couches where they stood. If the new house was close enough, we carried the small things by hand. We became a caravan of children, with lamps and end tables in hand, strung out like bedouins down the street.

The chaos swallowed things that would never be seen again. Family portraits. Volumes from the set of encyclopedias. Legal documents of every sort, including birth certificates, leaving some of us uncertain of when we were born.

Each new house was a change of skin. New creaking in the floors, new traffic noises, new voices passing beneath the windows. Some sidewalks were cement and some were brick. On cement, high heels clicked solidly by like the ticking of a clock. Brick sidewalks were ancient, their surfaces powdery and uneven. When high heels slipped in the powder, the sound was like the wrong-way screech of the chalk on a blackboard. *Skwitch, skwatch, skwawtch* was a woman walking.

In bed, I was shocked awake by groaning timbers or by voices that seemed to be in the room but were actually passing on the street below. The room would seem foreign at first. The shafts of moonlight would be wrong, as though the windows had suddenly changed walls. Then I would notice Brian and Bruce sleeping heavily on either side of me, and catch sight of Blake and Brad in the daybed across the room. I returned to sleep but woke up several times before dawn. Each time my brothers lay differently twisted in sheets, a new frieze cut from the dance of sleep.

At college I woke up alone in a room, for the first time that I could remember. I never slept with my brothers again. Months and then years went by without my even seeing them. When we met, I was often stunned by changes in them that seemed to have come overnight and were now irrevocable. What had been set in motion I was powerless to undo.

The moving left its mark. Grown and out on my own, I was phobically wary of possessions, of anything that would trouble me when it was time to go. My first apartment was an enormous five-room flat, with a dining room, a kitchen, and a walk-in pantry big enough to sleep one. I lived in that flat for six years with the walls barren of pictures and without a table of any kind. I ate from the seats of folding chairs or from beer crates while sitting on the floor. The move may have been years away, but when it came, couches and tables and bookshelves would be what they'd always been—encumbrances that had to be hoisted and dragged away. Time and time again I lived five years at a stretch without unpacking. The need to be poised for flight governed matters trivial and profound. I avoided magazine subscriptions; in them was the presumption that I'd stay put for an entire year. I disposed of friends and lovers without a thought.

I envisioned Blake's murder a year and a half before it happened. The image came from a letter he wrote me just after he'd ambushed Mark at a disco. Blake was on the run and in need of money. He denied having done the shooting and claimed that the police had fingered him for no reason at all. This was an obvious lie. I read the letter as an admission of guilt and understood that revenge was on the way. The first image of Blake dead on the ground came to me on its own. Later I summoned it up deliberately, trying to build a tolerance to the idea. There is no way to say this without its sounding callous and premeditated. In truth it was an act of reflex, no more thought out than pulling back from fire.

When Blake turned twenty-two years old he had three months to live. He and Mark were tearing at each other like warring dogs bound by the same leash. Blake reached for his pistol whenever Mark came into view. This gesture was often a bluff. It had to be. The police knew Blake as a drug dealer and shooter. He couldn't have carried a gun everywhere. Downtown, near the police station or the courthouse, he could have been stopped and frisked at any time. It was at these naked times that he would have reached for his gun with the most conviction.

As Blake's fear increased, his guns got bigger and more numerous. No longer content with pistols, he acquired the double-barreled shotgun and the gunbearer who carried it. I envision him wandering through the streets of Roanoke, thrusting a trembling hand into his gunbearer's bag. All around him are the means of escape, the buses, the trains, and planes that could take him anywhere. I whisper, "Leave this place." He never does. He never even hears me.

‖ The Hill

My parents married in Hollins, Virginia, a rural community in the foothills of the Blue Ridge Mountains, not far from Roanoke. It was January 1948. She was eighteen. He was twenty-one. The ceremony was performed in the log house where my mother was born and where she, my grandmother Mae Patterson, and my great-grandmother Luella Holmes Patterson still lived.

The way for this marriage was smoothed by a previous union between the Pattersons of Hollins and the Staples of Troutville. My mother's uncle Blaine had married my father's aunt, Ruby, in what was a step up for the Patterson family. In Troutville Blaine and Ruby lived prosperously on the farm they had inherited from Ruby's parents, my paternal great-grandparents, John Wesley and Eliza Staples. John Wesley was the son of a slave owner and a slave woman, and he was born on the Fourth of July 1865, just after Virginia ratified the Thirteenth Amendment. It is said that he was the first free black born in his part of rural Bedford County. In the 1880s he worked as a track walker for the Norfolk and Western Railroad, in which job he walked ten miles a day hammering down loose spikes. In 1892 he quit to start the farm. Though not an educated man, he could read and write. He was vain of his writing and scribbled even grocery lists with a flourish, pausing often to lick the pencil point. He and Eliza had eight children, including Ruby. There was no school for black children. The Staples joined with their two immediate neighbors and built one, at the intersection of their three properties. The teacher worked at least partly in exchange for room and board, which was shared among the three families.

In the 1920s when people still went about on horseback or in carriages, John Wesley burst on the scene in a Model T Ford with all the extras, and let it be known that he had paid for the car in cash. His faith in cold hard cash made him skeptical about things like insurance policies. Why pay the premiums when he could keep the nickel and the interest, too? He died in 1940, leaving behind the farm and $20,000 in cash, a small fortune for a man of his beginnings and by the standards of the time.

I visited the log house in Hollins as a small boy in the 1950s. The house stood just across the field from Hollins College, the fancy girls' school where my great-grandmother once washed dishes. My grandmother often sent me across to the college to fetch Coca-Colas from a soda machine. I remember Hollins as a place of women. My father was not included in these trips; he preferred to visit his family on his own. Mae was something to see on her way home from church. She was a tall, busty woman and wore dresses that showed off those bosoms. She strolled regally across the field, wearing a pillbox hat with a veil, trailing a string of fox furs from her shoulder. The beady glass eyes of the foxes were frightening as she bent to kiss me.

I remember little of my great-grandmother Luella, except

the mane of gray hair so long she had to move it aside to sit down. The hair was as thick as hemp. And I remember sitting on the back step watching her kill chickens for dinner. She whipped them in the air to break their necks, and then they ran wild around the yard and loosed their bowels. She dipped them in scalding water and plucked them naked.

At night we bathed in a metal washtub set near the big wood-burning stove in the kitchen. I watched as the women lifted the heavy iron lids and fed lengths of wood into the fire within. Once washed, I got into a white dressing gown and prepared to run the gauntlet to the outhouse. The path was long and dark and went past the cornfield where all the monsters were. My grandmother held a hurricane lamp out of the back door to light the way. The monsters shrank from the light, but I knew they were there, hiding behind the first row of corn. I could tell by the way the corn squeaked and rustled as I hurried by. The most feared of the monsters was the snake that turned itself into a hoop and rolled after you at tremendous speed, threshing the corn as it came.

The outhouse was dank and musty and surrounded by night. While sitting on the toilet, I tried to keep the lamplight in view through cracks in the wall. The trip back to the house was always worse. The monsters gathered in the corn to ambush me; their groaning and growling reached a crescendo as they prepared to spring. I ran for the lamplight as fast as I could and landed in the kitchen panting and out of breath.

Blaine and Ruby's place in Troutville had an indoor toilet. There was also an organ in the living room that I played while sitting on Ruby's lap. Then there was the food. Hams and pork shoulders hung by the ton in their smokehouse. Enormous tins of lard, more lard than I had ever seen, were lined up around the smokehouse walls. Ruby's table at breakfast groaned under serving plates piled high with eggs and sausage and pork chops and beans and grits and biscuits and pickled fruit and dishes too far down the table to identify. The food spread out for acres along a starched white tablecloth, breakfast grander than any dinner I'd known. After the meal we played with the horses and fed them apples from nearby trees.

The Pattersons were food rich, too, but the similarity ended there. My maternal great-grandfather, the Reverend Frank Patterson, had died prematurely, leaving Luella with five children to raise, which she did by sewing and washing dishes at Hollins College. Grandma Mae's preacher had also quit the family and walked away. The family's precarious fortunes must have made a second link to the Staples clan seem a fine idea. The good fortune that had been John Wesley's and Eliza's and Blaine's and Ruby's might then become Melvin's and Geneva's as well.

It didn't happen that way. I grew up with the household always on the verge of collapse, the threat of eviction ever present, the utilities subject to cutoff at any moment. Gas was cheap and therefore easy to regain. The water company had pity on us and relented when we made token efforts to pay. But the electric company had no heart to harden. We lived in darkness for days. While our neighbors' houses were blazing with light, we ate, played, and bathed in the sepia glow of hurricane lamps.

Domestic stability was not my father's experience. His father, John Wesley's son Marshall, had made a point of disappearing on payday and reappearing drunk and broke several days later. Marshall abandoned his family on the verge of the Depression, leaving his wife, Ada, with four children in hand and one—my father—on the way. Ada had no choice but to parcel out her children to relatives. My father missed the luck of the draw: He was raised in the home of Ada's father, Tom Perdue, a brown-skinned version of Simon Legree. My uncles hawked and spat when they spoke of him.

They remembered him lounging on the porch, his horse and buggy tied up in the shade, while his wife carried white people's laundry on foot beneath a blazing sun. Three wives preceded him to the grave, and the family line was that Tom had worked them to death. He hired out his sons for farm work, then collected their pay, leaving them with next to nothing. His children fled his presence. It was said that none of them were present when he died.

My father's childhood left its marks. He distrusted affection, and what there was of it he pushed away. He also changed his birth date from 1926 to 1925, which got him born before his father ran away. When my uncles disputed this date, which they often did, my father made a sucking sound through his teeth and said: "I should know when I was born. I was there." This was cynical in the extreme, coming as it did from the family's youngest child. He persisted in this fiction until he retired and claimed Social Security benefits. He needed a birth certificate to prove that he was old enough. The certificate came back from Richmond dated 1926.

I was probably six or seven when my mother told me that Grandma Ada had given her children away. The story as I recall it contains nothing about the Depression, nothing about my grandfather's abandonment, just the repeated and frightening claim that Ada had discarded my father and my uncles without a thought. "When things didn't suit her, she gave her children away and went on about her business," my mother would say. "What kind of mother would do that?" I knew from stories that Gypsies stole children when they could, and I assumed that it was to Gypsies that Ada had surrendered hers. I envisioned Ada by the side of a road, hurling children onto the wagons of Gypsies as they passed. My mother said she'd rather die than do what Ada did, and she promised to keep us together no matter what. The promise was too little too late. The scenes of Ada and the Gypsies had staked their claim.

My parents departed Roanoke by train on their wedding day, headed for Chester, Pennsylvania, a thriving factory town on the Delaware River, twenty miles south of Philadelphia. My father, his father, and three of my uncles had already settled there, drawn by the promise of work in an economy stoked by World War II. My father had found work in a factory that made parachute silk. WHAT CHESTER MAKES MAKES CHESTER. The sign in lights greeted the train as it rolled into town. Chester made paper, steel, aluminum, cars, and locomotives.

Beyond all these, Chester made ships. The Sun Shipbuilding and Dry Dock Company was a city of its own, sprawling along the river. The yard was bristling with cranes and steel, alive with fiery geysers that sprang from furnaces and arc welders' tools. What Chester made made Chester. The sign would seem a mockery when the yard was dead and the city was crumbling around it. But that was yet to come when my parents arrived. Chester was a bulging muscle on the Delaware, a place of promise and money and steel.

We lived through the 1950s in a neighborhood called The Hill. It was called The Hill because that was where we were: at the top of an elevation that began a mile below us, at the river, and reached to its apex just above 13th Street. It was hard to believe that the river really existed. What was said to be the river appeared as a shimmering silver band along the horizon. But the nearer you got the less of it you saw; fences, railroad tracks, and factories blocked it from view. The silver along the horizon might just as easily have been clouds.

The impulse that built the factories lost steam as it climbed Central Avenue. That impulse was dead by the time it reached The Hill. Unpaved, 13th Street was sown with miniature mountains that made driving difficult and games of tag downright dangerous. My sister Yvonne broke her arm on 13th Street. Back from the hospital in her gleaming white cast, she marched me into the street and pointed out the rock in question. It was an evil-looking rock. We lingered over it all summer, as though we expected it to speak.

Whole blocks in the neighborhood had been left vacant. In summer these fields either went to weeds or were turned into make-shift farms where corn, greens, and cabbage flourished. In winter the stubble of these crops, jutting up through the snow, sparked a constant longing for spring. The biggest of these fields featured a derelict house that had never been finished. The builder had poured the foundation, got partway up with the walls, and then given up.

Other houses had been quickly thrown up in the fading moments of the boom. The Neil family's house wandered randomly over its lot and looked to have been built from whatever Mr. Neil had at hand. The house seemed to rise from the piles of lumber and the rusting machines that littered the yard. By late summer the lumber and the machines had disappeared behind a forest of corn.

Mama and Daddy Jordan lived just across 13th Street in an ancient two-story house whose height made it seem palatial by comparison. The Jordans grew the customary cabbage and collard greens, but that was just in the front of the yard. The back of their lot held a glorious stand of peach trees whose peaches grew to mythical proportions. The branches sagged so wearily with ripening fruit that Mama Jordan had to prop them up with sticks. The peaches were heavy and beautiful by then. The skin was red where the sun reached it, and the red faded to voluptuous yellow that spread over the rest of the peach. Boys on The Hill were obsessed with fruit. We prowled hungrily at the fence, crazy for the peaches to ripen, crazy to have them even while they were small and bitter and green. But Mama Jordan's word was law. There would be no eating peaches until she said so.

Mama and Daddy Jordan were the most respected couple

on The Hill. Wisdom and authority seemed to radiate from them. Mama Jordan dressed like the women in wagon-train movies: in voluminous, ground-sweeping dresses and sunbonnets whose frilly brims fluttered in the breeze. Daddy cultivated a coarse gray stubble and wore a brown felt hat with the brim turned up in the front. Daddy passed afternoons sitting on the bench in front of his house, quoting from Scripture and addressing passersby as "son" and "daughter." "Good afternoon, son," "Good afternoon, daughter." To the "daughters" he tipped his hat.

The Jordans and their daughter Larry helped to raise my brothers and sisters and me. Their help was vital; babies were coming fast at our house. My mother's first pregnancy had ended in a miscarriage. The doctor told her she'd never have a child. She went on to prove him wrong, nine times. Blake was still six years away in 1955. Bruce was the newest baby, born that summer. He was big—nearly thirteen pounds and hairy. Dark curls covered his head and ran down the sides of his face and into the center of his back. I tried to hold him, but he was too heavy and unwieldy. Yvonne was six, Brian two. Brian was nervous, frightened of the dark, and angry that Bruce had displaced him. He repaid us with screams. He stood up in his crib, pudgy fists clenching the rails, and wailed to wake the dead. He screamed not because he was hungry or wet or because a pin had come loose in his diapers and was sticking into him. He screamed because he wanted my mother. I pulled the pillows over my head and prayed for her to hurry.

I came into consciousness at Mama Jordan's table, eating corn bread and peach cobbler. Larry and my mother were both teenage girls in bad marriages and took to each other right away. Larry visited us every day. She came helloing across 13th Street, calling out "Geneva, Geneva!" in a buoyant, laughing voice. She doted on us and took great joy in slipping us goodies that my mother had forbidden us to have. Larry was bold in this mischief. She hid the smallest children beneath her coat and passed them cake and candy, even while my mother was in the room.

The Jordans owned two enormous hounds, Boy and Brownie. We rode on their backs and played in their food until Boy in particular came to think of us as pets. He visited us often. One day he trotted across the street just in time to catch my mother spanking one of us. Boy didn't cotton to this. He barked and snarled at my mother and probably would have bitten her if Larry hadn't dragged him away.

Meanwhile the peaches grew more pendulous by the day. That I was an honorary Jordan did not improve my access. It only meant that I ached for the peaches at close range during my visits. From the back bedroom I could have stepped out on the roof and grabbed a peach from the tree. I held myself back, not wanting to risk Mama's anger. My face wet with peach juice would be my trial and conviction.

I watched the peach trees closely and was intimate with their secrets. Sunlight speckling through the leaves camouflaged the ground below. The dogs when they were sleeping were invisible until one of them moved and gave away their places. This effect could be frightening when it was windy and the light was churning as in a kaleidoscope. On one such day, I was watching from the fence, longing for a peach, when Mama Jordan in her frontier bonnet and dress suddenly appeared out of nothing, like a ghost become solid.

Eventually Mama gave the word. We lined up at the fence, and a fat, juicy peach was placed in each of our hands.

At the edge of our Eden men were building a highway. Machines as big as dinosaurs—earth movers, graders, and bulldozers—were roaming the upper end of Central Avenue demolishing houses and making hills and slopes where none had been. Then the roaring stopped and the machines disappeared. Central Avenue had been a through street. Now it ended at a gravel-covered embankment that supported the highway. I stood with the other boys watching as the workmen finished the job. They strung the steel cables for the guard rail, poured the last slabs of concrete and smoothed them out, then laid sheets of plastic to protect the concrete from the rain.

When the last trucks rolled away, we bolted across the street and scrambled up the embankment onto the broad strip of highway. The plastic coverings flapped and billowed in the wind as far as the eye could see. Those sheets that had held firm filled with air and rose like loaves of bread. The ones that had torn loose from the frames flew wild and ragged in the wind. This pattern repeated itself until the highway curved out of sight. The distance mesmerized us. We started eastward, drawn by the promise that the road would never end.

We had crossed the width of Central Avenue when we were taken by another marvelous sight: Mr. and Mrs. Prince's living room. The living room had a picture window on either side. One window looked out at where we were standing, in the northbound lane of the highway. The other window looked out onto Central Avenue. The gravel embankment ran right up to the Princes' aluminum siding.

We scuttled down the gravel for a better look. The room was clean and unlived in, like a model in a magazine. Doilies were neatly in place on the arms of overstuffed chairs. Across the room two chairs—Mr. and Mrs. Prince's—flanked the opposite window. Two of us climbed up on the other boys' shoulders and pressed our palms against the glass. The object of this quest was to see Central Avenue through the opposite window, just as Mr. and Mrs. Prince did when they sat in those chairs.

The Princes spent their days in their store, a block down Central Avenue at 13th Street. Knowing this, we went about our spying fearlessly, yelling and banging against the house, taking turns on each other's shoulders. Then Mrs. Prince was looming in the window, her gold teeth flashing angrily. "What are you boys doing? Get away from here! Get away, you hear!" We scrambled down the slope and fled for our lives.

Mr. and Mrs. Prince were rich by the standards of The Hill. In addition to the store, they owned several houses, including the one my family lived in. Theirs was the only house in the neighborhood that had a garage built into it. Each day that garage disgorged two gleaming Cadillacs—a black Fleetwood hardtop (his) and a blood-red Eldorado convertible (hers).

The Cadillacs were chrome and bigness; their soft, rounded lines made them seem pumped full of air. Cars had faces then. The hoods bulged out at you like the foreheads of whales. The headlights were dead ringers for eyes. The grillwork resembled a stylized human mouth. Buick Roadmasters were bucktoothed, their chrome row of ivories fixed in a perpetual grin. Cadillacs were dignified by comparison. The headlights were calming and widely set, like the eyes of sphinxes dozing. Their mouths, the grilles, had a bullet-shaped tusk at either side. The Cadillacs rolled with a heavy, zeppelin grace down the avenue. Every day the same stupid spaniel sped off the sidewalk and ran alongside barking furiously at his reflection in the chrome.

The Princes could easily have walked to their store. After all it was only a block away. But the Princes didn't walk, they drove. They drove to savor those sumptuous Cadillacs and show them off. Mrs. Prince's bad parking was made worse by the boys who gathered on the sidewalks to gawk. She either ran up on the sidewalk or parked miles out in the street. Mr. Prince had her fenders fitted with whiskerlike coils that made a pinging noise when they scratched the curb. The Princes tried to park within sight of the storefront windows. That way they could keep an eye on the cars and prevent us from fondling and leaving fingerprints on the chrome. Now and then they had no choice but to park out of view. Then we moved in, caressing the bumpers with lustful abandon.

Our gang was a stair-step bunch: Taller boys gave way to smaller ones and smaller ones still. For every one of us who was five or six there was one who was seven or eight or maybe even nine. Benny Jarrett was a year older than me, and his brother Roger was a year or two older than he was. There was big, burly Tyrone Finklea, and a few years later his little brother Woody. There was Bayboy Hamler and his younger brother Gene. And later, when Brian and Bruce were old enough, they came trailing after me.

The older boys knew things, and you could count on them for excitement. One day Roger promised to show me a secret about the black Prince Cadillac. He wouldn't say what the secret was; if I didn't go with him I'd never find out. The trouble was that Mr. Prince had parked that day so that the back half of the car was in plain view of the store window. With my heart racing, I followed Roger as he crept along the Caddy, keeping the car between the window and us. Roger felt along the left taillight, pushed a button, then lifted the light itself. There it was: the gas cap, ingeniously hidden in the taillight.

Mr. Prince was the blackest man in the world. His forehead was squared at the temples, as though a sculptor had chiseled him from obsidian. His mouth was ablaze with gold teeth that beamed mightily against his blackness. He was a perpetual smoker of cigars. The gold flickered as he rolled his cigar from one side of his mouth to the other.

Mr. Prince was an angry man. The muscles tensed in his forehead as he bit down on the cigar. He looked to be scowling even when he wasn't. It was hard enough to decide between a Hershey bar and a Baby Ruth, but with him looming over you, the decision was impossible. "Make up your mind and get out of here," he said. Mrs. Prince was nice to us. She was a short, plump lady, like my own mother, like every mother in the neighborhood. Her gold teeth were fewer and more discreet.

The Princes' son Junior had Down's syndrome. He was fat and affable and fully grown by then. His Mongoloid eyes were always smiling. We would say "Hershey bar." But what Junior said back to us was incomprehensible. His tongue was too big for his mouth and got in the way of his words. The old women said that Mrs. Prince had been frightened by a dog while she was pregnant, and that the dog had "marked" Junior, making his tongue hang out the way it did. It seemed more likely to me that Junior was a small boy in a grown man's body.

Next to see the miracle of paving was 13th Street. The boulder that broke my sister's arm was bulldozed up and hauled away. The smooth slabs of concrete went down. That summer we ran up and down the street joyously half-naked in the rain. The curbs doubled as altars, where we prayed for more when the storm was over.

One day a bulldozer turned up unattended in one of the fields. Naturally we considered it ours and climbed all over it, pulling clots of mud from its treads, commenting sagely on the workmanship. Alan Prattis climbed into the cab and fingered the levers timidly. We egged him on to give the levers an earnest tug and he did. The diesel engine roared into life. Alan bolted from the cab and jumped to the ground. He ran in place for several strides until his sneakers gained traction in the mud. We scattered in all directions, all of us bound for home. Running, I envisioned the bulldozer lumbering out of the field crushing houses as it went. At home I found my mother in the living room, sewing. I sat trembling in a chair just opposite her, and I stayed within sight of her for the rest of the day. She'd be my alibi when the police came knocking at the door.

The gang didn't get away with much. The women who crowded the windows, doorways, and steps along Central Avenue kept an eagle eye on us. The one block between 13th Street and the highway contained at least a dozen sets of watchful eyes. At the corner of 13th and Central was Mrs. Prince peering out through the windows of her store. Leaning from the window of an apartment above the store was gray-haired Miss Davis, the nosiest lady in three counties. Then came several houses that had about three women apiece: Roger and Benny's mother, Miss Pauline, and her teenage daughters, Paulette and Treaty; Miss Arlena Douglas and her daughters, Arlena and Selena; Tyrone's mother, Miss Sootie-Bell, and his grandmother Miss Eva. And finally at the other end of the block was the store of Mr. Prince's rival, Mose Lerman, and there another woman, his daughter Pauline.

Women on errands patrolled the sidewalk between Prince's and Mose's stores. This made it unsafe for cursing or fighting or playing with matches. Miss Helen, Miss Betty, Miss Susie, Miss Vi, Miss Estelle, Miss Costelle, Miss Mamie Bookman: any of them could happen by at any time. All of them were licensed to discipline us when they caught us in the wrong.

When caught, we feigned remorse, hoping to prevent a report to our parents.

Things we couldn't do in the street we did in the field. The field was at the western end of 13th Street. Weeds, wild flowers, and thistle grew in abundance there. The Queen Anne's lace, listing in the breeze, reminded me of the crisp white doilies that blossomed beneath my mother's vases. The weeds and flowers were waist deep even at the edges, but they deepened as you waded into them. From some places in the field only the very tops of passing cars were visible. By later summer, when the grass was tawny and high, we imagined ourselves in a jungle where boy-eating animals lurked beyond every bush.

The field was a hunting ground. We captured bees and yellow jackets and imprisoned them in jars. We caught Japanese beetles, tethered them, and flew them like kites. We caught butterflies, but they went to powder in our hands. Grasshoppers were the most unfortunate prey: We pulled off their jumping legs, cooked them between two matches, then ate them. They were crunchy and not bad at all once you got past the sulfur.

Dragonflies, which we called Snake Doctors, were the only insects that went uncaptured. Their stinger tails made them too dangerous to mess with. They sifted through the bushes right past your face as though daring you to have at them. The lidless domes of their eyes seemed dead and mechanical. The mottled scaling on their bodies made them seem for all the world like snakes. Snakes we caught by the dozen. Snake Doctors we left alone. Russell had told us a frightening story about them. Russell was a coal-black boy with wide eyes and big, horsey teeth. Russell had seen a Snake Doctor drill through a grown man's hand. The man had cupped his hands around a Snake Doctor as though it were a butterfly. Foolish, foolish man. "You shoulda seen him. He had it in his hands and he started screaming." I saw it vividly as Russell spelled it out: the bloody stinger bursting through the skin and whipping angrily at the air. The man's mouth open, his eyes wide with terror and pain.

The older boys had built a clubhouse in the deepest part of the field. The clubhouse was a windowless death trap, bristling with rusty nails and subject to collapse at any time. The "door" was a tar-paper flap nailed to the roof. With the door closed, it was midnight inside except when someone brought candles. The clubhouse was where we cooked and ate the grasshoppers. It was also where we plotted thefts of fruit. We didn't have to steal from Miss Arlena Douglas; she let us have all the mulberries and pears that we could eat. But the sour old lady on Central Avenue whipped boys with a broomstick when they tried to steal her apples. First she whipped them, then she called the police. The boys wore hangdog looks as the police marched them down the steps and drove them away. Meanwhile the lady scowled and waved the stick, as though challenging the rest of us to try.

And we did. We orbited the block, up Central Avenue and through the alley behind her house, aching for an opening and waiting for her to leave, which she never did. We sensed her crouched behind the shades, waiting to trap us in the tree, which was how she liked to do it.

There was easy fruit on the grounds of the abandoned Brinkley mansion. None of us knew who the Brinkleys were, but we knew that they were dead and that the place had ghosts. The apple trees there were nearly overgrown with weeds and creepers. The grape arbor had been completely submerged, but we waded in every year to dig it out. We also gathered blackberries in the brush and came home with our lips and fingers purple. My mother baked blackberry pies and dumplings that we ate and ate and ate. There were fruit trees of some kind in almost every yard. If the fruit wasn't ripe, we ate it green—bitter green grapes, unbiteable green apples—and got sick.

And when there was no fruit at all, we got perverse. One day we galloped down the alley to raid a certain lady's flower garden. In particular, we were interested in the orange trumpet flowers that climbed in a vine all over her back fence. The flowers were like honeysuckle, only bigger, with nectar enough to hold us until something sweeter came along. We pulled every blossom we could reach and sucked them dry. We were pulling and sucking noisily when a screen door slammed and a woman yelled, "Get outa my flowers!" We fled, leaving the alley carpeted with blossoms. When the lady complained to my mother, my mother shook her head in disbelief, "I know my children," she said. "They don't eat flowers."

The Hill was a very small world. Thirteenth Street was three blocks long (not counting the alleys), cut off by public housing projects at either end. On the east were The Bennett Homes, endless rows of red brick houses, every row just like the last. On the west were The Fairgrounds, where white wooden barracks repeated in the same dismal arrangement. Boys who lived in the projects were testy and prone to fight. One summer gangs from both sides marched into Central Avenue with bricks and bats and squared off for a rumble. My mother bundled us into the house and called the police. Kids from The Fairgrounds were the worst of the two. On Halloween they went in bag-snatching missions instead of trick-or-treating for themselves. Outsiders who crossed The Fairgrounds risked being stoned or shoved around. This I knew from experience. My mother's favorite hoagie shop lay at the far side of the project. The trip took vigilance and cunning. As a hedge against robbery, I carried the money in my shoe.

Near the sandwich shop was a slaughterhouse where pigs screamed all the time. The screaming came down in sheets. If you listened closely, you heard one pig above the others reach a wild crescendo and then fall silent. But that was at the slaughterhouse gate. From two blocks away the pigs sounded human. The squealing fell away, but the high notes carried on the wind. Walking home, with the slaughterhouse at my back, the screaming sounded like children.

Mother's brother, Bunny, came to live with us in 1958.

Bunny was big and athletic, with a quick, bouncy way of walking. I admired the way he walked through the house with a plate to his face, shoveling in the food. He snagged sausages just out of the frying pan, held them between his teeth, and dieseled in and out until they were cool enough to chew.

Bunny drove the way he ate—fast. So fast that I knew enough not to tell my mother how fast that was. We swept up onto the highway, the engine winding louder and louder, and swooped past the Princes' living room. I cheered to myself when the needle pressed past 80. This was like flying. I held my head out of the window until I was drowning in the wind, then collapsed breathless into my seat. A mile and a quarter slips by very quickly at 90 m.p.h. That was it. The road that had seemed headed into infinity was only 1.23 miles long. It ended at a barrier, dumping us onto a quiet residential street where the houses had aluminum awnings. Now we crawled stop-and-go from stoplight to stoplight; the heat cooked us as in a rolling oven. The highway was a gorgeous disappointment. It promised everything and took you nowhere.

Bunny changed cars as often as he did shirts. He went out in the morning in a Chevy and came back that night in an Electra 225 or in a Ford or in a pickup truck or even in a Porsche. Bunny drove incessantly: Five blocks or five hundred miles, it was all the same to him. He drove my mother, my brothers and sisters, and me from Chester to Roanoke, to visit my mother's family. I loved to ride. The idea of the long drive to Roanoke left me too excited to sleep. Riding that far changed the arc of the world. The flat became hilly. Straight roads curved and rose and fell. City smells gave way to the smell of farm animals. One place became another, right before my eyes.

I stayed awake all night to see the transformation, to catch the first whiff of the country in the air. I was Bunny's copilot and sat next to him, straining to see over the dashboard. I watched the taillights on the highway in front of us. I had discovered their secret: a car's true power came not from its engine, but from its taillights. Taillights were rocket engines that a secret science had rendered cool to the touch. That greasy mess under the hood was a ruse, to throw little boys off the track. I was certain of my discovery when we drove in the rain and the taillights seemed to melt and run like lava down our windshield. I knew that the grown-ups would one day take me aside and tell me the secret. When this happened, I'd tell them that I'd known it all along.

My mother and the rest of them were soon snoring in the back. But I stayed awake with Bunny into the night. The flat of eastern Pennsylvania gave way to hills and then to the mountains where the beasts lay. The mountains looked like dinosaurs in the night, brontosauruses mostly. Their humps rose everywhere, as they looked up from their grazing to watch us speed by. Bunny clowned to keep the two of us awake. He pulled the key from the ignition and stuck it in his ear. I held my breath, certain that the car would stall and die. It didn't; we sailed right along at 80 m.p.h.

Night turned to dawn and to day. The sun came blazing up over a field of corn. I dozed off, but woke up in time to see a man falling headfirst into the corn. He was a pale man, his hair the color of the tassels. I sat up and looked behind us. The man was getting up from a pile of corn husks: a farmboy practicing the high jump.

Bunny drove all the time. This meant that I could always get a ride with him somewhere. It also meant that he might move on and forget where he left me. One day he drove Brian and Bruce and me to a park and dropped us in a meadow by a wood. Brian and Bruce played all afternoon, while I watched over them. The sky began to darken. The shadows descended in the woods and crept out into the meadow. Evening pressed in, and still no Bunny. The vines in the woods had been vines all day. Now they were snakes that slithered down the trees and crawled out toward us. Finally it was genuinely, frighteningly dark. I pulled Brian and Bruce across the meadow to the road. The three of us huddled under a streetlight. Headlights appeared in the dark, then passed us by. Finally a car glided to a stop in front of us. Bunny at last.

My father earned a handsome living driving a truck for the Blue Line Transfer Company. Much of what he earned he drank up. My mother lacked the skill to stretch what was left. She had been raised in a barter economy, where neighbors traded their labor and what they grew for what they needed. The man who butchered your hogs could be paid in pork. Money was a mystery to her: she held the dollars in her open palm and stared at them, as though the bills themselves could give her advice.

The groaning tables of her childhood had forever determined her attitudes toward food. Even with a houseful of children, she cooked too much and had no idea what to do with the leftovers. Back in Hollins, leftovers had gone to hogs and come back to the table as pork chops and breakfast sausage. The hogs inhaled every bit of food that people left behind: They ate stale corn bread and cake; they ate beans and greens and rice; they gobbled up their own piglets when the frenzy struck them. In Chester we were hogless. Roasts of beef became dry and inedible when my mother stored them naked in the refrigerator. Leftover stews languished until they were covered with mold. Blaine and Ruby sometimes gave us hams and pork shoulders and enormous tubs of lard. These vast infusions of food reinforced my mother's belief that life was a horn of plenty. We missed the porcine part of the food chain; without it, we hemorrhaged food to the garbage dump.

My father raged about the wasted food but wasted quite a bit of it himself. He threw it when he was angry. He ripped food from the freezer and hurled it into the backyard, even as my mother raced out to fetch it. One of his tricks was pouring a can of coffee grounds over the kitchen stove, which he did conscientiously, sprinkling diligently so as not to miss a spot. He pitched raw eggs at the kitchen wall, and plates of food, too, when he found them objectionable.

My bedroom (which I shared with Brian and then with Bruce) was doorless and opened onto the dining room. I lay in bed at night listening to my parents argue, watching their shadows on the dining room wall. We missed school often, sometimes because our shoes had worn out, sometimes because my mother was too deflated to send us. After a rash of absences, the truant officer's shadow joined my parents' on the wall. He yelled at them. They yelled at each other. The voices rose in an angry braid. I drifted off to an uneasy sleep.

Acts of violence were mainly confined to the kitchen. This was futile because the kitchen was doorless too, and the entrance was only a few steps from my room.

One night I awoke to my father's cursing and my mother's muffled screams. In the kitchen my mother stood rigid and terrified against the back door, while my father towered over her, with one hand at her jaw, the other trying to stuff a washcloth down her throat. He struggled at this for several seconds until he noticed my mother's eyes locked on me. Then he turned and ordered me back to bed.

Night was another country, where a pile of laundry became a monster groping toward me in bed. The violence between my parents was like the beast in the laundry; I kept it confined to the night. One night my mother screamed again. This was not the muffled scream of the washcloth incident, but a scream that was full and harrowing and mournful. My father had drawn a knife and cut her. The wound took several stitches to close. Later, after it had healed, I helped her remove the stitches. The cut was awkwardly placed, toward the back side of her upper left arm. I held a mirror to the wound so that she could see to cut the suture knots. The stitches were black. A collar of dried pus clung to their necks as she pulled them out.

My mother grumbled, but her anger was directed more at the discomfort than at my father. She never criticized him in front of us. Later, when we were older and speaking badly of him, she would cut us short. "Don't talk like that," she'd say. "He's still your father, no matter what. You'll understand him more when you are older." My mother was resolutely forgiving. She smothered my father with forgiveness. The greater his sin, the more condemning the forgiveness. This drove him crazy, forcing him to acts that were ever more outrageous.

The stitches frightened me more than the idea of being cut. A cut took an instant; the sewing-up of the cut might have taken forever. The needle pierced the skin again and again, dragging the thread behind it. This I thought of as agony. My mother said the doctors gave you a shot that kept away the pain. I didn't believe her.

By daylight on Sunday morning my father was placid, the very portrait of composure. Gone were the sweaty work clothes. He had changed into his Sunday best, and the air around him sang with Mennon Speed Stick and Old Spice cologne. He was resplendent in pleated gabardine pants, his dress shoes buffed to a high sheen. His sleeveless summer T-shirt showed off his arms to advantage: He was thin but strong; the muscles moved visibly beneath his skin when he turned the pages of the newspaper or reached for the plate of sliced cantaloupe on the hassock in front of him.

On an end table nearby was a picture of my father when he was in the navy and not yet twenty years old. He was wearing dress whites with the cap tilted jauntily back on his head and his hand raised in a salute. He was happier than I'd ever seen him. He smiled a rich, expansive smile that spread to every corner of his face. I studied this picture obsessively. A hardness had undermined the smile and limited its radius in his face. His lips, full and fleshy in the picture, were tense and narrow, almost cruel by comparison. Back then I supposed that this was what happened when people got older. Now I see it differently. The picture showed a carefree boy for whom the world was redolent with possibility. A decade later all that possibility had been exhausted. He was knee-deep in children, in a foundering household, married to a woman he no longer loved but lacked the courage to leave. My father was ill at ease with the young, hopeful face in the picture. I suspect he was relieved when the picture disappeared. He might have been the one who got rid of it.

On Sunday morning he buried himself in the Philadelphia *Inquirer* and then the Philadelphia *Bulletin*. I was forbidden to touch the papers until he'd finished them. I waited just beyond the hassock for him to pass me the comics. Sometimes he peeked out from behind the paper and smiled affably. And other times he stuck out his hand quite unexpectedly and offered me a stick of gum. I took it, but the beneficence made me wary. Meanwhile my mother buzzed about the kitchen, baking biscuits from scratch, cooking sausage or scrapple for us, but salt fish for my father. Salt fish was his favorite food. The plate of it was placed on the hassock next to the cantaloupe. The blissful scene seemed irrefutable; the violence of the night before, no more real than a dream.

I craved my father's attention. But I kept a distance from him, even during moments of closeness. I watched for the scowl that might be brewing in his forehead or curling hardly seen at the corners of his mouth. I watched even on those rare occasions when he joined us in games of tag on the sidewalk along Central Avenue. His laughter was ominous. His mirth could give way to rage at any time.

My father wanted out. This was clear in nearly everything he did. Once when he was laid up with pneumonia he left bed and walked to work in a rainstorm. My mother stood at the door calling after him. "Melvin! Melvin! Come back here!" To no one in particular she said: "He's trying to kill himself."

I understood that my father had been sick. But what in the world was pneumonia? I went to the encyclopedias and took out the N. When I couldn't find *pneumonia*, my mother explained that it wasn't an *n* at all, but a *p* that was silent. She closed the door on the rain. We looked up *pneumonia* and read all about it.

By day the kitchen belonged to my mother and her friends, Larry, Miss Vi, Miss Betty, and the others who dropped by as the mood struck them. The rhythm of their voices comforted me. It was with them that I had learned to talk.

When I was ill, my mother pulled my bed into the dining room so that she could watch me from the kitchen. One night I lost a tooth, put it under my pillow as I fell asleep. I woke up to find a shiny new dime where the tooth had been. In the kitchen my mother and Miss Vi sat beaming at me. It was winter, and all the doors and windows were closed. How had the Tooth Fairy gotten in? My mother leaned close to me, and pointed to the faintest crack in the windowpane, a crack that you could barely see. "There, this is all the fairies need to come in," she said. My eyes still widen with this memory.

Some of my mother's friends were boozy. I registered their

boozy breaths and the half pints of whiskey peeking out of their bosoms. I noticed, too, that some of them spent their days with us even though they had families of their own. Later I found out why. They had husbands who beat them; husbands who took lovers within full view of their neighbors; husbands who drove them mad in any number of ways. The booziest woman had the worst story: Her husband had died in his lover's bed. The body was taken elsewhere to avoid a scandal. This woman was drunk all the time. My mother was the perfect comforter. She brewed coffee and listened. She stroked the woman's hand when she wept.

My mother's beautician, Gene, was the star of Saturdays. He didn't appear every Saturday but just when he was needed and when, as he said, "Some heads need doin'." Gene was a faggot. He minced and twisted as he walked. But his body had wrenched itself into a caricature of a woman's. His behind stuck out so that he seemed to be wearing a bustle. He chain-smoked as he walked, with his cigarette hand at a girlish angle in the air. His other arm pressed to his torso the brown paper bag that contained his curling irons. Gene's hair was patent-leather slick, pressed to his head in waves that made you dizzy if you stared at them. When the waves needed refreshing, he wore a silk kerchief knotted at the forehead, with a top flap that rose and fell as he walked. Teenage boys hooted and howled when he passed. Gene minced more brazenly then and blew smoke—POOF!—that curled over his head like steam from a passing train.

His voice was raspy and cawing and came out of him in a deep Georgia accent. He began his sentences with "chile" or "girl," as in: "Chile, guess who I ran into walkin' over here today?"; "Girl, I'm glad I got here when I did. This head sho needs doin'." His eyes were bulging and widely set, always bloodshot from drinking. The eyes, over his enormous mouth, made him look like a frog. He laughed with his head thrown back, and the froggish mouth open, showing the capacious spaces among his teeth.

Gene made his rounds to the rhythm of payday. And he materialized to do some heads just when heads needed doin'—and there was money on hand to pay him. He was an honorary woman, and the women greeted him warmly. Gene drank hard, harder when he had man trouble. Before he went on a bender he gave the curling irons to my mother and told her not to give them back to him until he was sober. He could drink himself into oblivion, spend every cent he had, but with the curling irons he could always regain himself.

These were the days before the cold permanent wave, when making kinky hair patent-leather smooth was hard work. Gene pulled a chair up in front of the kitchen stove and on that stove laid out his tools. The iron straightening comb with the wooden handle was standard equipment in almost every household. The curling irons were Gene's, and there were two sets of them. The first set was short and stubby for where the hair was longest. The second set was long and stilettolike, sharp at the tip like a knife. These were for curling the hair where it was shortest, at the temples and at the nape of the neck.

My mother sat down in the chair, with Gene standing behind her. He placed the straightening comb into the open flame. While it heated, he used an ordinary comb to separate the hair into squares at the scalp, pulling out a length of hair from each square. He dipped his thumb and index finger into a can of pomade and ran the length of hair through the oiled fingers. Then he picked up the hot straightening comb and drew it through the length of oiled hair. The comb hissed as it met the pomade. A perfumy fragrance suffused the air. Combful by combful, my mother's hair was made shiny and slick.

Gene was better with the straightening comb than women

were. This I knew from watching my mother straighten my sisters' hair. The teeth of our straightening comb were ominously bent from being left too long in the flame. My mother lifted the comb from the fire and waved it in the air to cool it, but still, when she started, you could smell the hair burning and see the billowing smoke. The girls fidgeted in the chair and were sometimes burned.

The hot teeth of the comb glanced the forehead, leaving teeth marks that were white at the start, but that turned black when scabs grew on them. These marks could usually be seen at the temple, where the hair was too short for the clunky iron comb to get at cleanly. These were brands from the painful ritual of beautification. Girl after girl was branded this way at Christmas and Easter, when the need to get dolled up was the greatest.

Even "tender-headed" women sat in Gene's chair without fear of burning. They swore by him: "Girl, you know I'm tender headed, but, honey, I never feel a thing with Gene." This was all the more fascinating because his hands were enormous and clawlike. His fingers were thick and grotesquely swollen at the tips. The nails were brown, as though painted from the underside, and grew downward over the swollen fingertips like talons. But, man, could those fingers fly. They moved swiftly, deftly, as he wound the hair into the curler's mouth. Meanwhile, the irons opened and closed, sounding like castanets. Soon my mother's head was covered with row after row of licorice-black curls.

Then came the styling. Gene picked out the curls with the tail of a styling comb. Patting and picking, he coaxed them into the arrangement that he wanted. The man was an artist, my mother always said, "A true cosmetologist!" When he finished, he gathered the excess hair from the combs and dropped it into the flame. Gene said it was dangerous to throw your hair away; voodoo people used it to cast spells on you.

My father didn't care for faggots. He spoke of them in faggot jokes that he'd brought back from the navy. (So-and-so was "as happy as a faggot in Boys' Town," or "as happy as a sissy on a troop train.") My father was jealous of the bond between Gene and my mother. He said to her: "You care more about that faggot than you do about me." He didn't know how right he was. Gene and my mother were bosom friends and stayed that way. His mincing walk and crowish laugh would be constants in our lives. He followed us from house to house around the city.

Prince cut off our credit. No one told me this. But it was obvious when my mother started sending me to Mose Lerman's instead. Prince knew exactly what was happening when I passed his window with the shopping list in my hand. He knew it was the list because as always it was written on part of a brown paper bag. That he knew made me edgy; this was, after all, a form of betrayal. Prince bit down on his cigar and glared. I stared straight ahead and rushed up the avenue.

Mose Lerman was a short, wide man, shaped like a brick stood up the long way. He wore a salt-and-pepper wool cap, indoors and out, winter and summer, and a long white butcher's apron, whose length made him look even shorter. He walked haltingly because half of one foot had been cut off in an accident. Miss Eva Finklea said that Mose had deliberately let a trolley car cut off the foot to get the insurance money. This seemed a particularly greedy thing to do. And painful too. But Mose was a Jew, Miss Eva said; Jews were so stingy as to be indifferent to pain. Yet Mose didn't seem stingy at all, at least to me. He gave me a piece of candy to wet my mouth while I shopped. He kept a cardboard box filled with fried pork rinds, which he sold by the pound but also encouraged me to eat, free of charge. And he let me shop on account.

Passing Prince's window with a list was one thing. Passing with a bag of groceries was something else. I couldn't do it. Instead I went the long way around the block so Mr. Prince wouldn't see me. Since his windows gave him a view of our front door, I sneaked into the house from the back.

My father stopped living with us in the spring of 1961, when Prince evicted us. My mother was pregnant with Blake at the time.

I came galloping home just as two men in uniform were carrying our furniture onto the sidewalk. The sheriffs' badges glimmered in the sun as they came and went. These were the badges that I had so often seen in the movies, worn by men sent out to set things right. The badges meant that we were the bad guys, and that evicting us was the right thing to do. Across the street Mr. Prince stood glaring at us from his window, his obsidian forehead glimmering with spite. People gathered to watch as the sheriffs did their work. I nearly wept with embarrassment. My mother arranged for us to move into a house that Mose owned. My friends helped us carry our stuff past Mr. Prince to the new house, which was a few doors from Mose's store.

On one of our first nights in the new house, my mother heard the clumping of feet downstairs. She didn't even bother to get out of bed. She knew it was my father. The next morning she saw that he had climbed into the basement through the window over the coal bin. He'd tracked coal dust up the cellar stairs through the dining and living rooms and out the front door. My father was trying to mark the place as his, even though he'd never live in it.

My father moved in with his sister, Susie, who lived forever away, in the Polish West End. He became the model father while we were apart. He took us on outings that we'd never gone on before and that we'd never go on again once he and my mother were back together. He showed up in my aunt Susie's Chevy and held the door while we climbed in. He drove us to the Philadelphia Zoo and bought us balloons and cotton candy. He drove us across town to the State Theatre, where a man in a red suit pulled back a red velour cord and showed us to our seats by flashlight. This was surprisingly unlike the Apollo, where the kids went on Saturdays for double-feature monster movies. At the Apollo our feet stuck to the floor; people screamed and threw candy at the screen. The State was as quiet as church. The whole picture went by without the manager shouting at us to shut up. Even the movie was different. The picture was in Panavision, so that the people were elongated and curved at the edges of the screen.

During these outings my father's face was dead calm. The only thing moving on that face was his mustache, which went up and down in its caterpillar way as he chewed his chewing gum. In retrospect he seems not to have been there at all. He was walking through the part, doing as someone had advised him to, but without feeling it. I made the best of these outings (what nine-year-old wouldn't?), but I was suspicious of them. Sooner or later he'd be screaming and raging again.

‖ The Perfect Father

I was happy during my father's absence. I had replaced him as king of the house.

On Tuesdays I sat out on the porch and waited for the mailman to bring the support check. Tuesday had become my family's Saturday. The other fathers got paid on Fridays, and the next day the whole neighborhood was alive with spending. Bill collectors made the rounds, knocking on door after door, fat receipt books in hand. Bags of groceries were hoisted out of the backs of station wagons. Little kids dribbled melting popsicles down their chins, their pockets jammed with candy. Kids walked down The Hill a mile or so to the Apollo to see the monster double features and throw candy at the screen. My family was out of sync with all this. Our day of celebration was isolated, lonely, without those other people's Saturdays to hold it up. And ours depended on the mail.

The house Mose had rented us was high above the sidewalk. The porch looked down onto the tops of cars and onto the tops of people's heads. My mother sat inside, near the window, a voice behind the curtains, waiting for the mailman. I manned my post on the porch.

On the adjacent porch, just across the railing, Tyrone's grandmother, Miss Eva Finklea, waited with me. Miss Eva was a dark woman with darker pouches under her eyes. The eyes rolled slowly in their sockets and lagged a beat behind her head when she turned to look at you. She spent hot summer days casting that slow reptilian gaze up and down Central Avenue and eating chunks of starch from a box on her lap. She crunched on the dry white chunks in her mouth as though they were candy. My mother used starch in our dress shirts, but never had we eaten it. Miss Eva seemed to enjoy it, so I thought, why not give it a try. She handed the box across the railing; I took a chunk. It was as nasty as chalk, nastier than milk of magnesia, and I spat it out. Miss Eva laughed and crunched merrily on.

The mailman appeared at the corner of 13th and Central. He went first to Prince's store. Then to the mean old lady who didn't like children. Then to Benny and Roger's house. Then to Miss Arlena Douglas's. Then to us. Inside, my mother grabbed the mail as it came through the slot, and sifted through it for the support check.

If the check was there, I got to enjoy my father's money without him coming between my mother and me. I went with her to the supermarket, and we breezed up and down the aisles, eating Oreo cookies while we shopped.

If the check wasn't there, or if the mailman passed by without stopping, my mother whispered through the curtain: "Go after him! Ask him to check the bag again." I did. We were crushed and hopeless when the check didn't come. When we were in desperate need of money, I undertook the walk to the Polish West End to get it from my father. I often walked long distances to borrow money from my mother's friends. But the trip to the Polish West End was the longest I'd taken. The trip took me through neighborhoods where I knew no one and where people spoke mysterious languages. My mother gave me bus fare, but I spent the money on a soda and walked. Walking, I daydreamed and let the town drift by me, house by house. The Polish and Ukrainian neighborhood began at St. Mary's Ukrainian Orthodox Church. Both church and rectory were made of stone. Their lot covered the better part of a city block and was surrounded by a wrought-iron fence. Just across the street was a store whose proprietor was missing all of one thumb and part of the second. His face was blocky, both long and broad. Like Mose Lerman he wore a hat indoors and moved about the store in his white jacket and apron. He seemed to limp, but on both feet.

I watched him wait on other customers, my eyes glued on the thumbless hands. He had improvised a way to grip the knife, using four fingers only. He handled the big slabs of luncheon meat by tilting them into the flat of his hand and hoisting them into the cradle of the electric slicer. It seemed impossible to turn the slicer dial without a thumb, but he did. Hungrily, I gathered up the facts of him. I sensed him watching me as well. He was proving to me what he had proved to a hundred boys before me.

A couple of blocks farther on, I passed the Polish American Citizens Club. Men stood outside, smoking and filling the air with the strange sounds of Polish. Then there was Kaniefski's funeral home, and then "Kyj's Bakery," though the people here pronounced it "Kay's." In that same block was the Lyric Movie House. The final corner was Highland Avenue. There I turned from 3rd Street toward 2nd and passed another knot of men speaking what I presumed to be Polish.

The twin boys and Studebakers were the last landmark before my aunt's house. Their cars were twin Studebaker Hawks, low-slung and racy, with hoods and trunks that both sloped toward the ground. The boys were bookends, with blondish hair that was greased back on the sides but flying in the air on top. They wore baggy jeans slung low on their waists, and loafers with white socks. They were conscious of how cool they looked and coordinated their actions to heighten the coolness: You came on them, one on the step, the other in the porch chair, one standing leaning against the wall, the other sprawled out on the banister railing. They were living sculptures.

Their father looked like them, only his body was thicker and he had more forehead than they did. The forehead was fixed in lines of surprise—as though he'd been startled by something and never gotten over it. He moved in quick steps from the front door, across the porch down the steps, and out to one of the Studebakers. The three of them were cool together, walking, the two thin ones on either side, the thicker one in the middle. I imagined that the three of them were buddies. I admired that. How neat it must have been to have a dad who wore the same clothes as you and even combed his hair the way you did.

My father answered Aunt Susie's door. He was polite but distant. He said, "How ya doin', boy?" but that was the extent of the conversation. He knew why I'd come; there was no need to talk. He turned and walked down the hallway to the dining room. I followed in the stream of Old Spice cologne and Mennon Speed Stick, the old weekend smells that trailed behind him. In the dining room he took a fountain pen from the sideboard and wrote out a check. He fanned the check in the air to dry the ink, and as he did this, he stared vacantly in my direction. His mustache crawled up and down as he chewed his omnipresent gum. He handed me the check and saw me to the door.

I went back the way I had come, reviewing the mysteries again.

*   *   *

Booker T. Washington School was just down the hill at 7th Street. One day a few of us returned early from lunch to an empty playground. Naturally we got up a game of tag. The game had three bases. Two were posts in the hurricane fence; the third was a square of cardboard well out in the school yard. Anyone tagged while not touching a base, became "it." Normally I thought of myself as a so-so runner, not fast, not good at dodging out of reach. But this day I had a new pair of sneakers. They were Keds, which was the cool sneaker then, optic white, and unmarred by dirt or scuffs. New sneakers convinced me that I could run faster and jump higher than anyone else. These gifts would fade as the sneakers got older and dirtier and lost their bounce, but in the first, fresh days I was superman.

I loitered in the base paths, bouncing on the balls of my feet, until the boy who was "it" was almost on me, then tore off for the safety of the base. Time after time, the hurricane fence rattled as I slid into it. Then I came in much too fast. The bottom of the fence gave way, my foot slid under, and I was caught on one of the sharp metal strands. I struggled fiercely, rattling the fence and pulling my foot. The strand cut through the sneaker and into my foot itself. By the time I pulled free blood was sloshing inside the sneaker. The slightest injury always sent me hurtling home to my mother. The sneaker was crimson, blood pulsing from the hole at every step. Run home! Run home! The message flashed from my brain to my legs and I was off.

Tyrone Finklea caught me as I was leaving the school yard. "Where you goin'?" he asked. "I'm going home," I said, dazed and afraid. Tyrone put a hand on my shoulder. "You can't do that," he said, "that's too far to go. Let's go to the nurse's office." His words carried weight; he was two grades ahead of me, one of the boys I looked up to. And he was right. Home was six blocks away.

Tyrone and another boy linked wrists, formed a chair with

their arms and carried me into the school. The nurse was missing from her station. The boys carried me up to the second floor and stopped at every room asking for her. Behind us I could see blood, my blood, marking the way we had come, collected in puddles where we'd stopped. We went down the rear stairwell and found the nurse back at her station.

The wound was big and deep: a vertical gash along the outer side of the foot. The nurse wrapped and wrapped the foot in a bandage until it was three times its normal size, then drove me to the hospital. The wound took eight stitches to close. My mother had misled me about how it felt to get stitches. It hurt. Each time I felt the pierce of the needle, the drag of the suture through my flesh.

Back at home, Tyrone and the other boys gathered on my front step while I told the story. I held up the bloody sneaker and took off the bandage so they could see the stitches. They were ugly stitches, black bristles growing out of the wound.

These communions with the older boys became fewer and fewer. They were no longer interested in hunting fruit or cooking grasshoppers. The spell that had bound us together in the clubhouse was broken. The older boys had discovered girls.

Tyrone and Roger began to drift off with a girl named Geraldine. She appeared among us and pulled them off to her house as though with a magnet. Bayboy and I tried to follow, but Geraldine yelled at us to get lost; we were too young, she said. We jammed our hands into our pockets and kicked at stones in the street. We weren't stupid: We knew that they were going off to do The Nasty. We knew only proximately what The Nasty was, but we knew that it was good and that older boys did it with girls. We had also seen the creamy stuff that older boys made with their dicks.

A girlfriend of Yvonne's was using me to practice kissing. One day when I met her for the next round of practice, I told her that I'd rather the other thing. The Real Thing that Roger and Tyrone talked about. Asking was all it took. We stripped down and hopped into bed for a game of "Doctor and Nurse." It was summer; we had the curtains drawn down and the windows closed. We were soon sweating heavily. The girl had breasts; the big brown circles around the nipples reminded me of bull's-eyes in a target. She smelled different than boys did, as the sea would when later I smelled it. I began to see dimly what the fuss was about, but still I wasn't sure. The fun of this was not the game itself. The fun was telling the older boys how I'd done it. They smiled wolfishly and leaned in to listen. For a moment I was a big boy, just like them.

My friends and I pursued this new interest the same way we hunted fruit. We worked diligently at it with girls, and just as diligently without them. One day we were undressed and playing doctor in my room when the back door opened and slammed. "Ginny, girl! You home?" It was Gene; a surprise visit in the middle of the week. We scrambled for our clothes, but it was no use. Gene was on us, at the bedroom door. I'd gotten only one leg into my pants. He hovered there, puffing his cigarette, a fist parked girlishly on his hip. "Where's your mother?" he asked. I told him that she'd gone shopping. He seemed not to notice our nakedness, or at least he said nothing about it. He turned and minced back the way he'd come.

For months afterward my heart would clench when Gene came through the door. I lived in terror that he would tell on me. I lingered in the next room listening for him to whisper to my mother that he'd seen me—and us—naked. After he'd done her hair and gone, I braced myself for a scolding. I braced and braced, but the scolding never came. I took this to mean that Gene had kept my secret. It was our secret now. We had an agreement.

My father was back. When I asked my mother why, she said: "The children missed him. They kept asking when Daddy was coming home." "*The children*"? I felt betrayed. I was one of the children and then some. I'd walked the width of the city to serve my father with the family's demands. I'd staved off bill collectors at the front door. My mother should have at least asked my feelings on whether or not to bring my father back.

It wasn't just "the children." My mother wanted desperately to believe that we could be the model family we'd been during the separation. I for one did not want my father back. Life had been blissfully quiet without him. The separation had lasted only through the summer.

We had moved down from The Hill a ways to a house between 11th and 12th. Even this short distance could cost me a day's adventure; expeditions began at 13th or above. Now that we'd moved, I arrived at 13th to find nobody around. I had missed a march into the brush beyond the highway or a retreat to someone's house where the parents were conveniently away for the day. And sometimes I came up the hill right into the middle of things—a card game, a ball game, one of the older boys telling a story about The Nasty.

Blake came along in November of 1961. This box-headed baby had the high, wolfish widow's peak even then. My father was on good behavior when there was a new baby in the house. He was giggly with excitement. He lobbied for names of his choosing, and these he put before us while my mother and the baby were still in the hospital. My father wanted one of us named for him. This he never accomplished. The middle name in Blake Melvin Staples was as close as he got. Still he lobbied and lobbied. When the next baby came, he tried for Melvina. He patrolled the house chanting it: "It might be Melvina. It just might be Melvina." My mother prevailed.

The baby was named Yvette. But that was yet to come. Meanwhile Blake was the fourth B in four boys. This meant terminal confusion for everyone.

My sisters, Yvonne, Sherri, Christi, had no trouble keeping separate identities. But the boys—Brent, Brian, Bruce, and Blake—were hopelessly tangled up.

My mother had sought a unique name for each of us. She succeeded. We were unique—to everyone except ourselves. Even my mother was confused. She stuttered through the whole list—"Brent . . . Brian . . . Bruce . . . Blake"—before getting to the boy who was standing right in front of her. Friends and neighbors had no idea who was who. To the list of names they added—Bart, Brett, Britt, Brandt, and so on. I gave up fighting for my name. I answered to anything that came close.

First love struck as lightning in the dark. It happened one night when someone knocked at the front door and I answered it. There stood Mattie Walker, the girl next door. She'd come to borrow a cup of flour and brought along the cup. Mattie was in fifth grade, a year ahead of me. I'd always liked her well enough, but no more than I liked Bayboy, Benny, or Roger. As we faced each other at the door, love of Mattie exploded in a fever. A shaft of light from the living room fell on her face in a way I'd never seen—in a way light had never fallen on the face of any girl in the world.

I stepped outside and pulled the door closed behind me, and in one motion encircled her waist, pulled her to me, and whispered breathlessly that I loved her. There'd been no rehearsing this; the thought, deed, and word were one. "You do? You love me?" This amused her, but that didn't matter; I had passion enough for the two of us. When I closed in for the kiss, she turned away her lips and offered me her cheek. I kissed it feverishly and with great force. We stood locked this way until I came up for air. Then she peeled me from her and went inside for the flour.

I hated the new house. It was too small and too dark. It was a straight-back stucco box, all of it on one floor. There were three tiny bedrooms off the hall, two of them for six kids, while Blake slept in my parents' room. There were too few windows and the place was depressingly dim.

      Mattie lived with her sister, Ethel, and mother, Miss Ethel, in a house that was identical to ours. The two houses shared a wall. It made me envious that the three of them had the same amount of space as my family of nine. I stared at the wall, imagining their rooms, where all their *things* were laid out just the way they wanted them. I envisioned Mattie and her sister Ethel tending rows of neatly stacked sweaters: gray ones, blue ones, the fuzzy kind with long hairs growing out of them. On our side of the wall everything was jumbled. My mother dressed us in interchangeable clothes from the day's pile of laundry. Nothing belonged to me; nothing belonged to my brothers; we wore what fit. If it was there, we picked it up and put it on. I longed for more space and for something, anything, that would be mine alone.

      Miss Ethel was young and shapely and pretty. I was partial to freckles, and she had a nice spray of them across the bridge of her nose and cheeks. One eyelid hung lower than the other, making her seem dreamy, even sexy when she looked at you. Once when boys came to woo the daughter Ethel, Miss Ethel posed in the window as well, pretending to be an older sister. I walked up just as the suitors were giving their lines. "Baby, I dig you in a big way." I started to laugh, but Miss Ethel shot me a look, then winked that dreamy eye.

The wink sent me, but sending me was not its purpose. Miss Ethel was telling me to keep my mouth shut, which I did. The boys wore themselves out, not knowing that it was Mattie and Ethel's mother that they were digging in a big way.

Miss Ethel's dreamy eye would have a dark resonance after she was murdered. It was said that she was killed on the way home from work and that people heard her screams but saw nothing. I was drawn to the spot of the murder and often stood there imagining the scene in great detail: The pair of hands around Miss Ethel's throat. The dreamy, heavy-lidded eye wide with panic.

That was yet to come when I fell in love with Mattie. The morning after our kiss, I searched her face to see how love had changed her. While I was searching, her boyfriend crept up behind me and got down on all fours. Mattie pushed me over his back into a pile of snow. The two of them waltzed away, arm in arm, laughing. I'd been caught in the oldest trick in the book. My love for Mattie was the suffering kind. The suffering was mercifully short because we moved. There were no sheriffs this time, but the suddenness suggested that we were leaving just ahead of them.

My aunt Susie had vacated the house in the Polish West End. We inherited it. My father's brothers showed up to help us move. Even as they lifted the heaviest things, my uncles talked in normal voices to show how little of their strength they were using. My father outdid them all: He strapped our enormous refrigerator to his back and carried it by himself. It weighed far more than he did. He was determined to show his brothers that he could do it all on his own. My uncles oohed and ahed as my father grunted beneath the load.

‖ Another Country

The new house was on 2nd Street, and 2nd Street was a truck route. Forty-foot trucks thundered by, spewing smoke, rattling windows, and sometimes breaking them. The trailers bore the company names in enormous letters: ALLIED, DAKOTA, MAYFLOWER, HEADLEY, MATLACK, and BLUE LINE, the company that my father and uncles drove for. Blue Line's trailers were the prettiest, at least when they were new. They were made of polished aluminum that shimmered in the sunlight, with BLUE LINE spelled out in dark blue lettering.

My relatives let rip with the horn when they saw me on the front step. Strangers had to be coaxed. This I did by tugging at the air above my head, pulling the chord on an imaginary air horn. The nice drivers rewarded me with a friendly blast of the horn. But most of them stared stonily ahead at the traffic light, gunning their diesels, eager to get under way.

I was sitting on the step watching traffic when three white kids appeared on the sidewalk in front of the house next door. The tallest one was oddly long from the neck up. His glasses were milky thick; the pupils splayed out enormously. With him was a thin, grasshoppery boy whose hair was cut like Prince Valiant's in the Sunday comics. The two of them were leaning in on the third boy chattering feverishly into his ears. The third boy stared fixedly at me with mournful, basset-hound eyes, and shifted slackly from one foot to another. He was trying to make up his mind.

I tried not to notice them, and soon enough I didn't. Then the mournful boy barged through the hedge around our yard and started tearing up the shrubbery. He broke off a piece of the hedge itself and tossed it onto the sidewalk. Then he ripped up a stalk of the snake plant and tossed that out too. He was clearly trying to provoke me to fight, but it was just as clear that this was not his idea. His movements were halfhearted, the basset-hound gaze resolutely sad. Between hands full of shrubs, he looked over his shoulder at Prince Valiant and the boy with the thick glasses. They gestured with their chins, egging him on. "What's the matter with you! You crazy?" I asked. He worked his way across the small patch of yard and slouched into my arms.

The fight was on. We rolled around on the steps, grunting and mauling each other, neither of us getting off a clean shot, neither of us really wanting to. We grunted and sweated for what seemed like a long time. Finally the pain of the steps cutting into my back got me mad. I freed my right hand and brought a fist up into his face four, then five times. We were still rolling when I saw blood on my shirt. I didn't know whose blood it was until we broke from the clench. Then I saw the twin rivulets running from his nose. He fell back, startled, and looked down at the growing splatters of red on his T-shirt. He retreated to his friends, and the three of them drifted away.

The boy with the mournful eyes and bloody nose was Albert Miller. He lived around the corner, a half dozen doors up Highland Avenue toward 3rd, past the twins and the Studebakers. Albert's family had an American name but they weren't American. His grandfather spoke Ukrainian. He was a solemn, brittle old man who paced up and down Albert's backyard, muttering in the foreign tongue. These mutterings reached a crescendo when I walked by, and I was certain that he was cursing me.

There were other clues to foreignness. The way Albert and his friends called out to each other during baseball games was one of them. On The Hill we complimented a good play by saying, "Way to go, babe!" or "Way to go, man!" The boys in the Polish West End said, "Way ta go, Stash!" or "Way ta go, Stashu!" How could all these people have the same name? They didn't. Years later I found that Stash and Stashu were abbreviations from the Polish name Stanislaw. This was the way the Polish boys said "man" and "babe."

The boy with the milky thick glasses was Gerry Wise. Gerry lived down by the railroad tracks with his half brother, Jimmy, who pronounced his name Bush but spelled it "Busz." (Phonetics meant nothing in the Polish West End. The corner store a few doors from my house was owned by Tommy Rzucidlo (pronounced "Roo-ZIDlo"). I knew that *y* was sometimes a vowel, but I had learned no rule that would permit the Hillwak family to write its name "Hly-wak.") Gerry was unprincipled and a marble shark. There were two kinds of marbles games: funsies and keepsies. Gerry won your marbles in a game of funsies, then refused to give them back. He caught me in that scam just once; I never played marbles with him again.

Prince Valiant wasn't a boy at all, but a girl named Helen. Helen lived next door. She was flat as a board, front and back. The only dress she seemed to own was the pleated jumper that was her Catholic school uniform. The rest of the time she wore boys' Levi's. The Levi's hung from the clothesline in her backyard, stretched tight on pants stretchers to keep them from shrinking. It was clear that Helen had put Albert up to fighting me. She was a ringleader and very big in boy politics, the driving force behind the marble games and the pea-shooting fights. The boys called her Hell for short.

The fight had won me the right to tag along with Helen and the boys. She acknowledged that I was alive, but that was all. Grace and favor were never to be mine. Helen shorted me when she handed out marbles for the funsies games. Same with the peas for the pea-shooting fights, which meant that I was the first to run out. It went hard for me with her minions, too. Gerry stared distantly from behind his milky glasses. Albert brooded and spoiled for a re- match.

The way I figured it, Helen and I had a lot in common: We both had fearsome fathers. Mine did me the decency of keeping his screaming fits indoors. Helen's father felt no such obligation. He screamed from the front door, even on Sundays, when there was no truck noise to cover him.

He was screaming after Helen's mother, who sometimes fled the house in her pajamas.

Helen's house and mine were separated by a narrow gang- way. When the shouting started I looked across into their windows and watched Helen's mother race through the house. When the front door slammed, I knew that she was out. I also knew where to find her: two doors away on the steps of Tommy Rzucidlo's store. It was almost bedtime, but that didn't prevent me from strolling to the corner for a bit of fresh air. There she was on Tommy's step, chin on fists, elbows on knees, crying into the sleeves of her pajamas. I leaned on the lamppost absurdly pretending that I'd happened by out of chance. I had followed her out of prurience, but when I saw how sad she was, I wanted to console her. I tried to talk with her, but she stared right through me. Eventually I gave up and went inside.

Albert had nothing to lord over me either. His family was as large as mine and poorer. He and his next youngest brother wore undershirts as shirts a lot, and often went without socks. Their homemade haircuts made them look like raw recruits in boot camp. My father kept a charge account at the barber shop and encouraged us to stay freshly cut at his expense.

Albert's grandfather sincerely hated me. This I learned by playing in the square just off Albert's backyard. The square was one of the few good places to play. The dump was littered with rusting cars; the boys who owned .22 rifles went there to shoot rats. The railroad yard had a solid constituency, but playing there was dangerous. The track switches opened and closed unexpectedly, and you had to take care not to get caught between the rails. The freight trains started up without notice. Somewhere out of sight, the engine moved and the boxcars screamed and slammed, one against the other, down the line. The scream and slam made me think of dismemberment. My legs twitched and numbed at the thought.

The grounds of the Ukrainian Catholic Citizens Society were safe and grassy. But only Ukrainian Catholics and their friends were allowed to play there. That left the square behind Albert's house. The square was an asphalt open space enclosed by garages and backyards, as good a place as there was for flying wooden planes. I was drunk with the idea of flying. At home I labored over model planes until the glue made me dizzy. At school I made planes from notebook paper and wedged them into my books and pockets. I was obsessed with movies about aerial aces. I studied their dogfights carefully, preparing for the acehood that I'd been born to and that was destined without question to be mine. I planned to join the air force as soon as I graduated from high school. They would already have heard of me and would have my fighter plane warming up on the runway.

The plane I took to the square was a wooden spitfire with British Royal Air Force markings and a propeller powered by a rubber band. I turned back the propeller until the rubber band was taut, then let her fly. The plane soared nicely, but landed in Albert's yard, in the vegetable bed where his grandfather was working. The old man snatched up the plane, muttered something in Ukrainian, and disappeared into the house. Several minutes later, one of his grandsons appeared at the door. He was in his twenties, and pudgy, with bad eyes and glasses as thick as Gerry's. He paused in the doorway, unsure of what to do. Then he walked to the fence and handed me what was left of the plane. He said nothing, but the redness in his cheeks told me that he was ashamed of what his grandfather had done. The plane had been destroyed with malevolent purpose. The wings and fuselage were broken the long way, twice. The pieces were the width of popsicle sticks. The old man had wrapped them in the rubber band and sent them back by a grown-up grandson whose nose I surely could not bloody.

I held in the tears until I had crossed the square into the alley. There I fell against a wall and cried for all I was worth. This was the deepest cruelty I'd known. A beautiful plane had been reduced to splinters by a grandfather. Grandfathers were supposed to be nice, especially to children.

I suspect that grandpa missed the days when black people were confined to small streets and alleys near the river; when the shipyard and the oil refineries were segregated, complete with supervisors for the colored; when the Poles and Ukrainians lived alone with their own, their schools, and their bakeries. Now black people were right next door. Grandpa needed someone to look down on.

My family had crossed the color line. My aunt Susie had

crossed it before us, but all of her children except one were adults. After Susie, my family must have seemed an invading army.

The Polish stronghold ended at Highland Avenue. One block east of that was Lewis Street, a black and Puerto Rican hovel that ran from 2nd Street to the tracks. The kids on Lewis Street were generally to be avoided. They were fight-prone, just like the kids in The Fairgrounds. These weren't namby-pamby fights like mine and Albert's, but brutal affairs where heads hit the sidewalk while roaring crowds looked on.

I made friends in the black streets beyond Lewis, but these friendships were largely disappointing. The kids were just like me; there was nothing exotic about them. Their names were Hudson, Hamilton, Wilson, and Jones. They ate fried chicken for dinner just like I did.

The Polish and Ukrainian boys were alluringly exotic. They had unpronounceable names and ate unpronounceable foods. They were Catholics, a new species to me. They smudged their foreheads with ash and ate fish on Friday. They told a priest their sins at confession and counted their prayers on beaded necklaces. I longed to see their houses and know their secrets. The Polish and Ukrainian boys didn't see it that way. They tolerated me, but in a way that made me invisible. When I think of the Polish West End, I think of a closed circle of backs, the reddened backs of necks and the greasy slopes of pompadours.

There were lots of things I needed to know. Where, for example, did the sixth finger come from?

The first case I saw was six-fingered Jack. He hung out on a stoop near 3rd Street, smoking a pipe, the brim of his cap pulled low over eyes that were never quite visible. The best look at the six fingers was obtained when Jack lit his pipe and held up his hands to shield the flame from the wind. Unbelievable. Jack seemed to have six fingers of equal length, not a thumb among them. His hands looked like a pair of pale spiders lying on their backs. The hands confirmed for me that the Polish West End was another country.

Yvonne made friends with a six-fingered girl named Pat. Pat visited our house and occasionally helped Yvonne wash dishes. I stood by the sink stealing glances at Pat's hands: The digit that was supposed to be a thumb was shaped like a middle finger. Pat noticed my curiosity and volunteered an explanation. She'd been born with a sixth finger, she said, but the sixth had been snipped off at birth. The nub on the outer side of each hand was all that was left of it.

She held still and let me look my fill. Then she finished the dishes. Six-fingered Jack rarely said a word. Then one day I strolled past his step counting a brand-new batch of play money. "*Six hundred. Seven hundred. Eight hundred.*" Jack groaned, then struggled to his feet and lumbered after me. I outran him easily. When I looked back, I saw him scoop up a rock and throw it at me.

My father laughed and laughed when I told him what had happened. "It's the money," he said. "He thought the money was real!" But that was beside the point. What if Jack had caught me? What if he'd clamped those spider-fingered hands around my throat?

Aunt Susie had left us quite a house. There were three floors (not counting the basement) and three bedrooms on the second floor alone. The third floor was a cozy setup with eaves and a second bathroom. The third-floor window offered a view of the power plant and the utility towers that marched out into the Delaware River and disappeared into New Jersey. The western end of 2nd Street ended in the oil refinery. The burnoff torch above the refinery burned steadily and at night cast a yellowish light over the neighborhood. The refineries stank; the smells they gave off were purplish and farty.

The odors that seemed to drift up from the river were worse than farty; they were evil. No one knew what these odors were. We named them for sharks, the most evil thing we could think of having to do with water. I assumed that fishermen were pulling malodorous sharks from the river. I could almost see the sharks split open and hanging from racks, like freshly slaughtered hogs on Uncle Blaine's farm.

Just across the street was a Sunoco station. The yellow sign that turned above the station carried the word "Sunoco" with an arrow shot diagonally through it. The cars that pulled in for gas rode over an air hose, causing a bell to ring inside the garage. The attendant who appeared at the door was a pale, rangy boy who looked to be in his late teens or early twenties. His hands were gloved in grease. He looked friendly, but this estimation was based almost solely on his feet. They were big feet, encased in greasy work boots. They seemed to burden him as he tromped across the lot to the pumps.

I wandered across to the station and found him bent over the engine of his car, an ancient Chrysler convertible from the forties. I circled the car, taking it in. The convertible top was rotten and riddled with holes. The rubber grips on the running boards were so buckled that they could trip you if you weren't careful. Lakes of rust had formed on the body where the paint had worn away. The leather seats were webbed with cracks. The rumble seat was split outright, with stuffing thrust up through the hole. That the car was up on blocks emphasized the devastation.

I asked a question or two about the car. The attendant launched into an extended discussion of how grand it would be when he'd fixed it up. He'd found it sitting in some old person's yard, going to pieces under the elements. Now the Chrysler's salvation was at hand. He wiped the grease from his hand and extended it for me to shake. His name was Eddy.

I was right about his friendliness. He saw that I was lonely and let me hang around as much as I wanted to. It didn't hurt that I was useful. The watchdog, a German shepherd, crapped all over the garage at night. In the morning I helped Eddy shovel out the shit.

I sat behind the wheel of the Chrysler, pretending to drive, while Eddy hunched over the engine. There were pivotal moments in the work when Eddy wanted to start it. I turned the key and held it and held it while he tinkered, but the engine never caught. Sometimes he focused on the steering column, in which case my job was to turn the wheel to one side and hold it, until my arms went numb from the strain. When he tired of this, Eddy joined me in the front seat and smoked a cigarette. Sitting in the Chrysler provoked him to ever more elaborate visions of what the car would one day be. His projections were quite precise: he'd figured out how fast it would do the quarter mile at the speedway. I dreamed the dream with him. I could see the Chrysler storming down the track, leaving the others in its smoke.

Eddy let me pump gas. These were the Sunoco pumps, with selectors that let you blend the specific octane that the customer requested. I felt more like a scientist than a gas station attendant. But my pumping days came to a close when the station owner drove by and saw me. He gave Eddy serious grief about this. From then on I stood by and watched while Eddy did the pumping. Customers sometimes tipped me for offering moral support.

The owner wanted me off the station, and he and Eddy occasionally argued about this. Eddy maintained to me that the owner was an asshole—an asshole's asshole in fact. "It's enough that I'm chained up here all day," he said. "I can certainly have company if I want to." The issue came to a head one rainy Saturday morning when the owner popped in and found me hanging around. I stood out in the rain while the two of them thrashed it out. The owner was a pinched-face man with angry, hunched-up shoulders. He scowled at me through the gas station window, turned to bark at Eddy, then scowled at me some more.

One day Eddy brought a trailer to haul the Chrysler away. The car still wouldn't start, and the two of us had to push it up the ramp and onto the trailer. This was a heavy car. A few times we got it halfway up, only to let it roll back at us. Finally we got it all the way up and battened into place. Eddy drove west toward the refinery and disappeared.

Then Eddy disappeared from the station. I came bounding down my steps, started across the street, and stopped cold. The owner was pumping gas and wearing the dark blue Sunoco jump suit that Eddy had refused to put on. The owner radiated meanness clear across 2nd Street.

Weeks later Eddy got the Chrysler started and dropped by to take me on a cruise. The car was as rusty as ever. And the rubber on the running board was still buckled. But the fact that it was running made it beautiful. Eddy had brought it back from the dead.

"Hop in!" Eddy said, and I almost did. Then I thought of my mother. She'd forbidden me to ride in cars without permission. I hated this: I was old enough to make these decisions on my own. Eddy said he'd wait while I went inside to ask. It took pleading, but my mother gave in. I ran back out and hopped in. Eddy nursed the Chrysler into first, clutch in, giving it lots of gas to avoid a stall. The engine rumbled and coughed, the car shaking with its roughness. Things calmed down as he ran through the gears.

This was my first ride in a convertible. I reached for the radio, but Eddy waved me off and yelled above the wind that it wasn't working yet. Not yet, but it wouldn't be long. The wind and the engine made a music of their own. We sailed east a few blocks, then looped around to 3rd and back down to 2nd again. Too soon, Eddy dropped me off at home. As he drove off, Eddy extended a fist toward the Sunoco station, unfurled his middle finger, pumped the arm for emphasis. I watched the Chrysler out of sight.

This was my last ride with Eddy. Without him, I was back at the mercy of the neighborhood.

I missed my friends on The Hill. But they weren't my friends anymore. The older boys had receded into early teenaged cruelty and taken the gang with them. The means for this cruelty was a card game called Knucks, so named because the loser was beaten across the knuckles with the deck. For this purpose the deck was bent into a U shape, the curve of which was hammered into the loser's hand a set number of times, depending on how badly he'd lost. Chopping —striking with the sharp edge of the deck—was usually ruled out because it drew blood. Usually but not always. The beatings left the knuckles swollen and painful. It was considered an excellent game when the loser was reduced to tears. The games were played on Tyrone Finklea's step, where once we'd contented ourselves with bees and Japanese beetles. The older boys played as one against the person they wished to punish. I was the outsider now and fair game. I was easy game, too; I daydreamed and lost track of the cards. Then I quit playing. When I came upon the card game in progress, I kept walking. I rounded the neighborhood and headed back to the Polish West End.

The Polish and Ukrainian kids went to one of three Catholic schools: Holy Ghost, Resurrection, or St. Hedwig's. I went to Dewey–Mann, a public elementary school well into the neighborhood where everyone was black. Passing by St. Hedwig's, I could see Catholic kids form lines and prepare to file into the building. Nuns in black patrolled among the lines keeping order. The nuns were fearsome custodians of discipline; boys who fooled around were snatched into line with neck-breaking force.

Catholic boys despised the nuns. Despisement of nuns became despisement of the religion and of all its precepts. Catholic boys boasted that they tossed used dick bags, and even girls' panties, into the rectory yard, with the aim of hitting the religious sculptures there. The boys made it seem a game of horseshoes: the closer they got to the saints, the more points they earned. This to me was courting a lightning bolt through the head.

Catholics said they were safe from lightning as long as they went to confession. The priest who heard the confession could absolve them of anything: Lying. Stealing. Sex. Even murder. It was a simple thing. You stepped into a booth, whispered your sins to Father So-and-so, and were forgiven, no questions asked. You could throw dick bags at saints for the rest of your life and never worry a second about hell. I suspected this easy out.

The nuns were said to possess a book that only Catholics were permitted to view, a book that listed hundreds of sins along with the punishment each would reap. There were sins for which you'd burn in hell for eternity. There were sins for which you served three centuries in purgatory and then were sprung to heaven. There were sins that brought mixed centuries, some in purgatory, some in hell. But even a minute in hell, and the doors of heaven were forever closed to you. A God who was that meticulous about punishment was not likely to be moderate when it came to throwing dick bags at saints. It seemed to me that confession was a trap, that the Catholics were building indictments against themselves that had to fall due sooner or later.

My mother's theology was easier to live with. Her view was that Christian spirit resided not in words or ritual but in everyday conduct. God was in people, she said, not in buildings. You didn't need preachers to live a Christian life; that you could do on your own. Hence we could miss church for years on end without penalty. If you lived a Christian life you could expect a Christian welcome when you died. If you didn't, you couldn't. Feed the hungry, clothe the naked, keep free of malice, and you had it made. I was uncertain of what malice was, but sure that I could keep clear of it.

Dewey–Mann was two buildings, a pair of nineteenth-century brick monoliths that sat on opposite sides of a macadam playground. The school seemed ancient compared to my school on The Hill. It was also dark and shadowy. There was one teacher for whom it was not dark and shadowy enough, though. He drew the shades, to shut out distraction, while the class ground out multiplication tables on brown paper bags.

The trip to the bathroom required vigilance because the boys' room was near the special education classes. The special ed boys there were bigger and surlier. They had been held back and bludgeoned with the idea that they were mentally defective. After an uneasy encounter with them, I limited my trips to when the bathrooms were full. Otherwise I held it in until I got home.

My welcome to Dewey–Mann was dramatic. It came to me from a boy who was tall and broad-shouldered, bigger than the rest of us, a boy you couldn't miss as he vaulted into the classroom, late. The coat closet was nearly full. Rather than search for a hook, he tore out a coat at random and threw it on the floor. The coat was mine. The other boys were watching. Either I made a show of resistance or I spent the rest of the year being picked apart. I settled on a token display, pushed out my chest, and stepped toward him. He took my move as real, and soon the two of us were rolling on the floor. The teacher hauled us up by the backs of our shirts and ordered us to the principal's office.

I made the mistake of going down the stairwell first. He kicked me in the small of my back, and I was falling. I reached out and was lucky enough to grab the railing. I stood there breathless, my heart racing. The steps were steel. The steel suggested broken bones, perhaps even a broken neck. I saw the danger, and I was only ten. He was at least two years older and should have known better. I looked up at him for an explanation, but none was forthcoming. He didn't even see me. He was scowling at his shoes. This indifference deepened my sense of danger. I held tight to the railing as he passed. I kept away from him for the rest of the way down, and for the rest of the year.

One day the principal appeared in class and called out three or four names, mine among them. "You have all been transferred to William Penn," he said. We were handed packets containing our records and dismissed. This was to be my third school in the space of a year.

I'd heard of William Penn the man. Chester was the first place he'd set foot in the colony after the King of England had granted it. Penn Street was named for him, as were the William Penn projects. Pennsylvania meant "Penn's Woods." I knew that I was living in his woods, but I had never heard of his school. So far as I knew, no one had. Those of us who'd been transferred were not alone in this. My uncle Bunny's wife, Margot, fresh from Cheyney State Teachers' College, had the same experience. At the end of her interview she was told that she'd be assigned to William Penn. She thought to herself, "Where is that?" She was the school's first black teacher.

＊　　＊　　＊

Getting ready for school was chaos, even under normal circumstances. Getting ready for William Penn was like preparing for an expedition. The school was more than a mile away, which meant that we had to pack lunches, thus adding one more step to an already strenuous routine.

I already had plenty to do. The coal-fired boiler that heated the house was a full-time job in itself. The fire often went out at night, which meant that I had to build a new fire that morning: chop wood, haul ashes, shovel coal. Then it was up from the basement to iron shirts, polish shoes, and make sandwiches. My mother was obsessive about personal hygiene. There was clean to meet the obsessive standard. Then there was clean to withstand the piercing scrutiny of white folks. Yvonne, two years older than me, had tired of housework and raising children. She balked at the drudgery. My mother railed and sometimes even slapped her around, but punishment grew less and less effective. Yvonne was slipping beyond my mother's authority. The extra work was falling to me. I brooded over this as I chopped wood and shoveled coal, and as I wrapped the peanut butter and jelly sandwiches and as I polished shoes and ironed shirts, and as I did hard time in the Laundromat, washing and folding clothes. Yvonne was doing more than brooding; she was planning her escape.

The walk to William Penn took us straight up Highland Avenue. There were no blacks once you passed 3rd Street. White men stepped down from their porches with lunch pails in hand. White women saw their children off to school. White crossing guards waved us across the streets.

At 9th Street I at last got a look at Resurrection, the Catholic school where Albert and his little brother began each day with something called catechism. One day three Resurrection girls in uniform came walking toward me on the sidewalk, singing in unison, their books clutched to their chests, their pleated skirts unfurling over their knees. They were singing "The Duke of Earl," which was just out that fall. I was well past them before I realized that they were singing "Spook" instead of "Duke": "Spook, spook, spook, of earl, spook, spook, spook of earl," in descending chords, to the tune of the song. This stung me, but there was nothing I could do; I couldn't hit girls. I entered Spook of Earl on Albert's side of the ledger. The Catholics were all the same: spiteful and mean.

William Penn was situated almost at the city limits, between 15th Street and Interstate 95, a long, low building, sleek and modern and lined with windows. The playground was enormous, with a small creek running through it. The school sat on the verge of a wild area that sprang up with a tall tawny grass. I was never wild about school. But this time I was elated. I had hit a jackpot.

The white students lived in the two housing developments that ran along opposite sides of upper Highland Avenue. McCaffery Village, on the western side, was a public housing project, and as such carried the stigma of poverty and second-class citizenship. It was clean and quiet as housing projects went, and this made it the most coveted housing project in the city. But these virtues were useless against the stigma. I had no right to look down on the people who lived there, but secretly I did.

Highland Gardens was brighter. The houses were also row houses, but they were white, with shutters. Their window boxes blazed with marigolds, violets, and geraniums. Their driveways showed a better grade of car. The mayor lived in the front row right on Highland Avenue itself, his windows overlooking the school. The Highland Garden kids were snottier and better dressed than the Village kids. The friendships among them were built on sports, Pop Warner football, Little League baseball, Biddy League Basketball.

The Gardens and the Village were alike in that they were for white people only. We knew instinctively not to detour as we came and went from school. Keep to Highland Avenue: the message was delivered to us on the air.

I had been transferred to William Penn because the school map had been revised. The new district spread down to the river tracks and took in three blocks east of Highland Avenue. That brought William Penn its first black students, but not many of them. There were a few kids from Lewis Street. The Wimbushes and the Hamiltons from Hayes Street, the Hudsons and the Wilsons from Wilson Street, but not many more.

The playground was a sea of white faces. The white kids held back at first, watching us. This phase passed quickly, and we were soon playing together as though we'd known each other forever. In my case there was one exception. The exception was George Kalodi. George took an instant dislike to me and put out word that he wanted a fight. I could see from his religious medal that he was Catholic; Polish or Ukrainian I couldn't tell. He was smaller than me, but that was no consolation. He was hunched and sullen, with a bit of the bulldog about him. The mask of freckles beneath his eyes only added to his menace.

Yvonne got word of George's intentions. She was thirteen, tall and rangy and strong, with bony fists. She landed blows that took your breath away. She blackened George's eye before he knew what had happened. Word went out that tough-guy George had been beaten up by a colored girl. That put an end to the threats against me. I even enjoyed a brief period of bullyhood, kicking the hell out of white boys who didn't hit back. I assumed that Yvonne's victory had placed me beyond all danger. In this I was mistaken.

School at William Penn was a whole new ball game. We read aloud in class from the *Weekly Reader* about John Glenn circling the globe. He advised us not to eat cookies in space; the crumbs floated around and made a nuisance of themselves. (There had been no *Weekly Reader* at Dewey–Mann.) William Penn was sleek and modern, and we were bathed in light all day. (Dewey–Mann was dark, ill-equipped, and old.) We could stay in when it rained and climb ropes or vault around the gym. (There had been no gym at Dewey–Mann.) When it was clear and bright outside, we ran all over the playground and jumped back and forth across the little creek. (At Dewey–Mann the playground extended into the streets.) At William Penn there was no need to fear meeting special-ed kids in the bathroom. As far as I could tell there were none. Anyway, every classroom had a boys' and girls' room attached to it, girls at one end, boys at the other.

The teachers set about getting me involved in the school's routine. The gym teacher drafted me into the safety patrol. The safety patrol was a big deal, a fraternal order of fifth- and sixth-grade boys on whom the safety of the student body depended. Each safety worked a corner either as auxiliary to a crossing guard or as a crossing guard himself.

The safety badges were shiny tin rectangles set on wide white straps that crisscrossed our chests from left to right. We were beacons of authority, empowered to break up fights and to report kids who broke the rules on the way to school. It pleased me no end that my corner was 9th Street. This put the kids from Resurrection under my control. I was rude and officious with them. I held them at the corner for a beat or two after the crossing guard had sounded the all clear. They couldn't ignore me because my authority stemmed from the crossing guards. They stopped at the corner when we said stop. They crossed when we said cross. *Spook of Earl*. I'd be their *Spook of Earl*, all right.

The post at 9th Street also meant I was close enough to go home for lunch. Invariably I found my mother still in her nightclothes. She lived in them now. Sometimes she was cross. Sometimes she was mute. After making my lunch she climbed the stairs and went back to bed. She was depressed, escaping into sleep. Blake's arrival had brought a short-lived peace between my father and her. Now the violence was back, as were the unpaid bills and, with them, collectors pounding at the door. My mother was learning how difficult it was to manage eight children by herself. On The Hill dozens of friends and neighbors had watched out for us. My mother had swept off on errands, confident that we'd be fine. In the Polish West End, she lived in terror of the trucks that rumbled by on 2nd Street. Before leaving on an errand, she herded us into the house and ordered us to stay there until she got back.

She missed her friends. Larry, Miss Betty, and Miss Vi rarely visited. We were too far west for them to reach us easily. Gene was a welcome sight when he came mincing out of the east. In the kitchen, he took my mother by the shoulders and sat her down. "Ginny girl," he said, as always, "I'm glad I got here when I did. This hair sho needs doin', chile. Chile, what chou talkin' about?" Gene livened us up. I hated to see him leave.

My father had become a series of sounds in the dark: the jingle of keys in the door lock; the *clump clump clump* of motorcycle boots up the stairs and down the hall to their bedroom; more jingling of keys and pocket change as he slipped out of his pants; the groan of the bedsprings as he lay down. There was one night when we were guaranteed a face-to-face encounter. That was report card night. My brothers and I went to bed early to be out of his way, hopeful that he'd let us sleep. Instead he hauled us from bed, sometimes at ungodly hours, and harangued us about our grades.

He was always drunk at the time. We stood in our underwear in the blinding light of the living room, asleep on our feet, as he thundered questions at us. "What about this 'C' in arithmetic!"

Then there was the teacher's written assessment, the dreaded, "not working up to potential," which they seemed to write on everybody's card, and against which there was no defense, even when you were awake. "What have I told you about all this!" He slapped and shook us, trying to wake us up. But the fog of sleep kept us from answering. By the time we woke up, we were back in bed.

It did no good to ask my father for money directly; he would only slink off to bed saying he'd think about it. The next morning was a grotesque version of Christmas: We woke up at dawn to listen to him leaving for work. Then we ran downstairs to see if our requests had been granted. There was no way of predicting. The money for the class trip or for the new pair of shoes was either there or it wasn't. When he came through, it was to the nickel and not a penny more. When he came through, the dollars and coins lay in the appointed spot (which changed with every house we lived in). When he didn't come through, the spot was heartbreakingly empty. The strategy then was to catch him in front of one of his brothers and shame him into it. "Go ahead, Melvin, give the boy the money," one of the uncles would say. And he would.

The surest way to get money was to steal it. This I began to do with regularity. My father, when we asked him for something, would say, "Christ, you all think I'm made of money!" In fact he was. His pockets bulged with the quarters he needed for tolls. He cultivated this stash of quarters, breaking bills whenever he could to get more of them. This habit got out of hand on Friday nights, when he got the drunkest. He came through the front door clinking and jinking like a sack of gold in a pirate movie.

I stole on Saturday mornings, when the drinking he had done would keep him sleeping soundly through the burglary, when the quarters that he had so manically collected were too sweet to resist. I crept into the bedroom, careful of the creaking floorboards, and went to the chair where his clothes lay in a heap. The pants could have fallen into the chair in any number of positions: bottom first; top first; heavy pockets perched on the edge of the cushion, ready to drop to the floor. I passed up the bills; they were too hard to get at. The chain on the wallet was noisy; the wallet itself was fastened with snaps that would make even more noise. Anyway, going after the bills would be stepping up from petty theft to grand larceny. That required more courage than I could muster.

I got down on my knees and snaked my hand into the pocket and down to where the quarters were. I stacked as many as I could between my thumb, middle and index fingers, then I drew the stack out slowly, carefully, applying just enough pressure to keep the quarters from slipping out of line. I transferred the stack to my other hand, and went in for seconds. Half-dollars could be used only at the base of the stack. If you inserted them into the middle, the stack could slip out of balance, even disintegrate, and fall noisily back into the cache. I sweated through this. Quarters hitting the floor would mean curtains for sure.

I left the room with the same caution that had brought me in: I stepped around the same creaking boards and hoped none of the little kids got up and bounded down the hall to jump into bed with my parents. Four or five dollars at a haul was common. My mother was a light sleeper, but I counted on her not to give me up. Though I was never caught, I suspected that, at least some of the time, my father lay there wide-awake, watching me steal from him. I especially thought this when he stopped snoring in the middle of my heist.

Then there was the way he brought up theft and lying out of the blue. "A thief and a liar are the two worst things in the world. Yes, sir, the first one is the thief, the second one is a liar. I can't stand either one of them." He said this as he leaned red-eyed into my face, reeking of booze. It was a mantra with him; I mouthed the words mentally as he spoke them. I couldn't tell if he knew I was stealing or if he was just playing a hunch. This didn't stop me. If he wanted to nab me, he'd have to wake up and catch me in the act.

I was a successful thief at school, too. My sixth-grade teacher volunteered me to sell milk and potato chips during the morning and afternoon breaks. The profits went toward our class trip, which that year was to New York City. When making change, I palmed a quarter at a time and slipped it deftly into my pocket. At first I stole just enough to pay for the milk and potato chips that I had no money to buy. Then I stole more, but just enough so that the shortfalls would look like honest mistakes. If caught, I was prepared to lie and cast suspicion on my fellow salesman. I enjoyed stealing for its solitary nature and because it was one of the few things I was good at. I was terrible at baseball, football, and gymnastics, but a regular whiz at pilfering.

My thefts left me flush at midweek, by which time my mother was broke. When she questioned me about my Coca-Colas and candy bars, I told her that I'd won the money on sporting bets at school. What a ludicrous lie. I knew nothing at all about sports. I had thus become the two things my father despised most: a thief and a liar.

‖ The Silver Surfer

Yvonne's blackening of George's eye put the white guys on notice. The notice never reached the black boys from Lewis Street; they lived on a different frequency. This came clear on the day of the ambush. I had fallen into step with a group of black girls who were walking my way. No amorousness intended; talking with them was just something to do for the long walk home. The group of boys that contained my assailant was walking a short distance ahead of us. We were abreast of The Village when it happened. All at once the boys stopped, knelt in a circle, and pretended to tie their shoes. As I stepped into the trap one of the boys jumped to his feet and shoved me heavily in the chest. Then he did it again, driving so hard that I nearly fell down.

"What?" I asked him over and over again. "What'd I do?" But the boy was mute; he bore down on me, pounding and pounding. His forehead had a strange convexity, like the forward end of a blimp. His eyes were slits on this blimp and menacing to look into. The girls stood by, grinning. Between shoves, he looked over at them and grinned back. One of the girls was this monster's girlfriend, but I had no way of knowing which one. I picked up a tree limb and waved it as convincingly as I could. The boy kept smiling, but he also kept his distance. I didn't know if I could actually brain him, but if he surged forward, we'd find out.

We stood frozen that way, not knowing how to end it. Then Bobby Hefner stepped out of the crowd. Bobby was one of the coolest guys in the sixth grade. He wore tight high-water jeans and cultivated a shiny pompadour through which he drew his comb in slow, measured strokes. His smile was not so much a smile as a smirk that had fixed itself to the corners of his mouth. There was an air of violence about him, but it was cool violence that wouldn't mess with you if you didn't mess with him.

Bobby came forward, reaching for the club. "Put that down," he said. "If you're gonna fight, fight fair." I didn't resist him. The Village was his turf; he had the right to break up the fight if he wanted to. He tossed the branch aside and clapped the rotten bark from his hands. Then he crossed the parking lot and disappeared into The Village. I was impressed. So was my assailant. The fight was over.

I made a friend of Bobby. He cooperated, but only in the coolest way, leaving most of the work to me. I visited his house for the first time on a Saturday. People in the village were accustomed to seeing blacks on weekdays, but only on Highland Avenue. I felt naked crossing The Village. Knots of boys fell silent as I passed them. Children came to their fences and stared. It set me on edge that every row of houses looked the same. There were no landmarks; you needed street signs to know where you were. The rows were claustrophobic, too close together. The staring, the tightness, and the sameness inspired a rising sense of panic. Bobby's next-door neighbor was hanging the laundry out to dry. She nearly swallowed her clothes pins when I stopped at the Hefners' door. I knocked. Bobby's mother looked through the glass, then disappeared briefly before opening the door.

She conducted a tactful interrogation. Where did I live? How many brothers and sisters did I have? Where did I meet Bobby? Then she retired to the kitchen and made us salami sandwiches.

Bobby had an older brother and a younger one. The younger one was a carbon copy of Bob, or at least tried to be. The older brother was almost a man, bigger than us by quite a bit, and cooler too. His clothes were James Dean clothes: tight jeans, with his thumbs hung in the front belt loops; a T-shirt with cigarettes rolled up in the sleeve. His hair was styled like cockatoo feathers, only black. The wry smile around his mouth was the same as Bobby's; clearly one of them had stolen it from the other. He looked at you with dreamy, half-closed eyes.

Bobby had only one toy, a cannon that fired shots the size of a softball. We blasted the bedroom wall until his mother suggested that we go outside. We made an expedition to the hill overlooking the school. The hill was covered with sweet grass; we broke off shafts and chewed them while we walked. At the top of the hill was a tree that had been nearly cloven in half by lightning. The lightning had carved a cavelike opening that Bobby said was home to a ghost and an owl. We took turns sitting inside the tree. Then, when we tired of that, we sat silently staring out at the school and The Village below.

I wanted closeness from Bobby. But what I got was silence. Not that I minded silence. In fact I sometimes preferred it. But Bobby's silences were different; I didn't know what they meant. He talked too sparingly for me to find out. I could never know him; very soon I gave up trying.

Hal Jordan was eminently knowable. Every fact about him was on record and discernible by me. Hal worked as a test pilot for Ferris Industries, a manufacturer of experimental aircraft. He flew the planes until the kinks were ironed out. His girlfriend, Carol Ferris, was the boss's daughter. Carol loved Hal, but she also harbored vague suspicions that he was hiding something. Indeed he was. When Hal wasn't testing planes, he was The Green Lantern, fighter of evil extraordinaire. The Green Lantern wore a mask that stayed put without an unsightly string. His uniform was a leotard with green body and black tights. His emerald ring emitted a green power beam that could take on any shape and function he wished it to. The beam could become a giant scoop to scoop up the bad guys, an enormous hammer to pound them into submission, an airtight bubble in which Hal flew to other planets.

The ring had to be recharged every twenty-four hours, usually before a mission. To charge the ring Hal touched it to the face of a lantern that he kept near his locker, in the airplane hangar. The hangar glowed with greenish light as Hal said the immortal words: "Through Brightest Day, and Blackest Night / No Evil Shall Escape My Sight / Let Those Who Worship Evil's Might / Beware My Power / Green Lantern's Light."

Hal was not your average playboy test pilot. He was earnest in a Boy Scout kind of way. He pondered weighty issues. Carol was naive. She should have seen in the first instant that The Green Lantern was actually her boyfriend Hal. The mask was scanty; it covered only his eyes and the area immediately around them, leaving his hair and his face exposed. But Carol couldn't see him. She couldn't see him even after he rescued her from villains and kissed her full on the mouth.

Hal was a martyr to his loneliness. He anguished over whether or not to tell Carol who he was but never told her. A hero's first duty was to his duty. Anything that might jeopardize that was out of the question. Hal talked to himself. On the way to battle he wondered if he'd survive. In the heat of the battle he wondered if there was enough power in his ring to get him through. I felt taken into his confidence. He spoke to my longing for flight and my wish for noble distinction.

Comic books were annotated. When a previous adventure was mentioned, the writer included a footnote and the relevant comic number so that the reader could catch up on pivotal moments in the hero's life. After reading a new comic, I went to the used-comic store and traded it for old ones. The store was run by a chain-smoking beatnik, whose graying hair was pulled back in a pony tail. The shop was quiet as a church, the books neatly stacked on a table in the center of the room. You could feel the beatnik watching. He was right to watch. Boys who loved comic books were potential thieves. He let you scan the issues, never pressuring you to buy. The deal was eminently fair, three old comics for one new one.

To enjoy a new comic book you had to read it when you were alone, and indoors, away from traffic noise and other distractions. The best place was the dining room table, which had to be cleared of objects that might detract from the book itself. First I fluttered the pages, breathing in the smell of fresh ink. Then I lay the book flat on the table and read it through, without stopping.

Thus was I reading the new Green Lantern when I felt a presence behind me. It was Bobby Hefner, spying and smiling that wry, derisive smile. I thought of Bobby as too cool for comic books and had never talked to him about them. I raised my hand in a motion for silence, and returned to the action. The story was coming to the usual dramatic conclusion, and there were only a few pages left. As I read, Bobby circled the room, staring down at me, then drifted into the living room. When I'd finished, he was gone. He wasn't in the living room, nor was he on the front porch. I trotted to the corner and looked up Highland Avenue. No Bobby; he'd disappeared.

Of all the lonely superheroes, The Silver Surfer gripped me most. He was bald and naked to his silver skin, and swept through the galaxy on a surfboard he controlled through telepathy. The comic's most perfect panels showed the seamless silver body swooping through the blackness of the board. No words; just the long view of The Surfer hurtling past stars and planets.

The Surfer looked free, but soon enough you learned that he wasn't. He worked for Galactus, the planet eater, and his job was to scout out the boss's next meal. The Surfer wasn't keen to do this, but he had no choice. He'd signed on to keep his own planet from being sucked dry, and was now stuck with the job.

This time The Surfer chose Earth. While waiting around for Galactus to show up, he developed sympathy for the human race and had a change of heart. He joined forces with Earth's heroes and sent the planet eater packing.

The Surfer was free of his endless shopping errand and could travel the heavens as he chose. But Galactus was not one to let betrayal go unpunished. He had placed a shield around the Earth to keep The Surfer imprisoned here. The Surfer tried to escape, but banged into the shield again and again. His was a wounded soul. The speck of dust called Earth was now his jail. I finished the book shaken and sad. The Surfer's sorrow had become my own.

Yvonne was slipping away. She stayed out later and later, then finally all night. She was thirteen. My mother raved and worried and strapped her. My father threatened juvenile detention. Policemen were brought in to intimidate her. But nothing worked. She stayed away for days at a time. My mother would get wind of where she was and send my uncle Bunny to fetch her. Bunny was the perfect runaway catcher: burly, strong, and quick. He chased her across rooftops, manhandled her into his car, and brought her home. Just in through the front door, Yvonne zipped out the back. Living with us seemed to suffocate her.

One morning, while we were getting ready for school, the back gate opened and Yvonne stepped through it into the yard. She'd been gone for two days. My mother was cooking breakfast. I was just across the kitchen watching Yvonne walk toward the door. She stepped into the kitchen, wary but still defiant. My mother surged forward and shook her until I thought her neck would snap. Then she threw her with such force that her head and elbows smashed through the wallboard.

Yvonne met my parents' anger with steeliness. When they interrogated her, she went dumb and stared into space. I knew this look; prisoners of war used it in the movies. "Do your worst," it said, "I will tell you nothing." This boldness was stunning to me.

My mother required me to be present and accounted for by dusk, when the streetlights came on, and I complied without fail. After dark I was allowed out on the front step but no farther unless I asked permission. "Mom," I yelled, "I'm going for a walk!" That meant a short jaunt west, toward the blazing torch over the refinery, or a quick turn through Lewis Street, where the steps teemed with big families, and Puerto Ricans spoke mile-a-minute Spanish. After a reasonable time had passed, I hurried back to my place on the step. "Mom, I'm back!"

I accepted my mother's word about the night. Girls got "in trouble" and were made into "sluts." Boys got into fights, got arrested, and lost their grace and goodness. This view of the night counted for nothing with Yvonne. She roamed as she pleased.

I began to shadow her. Yvonne lied casually and with great skill. But I was a skillful listener, determined to break the code. I broke it suddenly, after months of listening and watching. The lie had a strained lightness, a cotton-candy quality. I stood by, hearing as Yvonne told my mother she was going to a dance at William Penn. It was raining cats and dogs. That was a long way to walk in the rain. I gave her a decent head start, then hotfooted it to William Penn. I was soaked through by the time I got there. I circled the building in the dark, peered in through the windows. Of course there was no dance. The gym was dark, the school as quiet as a tomb.

I could have snitched that night, but I didn't. I came home drenched to the bone, slipped upstairs and changed into dry clothes. My mother was unaware of my spying, and I wanted to keep it that way. The bill of particulars was mine, to be delivered when the time was right. I didn't know when that would be, but I was keeping my eyes open.

I loved Yvonne—and resented her. My brothers and sisters and I stood in concentric circles around my father. The boys were in the outermost orbit, beyond reach of affection. The girls were the inner circle, to be doted on and bounced on his knee. Yvonne was innermost of all. He didn't just dote on her; he bought her things. He showered her with dresses and patent-leather shoes when the rest of us were threadbare. He kept it up even when bills went unpaid and we were on the verge of eviction. Yvonne had usurped my place. She traveled to Virginia with my father and uncles while I was made to remain at home. I was the eldest son, for God's sake. How could my father not take me?

The trips to Virginia began with the two of them getting up before dawn. In bed I listened to them bathing and scuttling around. Later I would find the two of them in the living room waiting for one of my uncles to pick them up. My father would have shed his musty truck-driver's clothes and become the self that we were seeing less and less of: His face was smooth and shaven; the air around him sang with Old Spice cologne. His dress shoes would be polished and shining. He'd have on his pleated gabardine trousers. On the chair beside him would be his Stetson hat, blocked in a gangsterish way. The sight of him all duded up was jarring. He rarely put on fancy clothes anymore. For Yvonne he broke out his long-lost finest.

My sister lay napping on the couch, done up as though this were Easter. To avoid mussing her freshly done hair, she rested her head carefully, using her forearm as a platform. Invariably she wore a flouncy new dress and new shoes, the soles of which were perfectly clean. One dress in particular is burned into memory: It was flouncier than usual, with flowers. It was short in a little-girlish way, too short for those very long legs. She looked like a woman posing as a child.

I watched them as they waited. This was supposed to be me. I was the one who should represent the household on these trips, wearing a suit and a hat, just like my father's. The car horn sounded out front, and they were gone.

Warmth was rare in my father. Yvonne was using it up. But the more he gave her, the more she fled his company. She ran away and ran away and ran away.

Finally she was missing for days that stretched into weeks and then into months. My mother was crazed with worry. By day she stumbled around the house looking dazed and beaten up. By night she paced the floors, jumping at slamming car doors and at voices passing on the sidewalk. My mother was afraid that Yvonne was dead. The car doors and the voices could well be the police bringing the news.

My mother was setting my teeth on edge. What bothered me most was the lack of precision in her speech. She should have said: "Brent, the kitchen floor is filthy, go scrub it." Instead, she said: "Brent, run the mop over the floor, won't you, please?" As though gliding across the room were all there was to it. The toughest chores she tried to sweeten by calling them "little." As in "Brent, build me a little fire to throw the chill off the house." There was no such thing as a "little" fire. Every fire required the same effort: Wad up newspapers. Chop kindling. Chop firewood. Shovel coal. Haul ashes. Come up from the basement stinking of smoke. To describe the job as "little" devalued my suffering.

My anger reached zenith one morning when we were getting ready for school. My mother was cooking breakfast. As I tried to slip out the door, she said: "Brent, put a little polish around the toe of your brother's shoe." I did just that: dipped the applicator into the bottle and dabbed one dot of polish on each shoe, leaving the rest as scuffed and dirty as before. This was a mistake. Yvonne's disappearance had left my mother another person. But I couldn't stop myself. I'd waited a long time for the right moment to make my point. My mother snapped angrily at me. In a mocking tone, I reminded her that she had said "a little polish around the toe." Then she hefted the serving platter and smashed it across my forehead. Fried eggs and bacon and broken glass rained onto the kitchen floor, the eggs going *blap, blap, blap* as they landed.

I rushed to the bathroom to survey the damage. There wasn't much; the platter had shattered cleanly. The splinters of white glass were easily seen in the lump that had risen on my forehead. I left for school thinking that Yvonne had the right idea. Maybe I should run away, too. But to where?

Florida. In Florida I could sleep out under orange trees, live on oranges and never have to work. I ran away on a Saturday morning in the dead of winter in the snow. My father had accused me of stealing a wad of bills that he had clearly misplaced while drunk and couldn't find when he was sober again. I was indeed a thief but had kept to the policy of stealing coins only, a few dollars at a time. I refused to accept punishment for a theft I didn't commit. I told my brothers and sisters I was running away and headed for the door.

There were three identical parkas—mine, Brian's, and Bruce's—hanging on coat hooks by the door. I grabbed Brian's by mistake. The coat was too small even to be zipped up. But there was no turning back; I pressed on into the snow wearing an open parka, my wrists and butt exposed to the elements. I ran west to the junk-yard and hid out near the railroad siding. The plan was simple: Hop the first train that moved and go wherever it goes, preferably to Florida. But the train didn't move. The snow thickened, the temper-ature dropped, my hands and wrists began to freeze, and still it didn't move. I decided to walk along the tracks to keep warm until it did. I walked three blocks west past Highland Avenue to Wilson Street. Then I stopped into Dickie Hudson's house to get warm.

Dickie shot me the look of recognition. "We know," he said. "They've already been here. You're running away?" I explained my predicament at home and my trouble with the parka. In the warmth, my feet thawed out and started to hurt. That ended it. I couldn't ride a boxcar to Florida with freezing hands and feet. I'd have to call it quits. But next time I'd take the right coat and my boots as well.

I walked home and put Brian's parka on its hook next to the other two. My mother was in the kitchen cooking. She didn't say a word. Later my father came home and was silent on the subject too. I'd scared them, and I was glad.

I was standing in the third-floor bathroom, drawing a bath and get-ting undressed, when I heard what sounded like a scream. I turned off the water, listened and heard nothing, then turned it on again.

What happened next was not so much a sound as a spasm that shot through the house, followed by running on the floors below me. I pulled on my shirt and trotted down to the second floor. There blocking the way was Elaine, a friend of the family who lived at 2nd and Lewis. "You can't go down there. Your mother said for all the children to go into her room and stay there." Elaine explained that Christi had set herself afire in the kitchen. I realized then that the scream had been real, that the scream was my four-year-old sister burning.

We huddled in our parents' room. The ambulance siren came closer and louder, then stopped in front of the house. I stuck my head out of the window just as Christi, eyes closed, lying on a stretcher, was hoisted into the ambulance. She looked dead.

But Christi wasn't dead. Her life had been saved, though just barely. She was badly burned over two-thirds of her body. My mother said that her chances were fifty-fifty, and that the doctors had given it up to God. Christi rallied. She lived in the hospital for nearly a year and had a dozen skin grafts.

I was the family's designated visitor. There was one problem with this: The hospital had signs aplenty saying that visitors had to be at least sixteen years old. I was eleven, big for my age, but still clearly a child. The fear that I'd be turned away seized me each time I entered the building. The hallway leading to the children's ward was the most treacherous. There was the nurses' station, and blaring from its window another sign that said: VISITORS MUST BE 16 YEARS OF AGE. I averted my face and veered to the far side of the hall. I turned up regularly for several weeks, well scrubbed and well behaved. The nurses murmured among themselves about what a good boy I was. I was home free.

Christi was wrapped in gauze, around and around the torso, around and around each leg, like a mummy. Blood seeped through the bandages where the burns were deep. A domed frame was placed over her bed to keep the sheets from touching her.

Eventually she was allowed to sit up. I would arrive to find her in the white gauze suit, in a child's rocking chair, beaming away as I came through the door. I had gotten used to the mummy suit, when they took it off. Exposing the wounds to the air, they said, to promote healing. Her body was raw from the breast to below the knee. The flesh was wet and bloody; I fancied that I could see the blood circulating beneath what had been her skin. The room wobbled a bit, but I kept smiling and tried to be natural. I walked in a wide circle around her, afraid that I might touch the wounds by accident. I got past this because Christi kept smiling.

In time I grew used to the sight of flesh without skin. The dozen skin grafts seemed to pain me more than they did her.

At eleven years old, I wasn't exactly brimming with conversation. To fill up the time, I rolled her wheelchair up and down the halls. We met other patients and spent time with them.

Christi's injuries were the worst on the ward. Next to burns everything else was easy to look at. I was especially interested in the boy with the steel rods jutting out of his leg. He'd been hit by a car, and the bone was shattered. He didn't talk much, but the rods in his leg were fascinating. The skin clung to them like icing to candles on a cake.

The children's ward was sparsely visited on weekdays. I cruised the room, cooing at toddlers and making jokes with frightened newcomers. On weekends the ward filled up with parents, highlighting the fact that my own parents were elsewhere. When real parents visited, I felt like a fraud, inadequate to the task. I clung to Christi's bedside and didn't stray. Often I wished that the scene at Christi's bed was like the scene around the other beds: fathers, mothers, relatives. But mainly there was just me.

I was having the wish when my father came reeling into the ward, drunk. The ward had a television set. My father changed the channel from some innocuous program to a horse race. Then he was down on his knees, beating his leg with his cap, shrieking for his horse to win. The children laughed, but their parents looked on in anger. I was mortified. I hid in the bathroom until my father left the hospital.

Debt was mounting in a familiar pattern. We pushed credit to the limit with one store, then abandoned the bills and moved on to the next one. Tommy Rzucidlo was first up for the treatment. I shopped with cash to soften him up and then began taking things on account. Tommy kept his accounts in a thick composition tablet, its pages butterflied from constant use. I read off my list: "A dozen eggs, two pounds of kielbasa, potatoes, flour, rice, a sack of coal," then reached for a Hershey bar to finish off the deal. Tommy smiled knowingly, and entered the total beneath our name. He kept his peace about the Hershey bar. It was an incentive to shop with him. The Polish and Ukrainian boys took it, too.

When credit at Tommy's was exhausted, I moved to another store directly across 2nd Street. There was nothing subtle in this. Tommy looked on from his window as my purchases were entered in his rival's book. When the second guy had been suckered to the limit, I moved a block east to Lewis Street and the store owned by Tommy's brother, Stanley. Stanley was onto us. Him we paid in cash.

One night a black girl dressed in only a slip came dashing along 2nd Street from the direction of Lewis Street. The girl was barefoot and running for her life. When she passed beneath a streetlight, we could see that it was someone we knew. She was pregnant. She'd hidden it well, but her mother had caught on and beaten her from the house with a stick. My mother knew a Christian test when she saw one. She bundled the girl into our house and comforted her. It was understood that she would live with us until the baby was born, even afterward if necessary. The baby would be born elsewhere than in the Polish West End. We were being evicted.

The man who served the notice wore an overcoat and an ordinary business suit. He was a portly man, with a face that was surprisingly kind. I peeked out from behind the curtains, watching him. He knocked and waited, then knocked again. Then he unfurled the writ and nailed it to the wall. When the coast was clear I went out to read it. Get out, it said, or prepare to be thrown out.

‖ Andy's Musical Bar

We bounced east out of the Polish West End and landed two doors from Andy's Musical Bar. At night the bar's neon sign bathed the building's upper windows in a pinkish glow. The words MERRY GO ROUND were spelled out in neon above a neon treble clef. Down the sides of the clef and beneath it were musical notes and the rest of the name, ANDY'S MUSICAL BAR. The sign had seen better days. Some of the notes didn't light up and others flickered and hissed. The whole sign sizzled dangerously when it rained; I avoided walking under it, for fear of being electrocuted.

I had passed Andy's many times in the past—on the way to and from the Dewey–Mann School, on the way up to The Hill, and running errands for my mother. One night while passing I'd heard polka music and an accordion. I pressed my nose to the glass brick for a look. Through the blur I saw white men drinking, raising their glasses in a toast. There was indeed an accordion. The man who played it sat on a stool, swaying, squeezing the bellows, and fingering the keys.

Things had changed by the time we moved in. The city had grown steadily more black, steadily less white. The Poles and

Ukrainians were yielding their bars and corner stores one by one. Andy's was a black bar now.

A block west at Ward Street were two establishments that the Poles and Ukrainians had not given up, the Ward Grille and St. Mary's Ukrainian Orthodox Church. The bar they would later part with, but St. Mary's never. The Ukrainians who had left town drove into the neighborhood on Sundays and double-parked in the streets around St. Mary's stone and wrought-iron fence. The grounds were beautiful and well kept. The space between the church and the rectory contained rose trellises and a garden. After services the parishioners walked to their cars and drove back to where they'd come from.

There was no longer any need to peer through glass brick to spy on Andy's patrons. The bar's three entrances—one main entrance and two "Ladies" entrances—were flung wide open during the summer. No more polka music. Ray Charles, Sam Cooke, and Brook Benton spilled out onto 3rd Street. Those Why-You-Done-Left-Me songs, with teary violins, struck me as dreary and old-fashioned.

The Beatles were more my speed. In the bathrooms at school, we huddled over transistor radios and went nuts for "I Wanna Hold Your Hand." Especially nuts when the Beatles screamed "OOOOOOOOOOOOOOOOOOO!" When I wasn't listening to the Beatles, I listened to WDAS, the soul station in Philadelphia, and learned the new songs as soon as I could. The jukebox at Andy's was a dull child that rarely learned anything new. It sang the same tunes over and over again, especially Ray Charles, moaning "I can't stop lovin' you, it's useless to say."

It disturbed me that I remembered the bar but not the house we were moving into. I should have remembered the house: Aside from the building that housed Andy's, it was the biggest thing on the block, a pale stucco ship whose prow jutted out from the rest. It was a storefront building with big plate-glass windows and an enormous front room that had housed a dry cleaner. I remembered no such building and no dry cleaner. I prided myself on cataloging even minor landmarks as I crossed town. But this one I'd somehow missed. I stood in the vacant living room looking out. I'd walked past these windows many times and been seen by people whom I'd never even glimpsed. I felt tricked and outdone.

Andy's was the center of the universe. Daily at about noon, the regulars slouched in to begin drinking. When the bar came to life, I joined the other boys who hovered on the steps, watching the drama within. We preferred the ladies' entrance on 3rd Street because it was shaded from the sun. The eavesdropping was best when it was very hot. That's when the patrons sat near the door to take advantage of the breeze.

Some regulars paid as they drank. Some ran tabs that were paid with welfare checks. Some ran tabs and were tardy about paying, so that the bartender refused to serve them. Love affairs waxed and waned. There were arguments, fights, and stabbings.

My mother worried about my safety and hounded me about spending so much time on Andy's step. But what else was there to do? The only other attraction was the abandoned brewery on 2nd Street. The building was many floors high, and all its windows were broken. Beyond the windows was only blackness, no matter what the time of day. A remnant of the company flag flew filthy and tattered over the street. An enormous colony of rats frolicked in the courtyard. Rotting stairwells led up and up to death by falling, or so it seemed to me. The brewery gave me the creeps. Andy's steps were safer by far.

The bartender was called Hump. He was a broad bull of a man in oversized shirts that made him look wider still. The bar was laid out in a rectangle, at whose center was a glistening tower of bottles. Hump moved heavily as he prowled the moat pouring drinks for his customers. His face showed profound boredom. Blood-houndish folds in the forehead; sad, sagging eyes: the expression never changed. Not even when he was stabbed.

It was Saturday, a big bar day. I heard the crowd from my living room and ran to see what had happened. At the center of the crowd were three people locked in a dance. Hump was staggering around, bleeding heavily from the back. Facing him was a taller, younger man, his head wrapped in a kerchief, his eyes wide with fear. Behind that man was the woman who'd put the knife in Hump's back. Hump staggered this way and that trying to get at her, but each time the younger man countered him. The woman taunted as she dodged around behind her protector. She was wild-eyed and rabid, pleased with her handiwork. Hump's shirt was a brilliant white. Down its back was a violent waterfall painted in blood. Hump shifted and staggered to one side; the man moved to block him; the woman yapped and yapped. They danced that way for a long time. Finally, Hump was coaxed into the ambulance and taken away. He was soon back at the bar. The knife had gotten only muscle.

Jimmy Burton was not so lucky. Jimmy was a handsome brown-skinned man who wore loud bowling shirts and looked to be in his early twenties. A hank of pomaded hair hung into his forehead like a cluster of grapes. He created a commotion among us when he screamed out of the east in his Mustang, turned a doughnut in the intersection, and parked facing east again—on the wrong side of the street. He was stabbed to death in an argument over a pool game. Jimmy lost the game and accused the victor of cheating. Jimmy was beating the man with his pool cue, more or less for amusement, when the man turned and put a knife through him. I was there when Jimmy's father, Johnny, screamed his car around the intersection just as Jimmy had earlier that day. Jimmy was a carbon copy of him —same shirts, same style, same strong arms and ropey veins. Johnny Burton walked through the crowd and into the bar, his arms hanging uselessly at his sides. You could see that he wanted to pull the place down. He was too late. Jimmy's body had been taken away.

The man who had done the killing was small and monkish. His jail term was brief and before long he was back on his stool at Andy's. I'd been raised not to stare but couldn't help myself. I searched his face to see if killing had changed him.

Yvonne was still missing and unheard from. I was first assistant mother. My mother took the infant with her wherever she went and left the rest at home. Yvette had replaced Blake as the baby, which meant that Blake stayed with me when my mother left the house. On those days I stayed put on our front step. My mother would have strangled me if she'd caught me with Blake at Andy's doorway.

Blake got ear infections. When they struck, it was my job to take him in for treatment. The nearest doctor was in the Polish West End. We owed him money. When the money got to be too much, we went instead to Triboletti, the pharmacist. Triboletti understood our situation; it was the same as everyone else's. We had a sick child; we had money for either medicine or diagnosis but not both.

Triboletti was a generous man and also a ham. Before examining Blake, he made a big point of telling me what was at risk. Yes, I said, I knew it was illegal. A pharmacist could lose his license for dispensing medicine without a prescription. Meanwhile, Blake tilted his head to one side, as though trying to pour out the pain. His big eyes were mournful and sad. Triboletti looked up and down the aisles to make sure the coast was clear. Then he stooped down, looked into Blake's ears and remarked at how bad they looked. He then went to his shelves and came back with the antibiotic. I thanked him, paid him (when I could), and walked Blake back home.

We had barely gotten settled when I recognized a face in a doorway across the street. It was Milton, the boy who had tried to kick me down the stairs during my brief stay at Dewey–Mann. He had grown a lot, but his face was unmistakable. He had the same downward-looking frown, the same brooding disagreement with his shoes.

His name was no longer Milton. Now they called him Goon. The name fit: It fit his gloomy disposition. It fit his broad shoulders and overly long arms. The air of danger about him was thick. I was courteous when we met, but preferred that we didn't. I gave him a wide berth, which wasn't easy, given that he lived just across the street. Soon enough I had an argument with his older sister. A girl knocked at the door and told me that a fight had been arranged between Goon and me. Goon had been asked, and he'd accepted. All that remained was for me to come outside. I hid in the house two or three days. Afterward I came and went through the back door, avoiding 3rd Street as much as I could.

A few summers later Milton fulfilled the grim promise I'd seen in him. He emerged from his house with a rifle and shot a boy with whom he'd had a disagreement. I saw the victim many times afterward. One of his arms was mangled and there was an ugly scar on his neck. That he was handsome, verging on pretty, made these wounds seem especially cruel.

Next door to Milton lived the Butcher family. Mr. and Mrs. Butcher were said to have had twelve children, but the children never stayed put long enough for me to count them. The Butchers were a family of extremes. For one thing, they moved more rapidly than we did. They had three different addresses during the time we had only one. I watched from my front step as they migrated out of a side street into a storefront on 3rd Street. I watched again as they shifted several doors west, to the house next door to Milton's. The houses they left showed the imprint of a large, hard-living family.

Mrs. Butcher was squat, with legs that were spindly and bowed. Her stomach was potted, as though she were permanently pregnant. The oldest of her children was tall, as tall as my father, and well built. But the children grew smaller as they went down the line; boys who had nearly reached full height were dwarfed by their older brothers. The last boy was frighteningly small. By then Mrs. Butcher had run out of pigment, too. The youngest girl had spots on her hands that were spreading and turning her white as snow.

Now and again Mr. Butcher asked me to take custody of his liquor to prevent his sons from downing it. He carved a notch in the label to mark how much liquor was left and made sure that I knew that he knew where the notch was. He didn't have to worry; liquor tasted hellish to me. My father's drunkenness had scared me; I'd sworn off liquor for life. But I sympathized with Mr. Butcher. We were both wedged into big families, and we both lacked places to keep our private things. I buried the bottle in one of my safest spots: in the basement under the kitchen, where the concrete foundation gave way to dirt.

I was sitting on my step one day when Mrs. Butcher and her daughter Marie came boiling out of the house, screaming and cursing. On the street they screamed and cursed some more, nose to nose. Then Marie slapped her mother's face and lit out down the street. Mrs. Butcher withdrew indoors for a minute and came back out. Walking in Marie's direction, she lifted her blouse, produced a meat cleaver from her skirt and threw it. The cleaver fell far short of the mark. The blade struck sparks as it skittered across the sidewalk. The sparks were bright as stars, one, two, three. Marie stood at a distance, laughing. Mrs. Butcher left the cleaver where it lay and stalked across the street to the bar.

On another day Mrs. Butcher walked out of her house in a silver-sequined skirt that would have been perfect for night but was blinding in the summer sun. The skirt would have been visible for blocks; drivers would see the sparkle long before they knew what it was. The skirt lit up the street as she made her way to the bar.

Leonard Butcher was in his twenties and still living at home. He was tall and slumped at the shoulders. His neck had a vulturous curve and an Adam's apple that went up and down when he talked. Marie was prone to trouble. I was hanging out in the pinball parlor when the next thing happened. Cephus Richardson was trying to play pool while Marie hovered behind him, tugging at the butt of his cue. She kept this up until Cephus slapped her. A few minutes later, Leonard stormed into the parlor, slapped Cephus around, then marched him outside hoping to give him a proper beating. But Cephus was a sprinter. As he passed through the doorway, he grasped both sides of the frame, leaned back to throw Leonard off-balance, then launched himself into the street. Leonard gave chase, but it was hopeless. Cephus was long gone toward home.

Not long afterward, Leonard was ambushed in the bathroom at Andy's and beaten so savagely that he lost an eye. My father said that Leonard's attackers had thrown a coat over his head before beating him. Leonard donned a black patch to cover the dead eye, thus burnishing his image as a bad guy.

Leonard's younger brother, William, was still in his teens. William's moonish face was ravaged by pimples, and his teeth were a mossy green. He was prime courting age, but poor hygiene kept him out of the action. The guys on the block called William's pimples "pussy bumps," and said that William was bumpy because he wasn't getting any. This abuse had left its mark. When he smiled he pursed his lips to hide the green of his teeth. William couldn't look you in the eye. When you called his name, he winced, as though expecting insult or injury. He covered his shame with swagger and drunkenness.

William became more popular after he was shot. He was trying to steal a car, or some part of a car, when he heard a voice say, "Halt," and took off, running. Then he heard the shots. The shotgun blast hit him in the shoulder. He knew he'd been hit when he looked out and saw his arm flying around like a rag doll's. He came home in a cast that covered much of his upper body. The cast had a strut built out from the rib cage to support the damaged arm and shoulder. Blood seeped out of the wound and stained the plaster. The smell was dank and scary. That summer was very hot; William's cast made him sweat and itch. He scratched beneath the cast with a straightened clothes hanger that he carried for this purpose. I worried that he would catch the hanger in his wound. We gathered around him as he told and retold the story of how he'd been shot. He enjoyed the telling and burnished the details. The bloody cast was his badge of honor.

Yvonne had left us as a spindly young girl, her hair pulled back in a ponytail. She was was gone for nearly a year and came back a brown-skinned version of Marilyn Monroe. My uncle Johnny's Lincoln Continental rolled up in to the door and a person I hardly recognized stepped out of the back seat. She was heavily made up. And no more ponytail. Her hair was fashionably styled, up and away from her face in curls. She was wearing a sleek black dress and clutching an evening purse. Already tall, she towered above us in high heels. The youngest children didn't know who she was. The feeling was mutual. Yvonne stared at them, trying to catch up with who they were.

Yvonne had been working as a waitress in Delaware when Uncle Johnny caught sight of her. I did not question her about where she'd been. A silent understanding put the subject off-limits. I knew the day she returned that there'd be trouble. There was an edge of jealousy in this prediction, but it was honest at its heart. Yvonne could never fit in among us again. Piling into bed with her sisters. Going without makeup. Going to school.

My father resumed his doting. One morning I came downstairs early to find Yvonne and him dressed up and sitting in the living room. They were waiting for one of my uncles to drive them to my father's family reunion in Virginia. Just as always, I was not invited.

Yvonne took custody of the enormous front room that had housed the dry-cleaning store. The room became a cabaret where her friends talked cryptically of sex and drinking and danced the evenings away. I'd arrived in the neighborhood knowing only Milton. Yvonne knew everyone, even Hump. The living room was jammed full of teenagers. They tolerated me, and for this I was grateful. I didn't have to compete with them as I did with the kids my own age. Hit songs blared out from the record player. My sister's friends danced nasty dances, the nastiest of which was the Philly Dog, so named for its resemblance to two dogs screwing: the boy pressed his crotch against the girl's behind; the two locked hands and rowed and bumped and ground to the music. My mother winced when she saw this but tried to pretend that it didn't offend her.

I liked Yvonne's music, but she didn't much care for mine. The Beatles didn't reach her. "She Loves You." "I Wanna Hold Your Hand." When these songs came on, I turned up the radio and danced around the room. When the Beatles screamed, my eyes rolled back in my head. Yvonne screwed up her face and asked me what was the matter. The matter was that the Beatles were electric. "Just listen!" I said. "Can't you hear it? Can't you hear it?" Yvonne couldn't hear it; she couldn't understand how anybody could. I kept my hand on the dial to keep her from changing the station.

The woman who stabbed Hump was a regular at Andy's bar. The guy who kept Hump from breaking her neck was Davy Robinson. Davy was the coolest of my sister's friends. He was at least twenty but worked only sporadically and lived in his mother's apartment above Andy's. He wore his hair in a process, as all the cool guys did. A process involved the beautician using a lyelike chemical to make your hair patent-leather straight. When the process was fresh, the hairdresser pressed in finger waves. The waves could be dizzying. When the process got old, it became tufty and hackled with new growth. Davy kept his process covered in a bandana that was knotted at the forehead. The bandana protected the process when it was new and hid it when it needed repair.

Davy was cool in every aspect. He wore Cuban heels. He stood with his left arm stiff at his side, its palm cupped and turned upward. The right hand provided cool gestures to go with his speech and came often to rest in his crotch. Davy walked with the stiff arm still stiff but with the other arm moving briskly back and forth, as though rowing him down the street. He hopped up a bit on one leg and dipped down on the other as he walked. The stroll was something to see when several cool guys walked by at once. Each strolled with his own set of flourishes, and each one's flourishes complemented the others. They dipped and rolled and glided down 3rd Street in musical motion. Strolling felt good to them, so good they could hardly stand it.

Davy and his boys sang the neighborhood to sleep with doo-wop songs. They sang Johnny Mathis's "Wonderful, Wonderful," or "There's a Moon Out Tonight" by the Capris, and kept time by snapping their fingers. The singing was best on Sunday nights. Pennsylvania was a blue-law state; bars and liquor stores were closed. This meant that there was no music blaring out of Andy's, no traffic, nothing to interfere with the sweet, high harmonies. No one called the police; the songs were too good for that. Davy's boys sang best on Sundays because they sang with their hearts. They sang to get through the dead boredom of a blue-law Sunday, and back into Monday when the bars and liquor stores opened again. They drank Thunderbird, two dollars a bottle. Come Monday, Thunderbird would flow.

During the election season Davy worked moving voting machines with my father. The pay was good, but such elections came only once every four years. Meanwhile Davy and the cool guys were truant from life. They slept till noon, fussed with the waves in their hair, then resumed the search for sex and Thunderbird.

My mother adopted Davy. He already had a mother, but now he had two. He had free rein of our house, even refrigerator privileges. It was O.K. if he made himself a sandwich of scrapple and egg on toast. He looked funny at the stove. The way he held the spatula changed him: the bandana knotted at the forehead looked like Aunt Jemima's then, and the high Cuban heels made his butt stick out in an almost feminine way. He flipped his eggs with the one cool arm stiff at his side: cool to the last detail. We clamored at his side while he cooked. We wanted to be around him, even when he was doing so humdrum a thing as flipping scrapple and eggs.

Davy taught me about sex. He explained in detail how you broke in a virgin. There was a barrier over the pussy that had to be pierced before you could slip it in. You had to be firm but careful. "You cut the nails on these two fingers so you won't hurt her," he said. Davy held up his right hand to show me the index and middle fingers. The nails were trimmed almost to nothing. Davy said he had just broken in a girl down the street. You pushed in the middle finger until you broke through the barrier. Then you worked the finger in and out until there was room for the index finger, too. You couldn't slip her the dick right then because she'd be sore. You came back later when the soreness was gone.

Davy pointed out the girl he'd just broken in. He told me he'd done it in her living room, while her family was out in the kitchen eating. It had to be done, he said. It was time: She wanted it; he wanted it. I took note of the girl. She was trim, athletic, and beautiful. She must have liked what Davy did. She draped herself over him whenever he came within reach.

The boys who lived around Andy's went to General Casimir Pulaski Junior High. But the same building did not mean the same school. Guys from my block I rarely even passed in the hallways. I had come to Pulaski from William Penn. They had come from Dewey–Mann. The William Penn halo had earned me admission to the academic sections. In the academic sections we studied Latin, French, or Spanish. Even the least of us were put through the rigors of algebra I and II. General Casimir Pulaski's name spelled out a student's worth, rank, and serial number: 7-P (Latin), 7-U (French), 7-L (Spanish). As an L, I had grasped the last rung of the favored. Below me lay the netherworld of A, S, K, and I. The boys down there were those of whom nothing was expected. They knew nothing was expected of them and so they gave nothing. Many of them were waiting to turn sixteen so that they could legally drop out.

The tracking system at school made it difficult for me to become part of the neighborhood. These boys were tougher than either the boys in the West End or the boys on The Hill. There was much more drinking among them, much more snarling and posing, many more fights, and a good bit of stealing. I stood out because I was new and because I was tall. I was an easy mark, for tough guys my age, and for younger ones seeking easy reputations.

*   *   *

Davy tried in vain to teach me to fight. He did this out of loyalty to Yvonne and out of pity at seeing me shoved around. I sparred well with him, but sparring wasn't fighting. There was one boy in particular who liked to hold a knife on me while he shoved me around. I caught him without his knife once, grabbed a handful of his hair, and pulled him to the ground. I was bigger and stronger. I could easily have broken a bone, except that I lacked the animus. My anger drained away as I held him down. I let him up without punching him even once. As he walked away he said: "That's the difference between us. You got some bitch in you, I don't." By "bitch" he meant that I lacked the courage to do serious bodily harm. He was right about that. Davy stood by, shaking his head.

My father found out that I was being shoved around. He walked into the living room one Saturday afternoon and found me in front of the television set.

"Come with me," he said.

"Where?"

"Just get up and come with me."

He stormed out of the house and headed toward the crowd of boys at the far corner. I thought: My God! He's going to make me fight this guy right in front of him. That wasn't what he had in mind. He walked full steam into the crowd, forcing the boys into a circle. Then he prowled the circle, threatening them.

"I understand that my son has been having trouble," he said, "I want it to stop. Tell whoever has been bothering him to stop. No one is to mess with him again. If there are any questions about what I mean, if anybody wants to try me, I carry my weight in my pocket. Is that understood?" Then he thrust his hand down in his pocket. Eyes widened all around.

Bursting with courage, I launched into a speech of my own.

"And you can tell . . ."

"Shut up," my father said.

"But . . ."

"Shut up," he said. "Let's go."

He was silent on the way back, just as he'd been on the way down.

The next day one of the boys who'd caught my father's act came up to me, still in amazement. "Man! Your old man was mad. He's gonna shoot the guy! We thought he was gonna pull out his gun right there!"

That ended my trouble in the neighborhood. I should have felt good about my father standing up for me. I didn't. I understood that it had nothing to do with me, that it had to do with the family name. The Staples boys were not to be fucked with. If you fucked with them, it was an insult to the old man. The old man wasn't going to stand for that.

I was nostalgic for the Polish West End and had developed warmth for the place that had no basis in the way I'd been treated there. I visited the used-comic store to pick up back issues I'd missed. While touring my old haunts I walked into Tommy Rzucidlo's store and chatted with him while he waited on his customers. I talked, he listened, wiping his hands on his crisp white apron as he moved back and forth from the slicer to the meat case. Tommy was cool and distant. This disturbed me because I imagined us as chums.

When the last customer was gone, Tommy asked about the money that my family had moved away owing him. I remembered the composition book under the counter, all the kielbasa, potatoes, sacks of coal that we'd taken and never paid for, all the candy bars I'd tacked on for myself. Tommy knew he had me. He settled into his priestly look. "Ask your mother to come back and settle the bill, won't you." He asked this calmly, with no hint of recrimination. I said I would and excused myself from the store. My face was hot with shame. How could I have forgotten the debt? From then on I stayed clear of Tommy.

My mother occasionally ran the kitchen at Andy's. I shopped for her, and delivered the groceries to the bar. She forbade me to enter the bar through the front door, as though walking through it would put me in spiritual jeopardy. Spiritual jeopardy was much on her mind. So was salvation of the fallen.

One night after closing my mother brought home a woman she'd found at the bar. The woman was very pregnant and very drunk. She was pale, with slanted eyes and a round, pie face. An easy mark for an Eskimo, I thought. I was wrong, but not by much. The woman was an Indian from Canada. She had come to town following the man who'd made her pregnant. My mother seemed to know him well. He was a dandy the color of deep chocolate, with a pencil-thin mustache and a Panama hat. He already had a family. And so the woman slept on our couch until she had the baby. She was little more than a girl, and we treated her as a new playmate. Talking with us improved her English. Soon after she had the baby, the dandy in the Panama hat had a change of heart. He came and took the two of them away.

The Canadian was the second woman to come to term on our couch. It had hardly gotten cold from the departure of the girl who'd come with us from the Polish West End. There were other guests as well: a girl at odds with her stepmother; a woman taking refuge from a miserable marriage. Some stayed the night, some a week, some a month.

My father grumbled that all this charity would sink us. These people used gas, water and electricity. They ate food. My mother's motto was that "Geneva's door is always open." When my father pointed out that he paid the rent and bought the food, my mother shot back: "What's it cost to add a cup of water to the stew?" Thus came moral checkmate: my father's complaint, reduced to a cup of water. We couldn't afford to feed the world. But neither could we abandon a lost soul for want of a cup of water.

My father was at war with a saint, if not the very idea of saintliness. This battle only a faultless man could win. The more he complained, the more ogreish he seemed.

My father had other complaints. He was against my mother working. He insisted that raising his children and keeping his house was enough work for anybody. He may have felt this earnestly, but he felt other things as well. One of them was jealousy. The bar was filled with men who liked my mother's cooking, men who walked into the kitchen and told her so. My father worried about where these exchanges might lead. He was right to worry; my mother attracted men. Some were genuine confessors looking for a sympathetic ear. Some were looking for advantage in an unhappy marriage. All of them knew that my father was almost never at home and usually out drinking.

At Andy's my mother attracted a gigolo. He even looked like a gigolo: slender features, pale enough to pass for white, with jet-black hair slicked back on the sides. He didn't have a job, but hung around our house during the afternoons on the pretext that he liked children. Then one day my father appeared in the front door in the middle of the afternoon. (The sound of my father's keys in the door at midday on a Tuesday or a Thursday was just wrong. It had a bad feel to it.) A spasm moved over the gigolo's face and for a moment he looked as though he had swallowed a frog. My father glared at him, walked into the kitchen, and ran himself a glass of water, then disappeared out of the door again. My father hadn't gone to the trouble of parking his forty-foot semi for a glass of water. Not when he was five minutes from the garage. The gigolo got the message.

After the gigolo there was an aging softball player. He was suspect, too, but in a quiet way. He had an unhealthy interest in my sisters and spent far too much time roaming our house. Then there was Mr. Tommy, a mountain of a man who became a good friend of the family. Mr. Tommy worked for the Diamond Ice and Coal Company. He had only one hand. Still he drove trucks, pumped oil, and hauled coal with the best of them. He lavished attention on my mother and sent us fuel to heat the house when we were broke. My father tolerated his presence without complaint.

I crossed town all the time, to the movies, to face the utility companies, to shop for the week's groceries. I walked gerrymandered routes to avoid housing projects and the tribal anger of those who lived in them. I cut from 3rd Street to 4th or even 7th to avoid the winos who panhandled outside the liquor stores, eyeing you murderously when you didn't come across. This day I was daydreaming on the 3rd Street bus, on my way to do the weekly shopping. I pulled the cord and stepped from the bus into a crowd of loud, red-eyed characters clearly drunk. It began to rain punches as soon as my foot touched the sidewalk. I kept my hands up to protect my glasses, and backed away, looking for daylight to run. Then I was rescued. A man with a froggish voice shooed the others away. "Leave him alone! Leave him alone!" he said. They giggled and backed away. As I turned to run, I felt a warm, stinging sensation behind my ear. The warmth spread over my head and the sun went out. Then I heard laughter from the blackness above me. My rescuer was an awesome puncher. He'd gotten the drop and knocked me out.

I woke up lying in the dirt, not more than a dozen feet from where I'd gotten off the bus. I felt my pockets; the grocery money was still there. They didn't want money, just a little fun. I took off toward the market, still unsteady on my feet. A car pulled up beside me, and it was Davy's girlfriend, the virgin he'd broken in. She'd seen the whole thing and driven around the block to pick me up. 'I don't understand you, Brent. How come you didn't fight back!" She was a tomboy and believed in slugging it out to the last.

I kept silent. I was ashamed that she'd seen it, but not of what I'd done. The logic was clear. The more I fought, the greater the possibility that I'd be hurt. The blow that had landed behind my ear and put me to sleep could easily have hit my face, scarring me for life. I was right not to resist but didn't dare defend cowardice to a girl.

My attention turned to weapons. A straight razor was just the ticket. It was fearsome and just short of a gun. The one I settled on had a mother-of-pearl handle. It was given to me by a barber who said that the blade had grown too thin to use in the shop, but was fine for use at home. I was supposed to give the razor to my father, but I kept it.

I fingered it in my pocket as I walked. It was light, but still had an impressive heaviness. It was dangerous, but mainly to me. Opening the razor with one hand was a complex maneuver that often ended in cut fingers. To surprise an attacker, the razor had to be opened partway while it was still in your pocket. To do this, the thumb, middle, and index fingers worked together, gripping the fat part of the blade and pulling it out of its slot. Taking the razor out of the pocket, you placed your thumb onto the flat of the blade and pivoted the razor fully open, while whipping back your wrist to make use of gravity.

A strap-sharpened razor slips imperceptibly through the flesh. I didn't know I was cut until the bleeding started. The cuts were deep and streamed gouts of blood. The linings of my pocket were strained from these accidents. I washed most of my clothes myself, but still it was a matter of time before my mother turned a pocket inside out and saw the stains. And I was tired of cutting myself. I ditched the razor and took up a knife.

I saw little of my cousins while we were growing up. We never took meals at one another's houses. There were no family outings or picnics that would let us get to know each other. I resented this lack of closeness. It had robbed me of allies. My cousins Wesley and Stephen should have been my allies, but they weren't. Stephen was one year older than I, and Wesley was two, and both were one grade ahead of me at Pulaski. School was an endless popularity contest that Wesley and Stephen won without trying. The school yearbook documented their victories: Most Popular, Most Talented, Best Dressed. Stephen and Wesley traded off these honors while an admiring public basked in their radiance.

Wesley was the jock. His laughter was rough, braying. He cut his hair short so that the scalp showed. He had a brawling walk: legs set wide apart, arms out, as though ready to tackle someone. He never stood still; his arms stayed in motion, swinging, swinging, one hand beating a tattoo on his thigh. His fame was solidified when his basketball team had won the state Biddy League championship.

Stephen was soft and girlish. His hands hung limp from his wrists. His pomaded hair broke in waves, left to right, across his handsome forehead. He glided across rooms with the self-conscious ease of someone who knew exactly how others saw him. He walked with a rhythm of his own: shoulders hunched, with dramatic strides that ended in a kind of slow drag, as though he were moving through ankle-deep water. Girls were mad for him. He was getting it all the time.

I fell short of Stephen and Wesley's mark. I was chubby and

knockkneed. My dream of becoming a fighter pilot had met the reality of nearsightedness. A fighter pilot needed 20/20 vision. I needed glasses to see the blackboard.

I wasn't getting any. In gym class you could see who was getting it and who was not. The guys who were getting it had muscles and moved with a smooth, easy grace. Hair crept in a smoky fire out of their underwear and down the insides of their legs. They smelled different. It was an erotic smell that drew you in and repelled you, both at once. It set your teeth on edge. It trailed thickly behind them and marked a path in the air where they had walked. I was certain that the smell, the muscles, and the body hair had come from sex. I avoided undressing with these boys. I fiddled with my locker until they went to the showers, then scrambled into my clothes and fled.

I evaded public nakedness even after I'd made the football team. I went out for the team because I was desperate to belong. Football required athletic skill and viciousness. I had neither but prayed for both. I was big enough but couldn't keep my mind on what I was supposed to do. The action on the field mesmerized me; I played as though sitting in the stands. When the opposing runner made a nifty move, I'd say to myself, "Man, what a move." But I was supposed to be stopping the runner, throwing myself into his armada of blockers.

After a few days of tryouts the coach cut me from the team, but brought me back after he saw how miserable I was. I was moping around the halls when he pulled me to one side. "Keep coming to practice," he said. "You can make it. Come this afternoon." I did, but I stayed in limbo, not cut, not officially on the roster. The defining moment came when the school district dentist came around to make mouthpieces. The dentist could make a specified number of them and no more. The coach told me to lie low during the fitting. I was kept on the team and played without a mouthpiece.

The mouthpiece wasn't necessary. I spent most of the season on the bench. Now and then I went in carrying a play from the coach, stayed for a down or two, then returned to the sidelines. After the games my fellow bench warmers wallowed in the dirt to make it look as though they'd played when they hadn't. This to me was excessive subterfuge. The approval I coveted was not that of the classmates who met the bus when the team returned to school. What I most wanted was the approval of strangers on the street. I wore my jersey home on evenings before the games and back to school the next day. It was a snappy jersey, blue and gold with "39" emblazoned across the chest and back. Strangers on the street had no way of knowing whether I warmed the bench or was the team's most valuable star. They smiled as warmly on me as they would on an All-American. No need to muddy the picture. Best to keep that jersey sparkling clean.

The players knew that the coach had kept me on out of charity. But on the whole they were nice about it. I came away from that season with a pair of Stephens as friends. Stephen one was Stephen Dale, a smiley, cricket-faced boy who lived near Andy's. Stephen two was Stephen Watson. He didn't play ball with us, but came with the package.

The two Stephens and I passed time at the Coffee Cup restaurant on 2nd Street, not far from the abandoned brewery. We played the jukebox until we ran out of dimes and then were obliged to leave. On one such day we got kicked out into the rain. We stood under the eaves, trying to keep dry. The trucks rolled by, their tires hissing and throwing up spray. Still, we would rather stand shivering in the rain than give up and go home.

A police car rolled out of a side street and turned onto 2nd.

Without saying a word, the two Stephens locked eyes and vaulted over a stone wall, into a yard next to the restaurant. I jumped just after them, and all three of us hunkered down out of view. The cops wheeled around into an alley, blocking our escape. We went back over the wall and darted into traffic, then into another alley on the other side of 2nd. We ran breathless to the back door of Miss Geraldine Cooper.

Miss Geraldine opened up and the three of us tumbled into the kitchen. The kitchen was steamy from the industrial-sized pots she had going on the stove. Miss Geraldine cooked in industrial-sized pots because she had a dozen or so children. She was a patient woman. I was always welcome at her house when there was trouble at mine. "What the hell are you boys runnin' for?" she asked. I didn't know; the two Stephens wouldn't say. This was how it went with me. There was always some vital bit of history that I'd missed. Miss Geraldine gave us paper towels to dry ourselves. The two Stephens disappeared out the front door onto 3rd Street, but I lingered for a while in the friendly kitchen. By then I had spent quite a few afternoons there, chatting with Miss Geraldine and her two eldest daughters, Margaret and Titty.

Margaret and Titty were older than I, Titty by only two years. Margaret, though still in her teens, had false teeth that seemed not to smile when she did. Titty's real name was Ethel, but nobody called her that. She was dark, slender, with a sharp, striking face. She went to Catholic school, and her plaid Catholic school jumper didn't fit. None of her dresses did. They all slid off her shoulder, leaving the shoulder excitingly bare.

One dress she wore was much, much too big. It was gray, made of heavy material, and hung well below the knee. It revealed the luscious darkness of her chest, in addition to the shoulder. Girls laughed and said mean things about the dress. It may have seemed dowdy to them, but not to me. I was on the verge of something. The voluminous dress made me think of nakedness. I could almost feel Titty naked against me.

But Titty had a boyfriend. I didn't much care for him. He was benign and dutiful. The two of them sat on the couch together, not holding hands or touching. They lacked the breathless wildness you saw in other pairs on the block. This I interpreted as a hopeful sign. I stayed close and bided my time.

Yvonne was slipping away again. I heard it in her voice when she said: "Mom, I'm going across the street to the store." I pulled back the curtain to watch her, as she passed the store and headed toward 2nd Street. I caught up with her near the brewery and followed at a distance, firing questions. "Where do you think you're going? What is on your mind? What are you trying to do to yourself?" She ignored me and walked on. Night was falling and it was getting cold. Yvonne was warm in her coat. I had run out of the house in my shirtsleeves. She smiled and kept walking, figuring that I'd give up and go home. Then I yelled, "Slut! Street dog!" She lunged at me, and I dodged out of reach. "Street dog" was an original; I had made it up on the spur of the moment. "Slut" I had taken from my mother.

I dogged Yvonne for several blocks. Past the crab shack, past Shilo Baptist Church, past Central Avenue, all the way to Diamond Ice. There I found what she was after. An older boy and his gang had staked out the corner and were waiting for her. The boyfriend was many years older, probably in his early twenties. He folded Yvonne into his arms and turned his face away so I couldn't see him. She lay her head on his shoulder and smiled smugly at me. And there I stood, coatless in the cold, looking stupid. I felt the freeze and trotted home.

I had become my mother's agent. I nagged, looked on disap-

provingly, and took mental notes on the wrongs that were committed. I relished that role; it allowed me to be superior to my sisters
and brothers, to the boys and girls I envied but lacked the courage
to imitate.

My father warned Yvonne over and over: "If you don't let us know
where you're going, we can put you somewhere where we won't
have to worry about it." And so they did. Yvonne was shipped away
to a "girls' home." I envisioned a farm, with cottages, where the girls
wore pleated Catholic school jumpers. The pleats unfurled gently at
the knee as the girls tended their tomato plants.

The "home" was in Muncy, Pennsylvania, way out in the
middle of the state. I visited with my father and my uncle Calvin.
There were no Catholic school jumpers or tomato plants. The
sprawling brick structure was surrounded by a chain-link fence
topped with razor wire. Inside the fence was a runway where they
probably let loose dogs at night; then another fence beyond that.
Outside the fence was a perimeter of gravel that crunched thunder-
ously underfoot and sent echoes through the surrounding valley.
Trees crept down from the nearby hills but ended abruptly in grass.
The grass zone was vast. A girl who scaled the fence would have a
long run before she reached cover.

My father and Uncle Calvin crossed the gravel track and
disappeared behind the fence. I had to wait in the parking lot because only adults were allowed inside. The parking lot was empty
except for my uncle's Buick Roadmaster, a clear sign that no one
cared about the girls inside. I stepped on and off the gravel, marvel-
ing at how loud a footstep could be. I amused myself by throwing
chunks of gravel out into the grass. Then I heard voices on the wind.
The voices were faint, and at first I thought I was imagining them.

When the wind died down and I could hear them clearly, inmates were calling out to me from inside the building: "Hey, honey, you come to see me?" "Hey, baby, come on in here and give me some of that." "Hey, darlin'." "Hey, baby." I could see no faces; the windows were barred and meshed.

‖ The Knock Out

The sky over Miss Pell's algebra class saw heavy traffic in paper planes. The needle-nosed gliders flew beautifully—when they flew—but often spiraled straight onto the floor. Box-nosed planes showed better loft and distance. The folds that squared off the nose displaced weight toward the front of the plane and made all the difference. I made the planes, but left it to braver boys to fly them, which they did, with great regularity, when Miss Pell turned her back to write on the board. Good planes reached her desk or landed on the floor near the wastebasket. The best and most glorious plane banked off the blackboard and floated to a perfect landing on the ledge, with the chalk and erasers. The room exploded in cheers.

The class tortured Miss Pell in ways that were unheard of at Pulaski Junior High. Hatred of her burned especially bright in two Polish boys who were said to have been booted from Catholic school for monstrous behavior. They were a pair. Both short, they sported glistening pompadours, one dirty blond, one black. Miss Pell reminded them of the nuns, which was unfortunate because she lacked the habit and crucifix that would have kept them at bay.

Planes were the least of it. The boys rose as twin assassins when she turned her back, hurling erasers and lengths of chalk that thumped and thwacked off the board near her quaking hand. The room neared riot and stayed that way until the principal, Mr. Rhoades, thrust his balding dome through the door and scowled us into submission. Miss Pell put on a show of sternness for him, but the sternness never reached us. We tore at her with smirks, even while Mr. Rhoades was present. The wildness started to build again as soon as he withdrew.

Miss Pell's fear of us incited cruelty and belligerence. I felt the lure but resisted as much as I could. I was always on the brink of failure and needed the mercy that good behavior would bring.

My mind fled the room when Miss Pell filled the board with equations. I punched through the windows, through the blue roof of the sky, and into deepest, darkest space, where I roamed the void with The Silver Surfer. Space travel left me ignorant of algebra, hence the need for mercy. Civics and English I could pass even with poor citizenship, so I howled with the best of them. But in algebra I was a saint. My soul leaped to its feet when others got up to bombard Miss Pell, but my body stayed firmly in its seat. Good behavior could transform an "F" into a life-saving "D."

The burning plane placed me beyond redemption. I made a plane with my usual care and passed it to David, who sat in the next row, a few desks behind me. This time David put a match to the plane before he launched it. The plane limped across the room, trailing smoke and ash, and crashed in the aisle a few desks ahead of me. Miss Pell whipped around and burned her eyes into mine. Perhaps she'd seen me make it. Perhaps she'd traced the line of flight to me. Whatever the evidence, she clearly thought me the culprit.

Only candy asses squealed. The code of the class dictated that I keep my face barren of emotion, except for a smirk that said, "Torture me, I'll tell you nothing." My resolve evaporated as Miss

Pell's gaze burned into me. Her eyes were slits, her face red and heated, her hair plastered in damp hackles to her forehead. This burning plane had tapped a rage that we had never seen. She accused; I pleaded: neither of us said a word. The year was nearly finished. There was no time to redeem myself by studying and paying attention. Silently I screamed: "It wasn't me. It was David!" I motioned with my eyes to the next row. "I made the plane! But I didn't set it on fire! It was him!"

My telepathy went unheard. I failed algebra and would spend the summer in summer school. I'd be sweating over equations while everyone else slept late and ranged free in the streets.

The first day of summer school I stepped out into the barren morning feeling sorry for myself. Then I saw Wesley standing at the bus stop, his sneakered feet spread wide apart, his arms swinging, the fist of one hand punching the open palm of the other. There was only one reason for him to be there: He was going to summer school, too. That made failing seem like good luck.

Wesley was beginning his junior year at Chester High. Hanging out with him would give me a boost and insight into the mysteries. Girls would be sympathetic to another boy named Staples, even if he wasn't as handsome as Wesley and had never played on a championship basketball team. Tough guys who ruled the territory near the high school would certainly have failed as well. I'd be introduced to them as Wesley's cousin and thereby receive immunity. All this I calculated in the short distance between my doorstep and the bus stop.

The summer school was held at a junior high school on the far east side of town. Wesley moved easily among the students. Girls threw themselves in his path. Time after time, he introduced me as his cousin, and each time was a baptism, like being born again.

Wesley and I met after school, lingered too long in the crowd, and ended up running for the bus. His strides were smooth and powerful, and I could barely keep up with him. He mocked my awkwardness, but there was gentleness, and even something like love in the way he did it. Normally I was deeply embarrassed at any reference to my body, but from Wesley I welcomed any attention at all. We caught the bus and collapsed breathless into our seats. Sometimes we talked, but mainly we didn't. I sat across the aisle and slightly behind him, so that I could watch him without his knowing. He looked out of the window, lost in his own thoughts. When we were together, my thoughts were always with him.

Wesley was killed after summer school ended. The weekend that killed him nearly killed my father and Brian and me as well. My father was taking Brian and me on a trip to Virginia. This was unexpected, since the honor of traveling with my father had always been set aside for Yvonne. Mr. Tommy was our driver. He owned an enormous Mercury Scenicruiser, as big as a Pennsylvania Railroad boxcar, with power everything. The trip seemed wrong. My odysseys to Virginia had always included my mother and my uncle Bunny. We always left in the late afternoon and drove at night, with me riding shotgun. This time we left early in the day with Mr. Tommy behind the wheel and my father riding shotgun in my place. Brian and I rode in the back seat. My mother stayed behind, thus adding to the strangeness.

We were driving toward the highway when the black Crown Victoria came roaring toward us, its front end high in the air. Mr. Tommy veered to the right, but the Crown Victoria veered with us. There was an explosive crunching of metal, and I felt myself being slammed around against the seats and ceiling. I came to sitting on the curb, blood running into my eyes from a gash in my forehead. Brian was clutching a broken shoulder. My father and Mr. Tommy were barely scratched. The Crown Victoria's windshield was smashed, the driver's head a mass of cuts.

I was lying on the table awaiting my stitches when I saw that the doctor was not a doctor at all, but an intern. A spasm of terror ran through me. My face would be ruined. I could see the sausagelike scar ballooning out of my forehead, girls at Chester High averting their eyes in horror. "Go away and send me back a real doctor," I said. The intern frowned and leaned in for a closer look. His hand touched down beside my face, smelling of soap. I grabbed at his wrist, and just missed, the hair of his arm like sandpaper on my fingertips. He stalked out of the room and came back with a bigger, hairier man, also in surgical greens. "This man is an orderly," he said. "You can lie here and be treated of your own free will. Or he can hold you down. Which would you prefer?" The intern scowled and awaited my answer. There was an animal force about him. Hair grew uninterrupted from his head, down his neck, and onto his upper arms. Fighting him would worsen the disfigurement. I agreed to lie still. The intern threaded his stitch hook and sewed me up.

That night Wesley was shot to death. My thoughts were still blurred from the blow to my head; people and buildings floated at odd angles. The phone rang with the news. Whoever answered it repeated to those of us who were in the room: "Wesley has been killed. Someone shot him. It happened down at the corner of 3rd and Reaney." That was three blocks from our front door. Earlier in the evening I'd heard an ambulance and wondered what hapless soul it carried. Now I knew.

I stepped outside onto the porch. I squinted, trying to make tears, but none would come.

Wesley was sixteen years old. Hubert Dixon, the man who had killed him, was twenty-one. The death was ruled an accident. The police said that Wesley and Hubert were passing a gun back and forth when the gun went off. Later I heard that Hubert had jokingly held the gun to Wesley's chest and that Wesley had said, "I dare you." The gun went off and he was dead.

My father and his brothers went with my uncle Paul to identify the body. By the time my father got home, he had reduced Wesley's death to handleable facts. The hole over Wesley's heart was rimmed with powder burns, he said. This meant that the gun had been held close, probably right up against him. The image of my father and his brothers surrounding Wesley's slab came into focus. They circled him in silence. None reached out to comfort the others. They stood separately, trying to sum up the scene in sentences like my father's: powder burns; no blood; dead before he hit the ground. "There was very little blood, almost no bleeding at all. He was probably dead before he hit the ground. Yep, dead before he hit the ground." What my father meant was that Wesley had not suffered, that the end had come swiftly. But that's not what I heard. What I heard was my cousin shuffled off to the grave without a proper show of grief.

I had always been startled by the way my father dealt with death and damage. I was a small boy of eight or nine when I first heard him tell the story of the gabardine suit. The story begins with my father putting on a custom-made suit that he's just picked up from the Chinese tailor. My father is walking into the Seven Seas bar on 2nd Street when a man who has been gashed across the abdomen comes running out. "He came runnin' outta the bar with his arms across his stomach holding his intestines in," my father said. "When he ran into me, his arms came away and all that stomach came flying out onto my suit. Don't you know I'd just picked up that suit from the Chinaman. Hand-made! And there was blood all over the damn thing." At this point the man with the intestines disappears from the story. What happened to him? Did the ambulance take him away? Was he dead or alive? It seemed pointless to ask. This story was about a ruined suit.

"He was probably dead before he hit the ground": The sentence stayed with me. My father's voice neither cracked nor wavered

as he spoke it. He seemed to smile as he described the body. It was not a happy smile, but the slow involuntary smile that came to his face when he'd rendered a tragic scene down to a few, pithy details. Wesley was my own flesh and blood. Surely his death called for more than a shrewd summary. I charged my father with cruelty. In doing so, I forgot about my own dry eyes on hearing of Wesley's death. I'd forgotten, too, that Wesley and I had been strangers before that day at the bus stop.

The funeral was filled with weeping girls who wailed throughout the service. Their wailing came in sheets, like rain. They strained forward in their pews, stretching toward the coffin. One girl in particular stood out. Her eyes had an Asian slant and were nearly swollen shut from crying. Her shapely, hourglass frame shuddered marvelously as she sobbed. She wailed until she was out of breath, moaned into her own throat as she gasped for air, then spent the air in sobs again. The moan of her inward breaths made her weeping stand out. I turned toward the stained-glass windows and squinted and squeezed, but still my eyes were dry. I could hear the moaning girl and see her shapeliness in my head. Several times I turned to look at her. I wished that she was weeping for me.

Hubert Dixon was helped forward to the coffin, barely able to keep his feet. His shoulders rose and fell, heaving to match his sobs. I suspected him of faking it. My suspicion was really guilt and envy: Guilt at my own tearlessness. Envy at Hubert's magnificent show of grief.

Hubert was found innocent and given two years' probation. I embraced the court's judgment, but not because of the facts that had been presented. I embraced Hubert's innocence because it was safe.

I had in me two versions of Wesley's death. In the first,

Wesley and Hubert laugh and joke as they pass the gun back and forth. The gun goes off; Wesley collapses; Hubert falls upon him in genuine grief. In the second, a scowling Hubert guns Wesley down, then fakes a pose of grief for the police.

I preferred the benign version to the malicious one. To believe that Hubert had wantonly murdered Wesley obligated me to hate Hubert and wish him dead in return. People felt it when you hated them, and sometimes they hated you back. Hubert was a grown man, and he had already caused someone I knew to be dead. Hating him seemed a risky proposition. It was safer to assume innocence and move on. Elsewhere in my family people talked of taking an eye for an eye. The talk persisted on and off for years.

We had fled the house near Andy's, hastily and at night. The house we moved to was three blocks east, but those three blocks had landed us in a different world. The families on this new block were smaller, the households more middle-class. We were renting, but most of the others owned their houses. Among the neighbors were a nurse, two teachers, a foreman at the Sun Oil refinery, a welder at Sun Shipbuilding, and a dry cleaner. There was a speakeasy two doors west and a number writer two doors east, but the men who ran those businesses were discreet and well liked.

Our front porch faced the Community Methodist Church, a handsome brick building with a vaulted roof and good-sized bell tower. Like Andy's Musical Bar, the church had been bequeathed to us by whites who'd fled the city. The church looming at our front door made every day seem like Sunday. My mother leaned on us to go. "What's the big deal?" she said. "It's right outside your door." When I balked, she said: "You mean you wouldn't walk 'cross the street to serve the Lord?" I went to church.

The size of the place impressed me. The aisles descended through pews enough for four or five hundred people, but the new congregation numbered no more than forty, a scattering in the vast space. At the end of each sermon the pastor came to the communion rail and extended his hands in an appeal for new members. He held his hands palms up, reaching, as a pianist played soul-stirring music. That he walked with a limp made his reaching more poignant and compelling. The pull on me grew stronger every Sunday. One Sunday it got to me. I walked down the aisle and took his hand and officially joined the congregation. The music rose to a crescendo. The pastor turned me around to face the congregation. Thus was I saved.

As the congregation's senior boy I was made an usher. Good service gave me first dibs on a summer job at the church center. I was hired as a counselor, to supervise and instruct a classroom full of eight- to ten-year-olds. The other instructors were either in college or seniors in high school. I was fifteen and I felt fifteen. The children's silliness was contagious. When they started a game, I dived right in and had a ball. The class dissolved in chaos.

Two women from the white congregation had stayed behind at the church center to help out. One of them belonged to the local theater group, The Chester Repertory Theatre. The CRT was putting on a play about Gideon, the Old Testament general whom the God of Israel raised from modest origins to greatness. The cast lacked a boy to play Gideon's herald, and I was he. My mother approved because the play was biblical. I was in favor of it because rehearsals would get me out of the house.

Rehearsals were held at the Crozer Theological Seminary, the alma mater of Martin Luther King. My part was simple. I ran onstage, blew the ram's horn, and announced that his greatness Gideon was on the way. For the rest of the time I watched.

The CRT was integrated. The General Gideon was black and had a business job in Philadelphia. God was a British bricklayer. The wise men were played by a hairdresser, two teachers, an insurance executive, and a salesman from the Strawbridge and Clothier's department store.

The men's dressing room was a small bathroom at the rear of the auditorium. There we hopped from one foot to another, getting out of our pants and into our biblical clothes. Gideon's jockey shorts were blue with horizontal stripes. (Until then I'd seen only white ones.) They were also scant and tight. One of the wise men was a faggot, not quite as flaming as Gene, but nearly. Gideon slipped out of his underwear and stood naked next to the guy, taunting him. "What do you think of this?" he said. "This" was Gideon's dick. It was an enormous dick, with pendulous balls. Gideon dangled "it" in front of the guy and teased him relentlessly. This unnerved me. From then on I arrived early so that I could change alone.

God wore boxer shorts. While Gideon raved, God stood quietly, gathering himself for the performances. Gideon was a ham; he flew all over the stage, even changed his lines when it suited him. But God was the picture of discipline. He had the most precise diction I'd ever heard. His words were discrete, like his bricks; he slammed them one by one into Gideon's face. My favorite scene was the one where Gideon gets sassy and God sets him straight. God's rage was something. His voice was big and came from deep within him. In the footlights his breath was vapor and spittle, a stop-action photograph of a sneeze.

I was the only teenager in the group, and people went out of the way to make me feel welcome. They drove me to and from rehearsals and smuggled me into bars for after-rehearsal drinks.

The cast parties were all in the suburbs. At these parties I was introduced as an adult and given bonus points for being only fifteen: It was looked upon as miraculous when I said anything even moderately smart. Adults had no reference for what was cool and what was square. Life with them was considerably easier than life with teenagers. Among them I was free to put forth any version of myself that I chose. I chose the ladies' man, worldly-wise and urbane.

The job of driving me around fell to a young woman in her twenties named Sayre Dixon. The arrangement was convenient because Sayre and I lived only two blocks apart. Sayre was the group's aide de camp. She was also Hubert Dixon's sister.

The air between us was heavy with forced cordiality. We talked about diction. We talked about why it was important to maintain a constant speed when driving. We talked about a guy she had a crush on. We talked about the missing tips of her two little fingers, which had been cut off in a fan. We talked about her hair, which had fallen out due to nervous trauma, causing her to wear a wig. We talked about everything under the sun except that her brother had caused my cousin's death.

At first I waited on my front porch for Sayre to pick me up. But waiting made me restless, so I walked to her house and we left from there. I knew what I was doing, that Hubert and I would eventually come face to face. I was eager for it, and I dreaded it. We met one day in the long hallway that led from the Dixons' front door into their dining room. The hallway was so narrow that Hubert and I had to turn sideways to get by each other. For a second we were chest to chest, close enough to feel each other's breath. We went rigid with recognition. I was looking at him, but he was looking insistently down the hall toward the door. His face was hard, even angry, more like the murderous face than the grieving one.

*   *   *

I never tired of the beauty parlor Gene created in our kitchen on Saturdays. The laughter of my mother's friends, their voices husky with drink. The perfumy smell of melting pomade. The castanet clicking of the curling irons. I stood in the kitchen doorway, taking it all in. Among the women were Miss Vi and Miss Betty, both of whom had held me to their bosoms when I was a baby. Eavesdropping on them was a sweet addiction. These were the voices from which I learned to talk. The voices and the smell of pomade kindled a dreamy warmth in me.

I was standing in the doorway, listening to Gene chatter away, when things turned serious. Gene had something delicate to say, and he motioned with his eyes that he wanted me to leave. "Go on, boy, get out of here," my mother said. "Stop starin' down grown folks' throats."

I retreated to the living room and put on the new record by the British singer Dusty Springfield. It was a sad record. The voice was smoky, soulful. The song was about a girl who begs her boyfriend to stay even though he doesn't love her. "You don't have to say you love me, just be close at hand. You don't have to say forever, I will understand. BELEEVE ME! BELEEEEEVE ME!" Gene called out from the kitchen: "Chile, take that off, I cain't listen to that today." I lifted the needle from the record, then thought, what the heck, why not torture him, and put it down again. Dusty Springfield pleaded on: "BELEEVE ME! BELEEEEEVE ME!"

Gene came whirling out of the kitchen with the hot straightening comb in his hand. I leaned back in my chair to avoid being burned, as he pushed past me to the record player. He grasped the arm between a bearish thumb and index finger and lifted it from the record with startling delicacy. "Please, chile," he said. "You cain't play that. I told you I cain't listen to that today." The livery whites of his eyes filled up with tears. He wiped them away with the heel of his hand, then minced back into the kitchen. Gene was having man trouble again; the torch song was killing him. I put aside Dusty Springfield and put on the new record by The Byrds.

I'd known for a long time that Gene was a faggot. I'd known only roughly what faggots did until Davy and the cool guys laid it out for me. Faggots sucked dick. Faggots took dick up the ass. This made them freaks. The cool guys supplied the dick, but not because they enjoyed it. They did it for money. It was a rental proposition: dick in exchange for dollars. Fucking a faggot didn't make you one. Sucking dick and taking it up the ass did.

My affection for Gene had begun to trouble me. I was friendly with him in the kitchen but ignored him on the street. In the kitchen we were both honorary women. But the cost of being seen with a faggot on the street was much too great. When Gene walked by, the cool guys hooted and howled: "Hey, honey, want some of this?" and grabbed their crotches. Hooting was as far as they got. Gene was strong, his forearms and hands cartoonishly overlarge. The greasy paper bag tucked beneath his arm was made lethal by that stiletto curling iron. Once, when I threw a mock punch at him, he lunged at me with the bag, twisting it as he came, stopping just short of my chest. "Chile, these irons a go right through you, don't you know that." He held them there for a long time to let the idea sink in: the curlers doubled as a dagger. With them Gene walked the toughest parts of town unafraid.

One Saturday after finishing my mother's hair, Gene remembered a lamp that he wanted to give her. "Ginny, girl, I got this lamp at home I wanna give you. You gon' love it, girl," he said. My mother told me to go with him and fetch the lamp. I pleaded with my eyes, but was too cowardly to say right out that I was ashamed to be seen with him. My mother flashed a menacing glance, and I did as I was told.

We'd gone only a few blocks when I saw the crowd of boys milling around on the corner. "Hey, baby, want some of this?" Gene just wiggled his ass with more conviction. He smoked as he walked, the cigarette hand floating girlishly in the air. He exhaled violently and smoke curled over his head like steam from a passing train. Then the boys zeroed in on me. "Hey, Brent," one of them called out, "that your new girlfriend?" My heart sank. I looked for a place to take cover, but there wasn't any. I slowed down and watched Gene disappear down the street.

Gene lived above a bar at 3rd and Flower. I caught up with him at the mouth of the alley that led back to his stairwell. Up the wooden stairs we went, past the sullen faces of people who cooked on hot plates, past rooms with bare bulbs strung by wires from the ceiling. Gene's apartment had a hot plate and a naked bulb, too. The place smelled of hair and pomade. I was ashamed of deserting him, and he was hurt at being deserted. Neither of us spoke and we avoided each other's eyes. I took the lamp and bolted down the stairs.

A few months later, Gene's mother died. He set off to Georgia for the funeral and was never heard from again. Perhaps he was murdered by a numbers racketeer whom he had crossed several years earlier. Gene told my mother that he'd been stabbed nearly to death. The man who stabbed him was said to be waiting in Georgia to finish the job. Gene hoped to slip into town unnoticed and watch the burial in secret, from a hill overlooking the graveyard. "If I don't come back, you'll know I'm dead," he said. "But I must go to see my mother buried." This was the last we saw of him.

Chester High School was a spectacular building that had once been displayed on postcards of the city. It had a grand gothic entrance with several enormous arches. Above the building soared a majestic bell tower. The high school was where everyone wanted to be. The sidewalks were brimming with people—students and hangers-on who'd graduated or dropped out. Racing-caliber cars moved in orbit around the block, glass-packed mufflers growling. These cars were driven by graduates who showed up daily to impress us. Some drivers lifted their hoods and tinkered with their engines while the carless among us looked on in pain. Now and then a circling car stopped to pick up a girl, then broke from orbit and roared away.

Chester High had two thousand students. The student body was about 70 percent black and growing blacker every year. The first days of high school were a fashion show. The school dress code forbade blue jeans and required boys to wear ties. We dressed to the nines in fine trousers, bright white shirts, handsome cardigan sweaters. The hallways sang the men's colognes, Jade East and English Leather. As people climbed the stairwells, you could see the bottoms of their feet. Many of them were wearing new shoes.

Chester High was a basketball power. The team was called The Clippers, and the school crest showed a clipper ship under full sail, a homage to the shipyards around which the city had been built.

The Clippers frequently advanced to regional championships in Philadelphia, and occasionally to the state championships in Harrisburg. Away games were relaxed and carefree. But at home games I left early to avoid the fights that sometimes broke out afterward. Outside the gym I walked briskly through the crowd and broke for home.

High school was a caste system. College prep students were the elite. They dominated student government. They appeared in yearbook photographs of organizations that seemed to exist for them alone. They were the principal actors and actresses; the rest of us were the crowd scene.

The bottom caste were those who studied the "industrial arts" (welding and metal work) and the "practical arts" (cosmetology and cooking). I was eligible for the college prep group, but the risk of failure was too great. Instead, I opted for the commercial studies, midway up the status chain. Commercial students would work as clerks and tellers and secretaries, not stellar jobs, but at least we'd wear suits and leave work with our hands clean.

My cousin Stephen was exempt from the rigors of caste. Stephen was studying the "practical arts," but chose his girlfriends from the elite. He was soon going out with a stately beauty named Regina Raymond, a college-prep student, and queen of the unattainables. Stephen was much desired. Girls who craved his notice cornered me and poured out their love for him, hoping that I'd convey the message.

I was the wrong messenger; Stephen and I rarely met. About the only time we saw each other was when he cut my hair in the makeshift barber shop he'd made in my aunt and uncle's basement. During the haircut I suffered Stephen's beauty at agonizingly close range. He passed barely scathed through the pimple phase that had ravaged the rest of us, or so it seemed to me. No pussy bumps for Stephen; he was *getting it* all the time. His hands were manicured, the nails glistening with transparent lacquer. His wrists broke with a Balinese grace. While one hand guided the clippers through my hair, the other hung as limp as a flag on a windless day. "Girls don't like that tough guy thing," he said, "they like the soft thing. As close to a faggot as you can get without being one." He went on heartbreaking missions, not in a hot rod, which he surely could have had, but in a car that was soft like him: a baby-blue Ford Galaxy with a white convertible top.

Around Stephen I felt compelled to lie, to invent constantly cooler versions of myself. This was a losing proposition. Stephen had already won everything—any girl he wanted, a huge following of friends. He tried to be friendly with me, but I couldn't see it then. I thought myself unworthy of his friendship and read reproach into everything he said. When he complimented my clothes, I was certain that he thought them rags. When he said nice things about a girl I liked, I was certain he thought her Medusa.

Stephen was the focus of my discontent. Had I looked beyond myself I'd have seen that he had worries of his own. Wesley had been a clean-scrubbed counterweight to Stephen's rakishness. But Wesley had died, and with a short list of faults. He had slipped the bonds of earth and would stay forever young and full of promise. Stephen accrued shortcomings just by staying alive and was suffering in the comparison. A weariness was settling over him, but I couldn't see it then. I treated him warmly, but secretly I wished him ill. Ideally, I wanted his fortunes to decline in a way that would boost my own.

My courses were mundane and utilitarian: typing, shorthand, bookkeeping, business machines.

Miss Adams taught Gregg shorthand. The Gregg system substituted circles for vowels, and curved and straight lines for consonants. A small circle was an "e" and a bigger one an "a." A short line was "n" and a longer one "m," and so on. Miss Adams dictated letters, which we copied down in shorthand and read back the next day. These letters were always to "Dear Mr. Jones" or "Dear Mr. Brown." They were boring letters referring to other boring letters that one of them had received from the other. Dear Mr. Jones and Dear Mr. Brown seemed always to work at IBM. The steno pool was big at IBM, and if we all were lucky, that's where we'd end up. The real Mr. Jones would call us to take a letter and *whammo!* we'd be vaulted into great jobs as secretaries to vice-presidents.

Miss Adams was a portly woman. The spikes of her high heels were frayed like the tips of exploding cigars. There were two boys in the class: me and a mild-mannered boy who scarcely spoke because he stuttered. Miss Adams treated us like visiting royalty, and regaled us with tales of how well we'd be treated because we were men. "Executives in the big companies prefer male secretaries. You watch. You'll start out in the secretarial pool, but you won't stay there long. You'll make a lot more money than women. Think IBM! They'll snatch you right up!" She said this grinning, oblivious to how it insulted the girls and herself.

Miss Hall taught typing. She walked the aisles with a pointer that she used as a combination swagger stick, instructional tool, and sexual instrument. We were supposed to keep our wrists up when we typed. When wrists fell, she slipped the tip of the pointer under them and said, "Wrists up! Wrists up!" Here, too, boys got more attention than they deserved. Miss Hall continued the chatter about the royal treatment male secretaries were given.

I couldn't see it. All my secretarial images came from Eve Arden movies. Eve played the brilliant executrix who took great letters and handled the office in genius style, but could never get the guy. The guy preferred the dumb blonde who couldn't type her own name. Still, I struggled to bring my secretarial future into focus. I saw the vast hall of the secretarial pool, filled with scores of eager young secretaries. When I was called to take dictation, it was always from a man in a brown suit. I hated brown suits; they were the ugliest suits under the sun. The man's voice was nasal, like Miss Adams's: "Dear Mr. Jones . . ."

My steno pad and pen became manacles, the typewriter the ball at the end of the chain. I was on a forced march to IBM, an entire company of men in brown suits.

Miss Beldicose taught bookkeeping. The class involved a

semester-long project, keeping a ledger and journals and balance sheets and assorted financial documents for an imaginary business. Bookkeeping was mind-numbing work. I gave up and let the project lapse. A few nights before it was due, I copied the totals from someone else. The entries that were supposed to add up to these totals were incorrect. Hence I had committed the mortal sin of *forcing a total*. Miss Beldicose scourged me before the class and let me off with a "D."

Clara P. Riley taught English. Miss Riley had graduated from Chester High in the twenties. She went off to college, then graduate school, and came straight back to teach. She was a broad, matronly woman, her feet encased in the orthopedic high heels that were known as nun's shoes. Her voluminous print dresses showed just a bit of the calves, and her old-fashioned seamed stockings.

Miss Riley recalled a time when teachers were morally superior beings. No longer. A woman in Miss Riley's own department was sleeping with a student and was being hissed and stared at in study hall. Another teacher had been convicted of fencing stolen goods for a student burglary ring. The ring had been the scourge of the suburbs for months and was masterminded by two boys I'd known in the Polish West End.

The students were changing too. Girls had once dropped out of sight when they got pregnant. Now they walked the halls as big as day. By the time I'd arrived at Chester High heroin users had appeared. Miss Riley became aware of the drug through a student who couldn't stay awake in class. Heroin was the ultimate cool. Smackheads nodded out on their feet—bang, gone in the middle of a sentence. They slept standing up.

The most dramatic evidence of change was the arson fire that destroyed the school's tower wing. The city went into shock. People wept as the burnt-out tower fell to the wrecking ball. We were split up and sent to the junior high schools on half-day sessions until the remaining wing was again made habitable.

But Miss Riley was married to Chester High, and we were the children of that union. She had a talent for reaching us. One day while reading to us she came across the word "rhubarb" and was stunned to find that none of us had ever tasted it. Her eyes flashed amazement; you could see a novel solution taking shape. Later that week she came to class with a tray of rhubarb pielets, one for each of us. As the tray went around the room, she held aloft a stalk of rhubarb and talked about its origins. We bit into the pies in unison. "Taste how it's sweet and tangy at the same time," she said. She watched intently, as though tasting the pie through our mouths.

English class was an oasis. I enjoyed writing and experienced as pleasure the words flowing out of me. I loved words, but primarily for use as weapons. I preferred my adjectives British, like "veritable." People were no longer just idiots, they were veritable idiots. My father was "a veritable monster." I fancied condescension; it came trippingly off the tongue.

The high point of the year was when we read aloud from *Macbeth*. At first I thought, Oh, God, a creaking relic spoken in 'thees' and 'thous.' It wasn't that way at all. There were ghosts, witches, prophecies, and murders aplenty. I was at the edge of my seat when Birnam Wood got to Dunsinane.

Chester High was a high-fashion place. To keep myself clothed, I needed a job. I landed one at the shipyard, as had thousands of young men before me, dating back to Colonial days. The Sun Shipbuilding and Dry Dock Company was still being called the largest in the world, but was actually a waning shadow of its former self. At its busiest, during World War II, the yard had employed nearly 40,000 workers, a dramatic number in a city of 60,000. The prosperity of war was brief, so brief that it would later seem a hallucination. Among the first fired were blacks who'd worked in Sun's segregated section for Negroes. The yard lost an average of 10,000 jobs a decade. Finally it was reduced to a skeleton crew and taken out of shipbuilding. Steel and other related industries had suffered in the same vein. When the yard breathed its last, Chester was well on the way to becoming a ghost town.

But that was still to come when I got the job. The streets were thickly parked with big, new cars, many of them bought with Sun Ship paychecks. Shift change at the main gate was a cast of thousands. When the whistle blew, the gate disgorged a sea of men, as many abreast as the street could hold. Their boots churned up a fine metallic dust that billowed around their knees. The welders had flipped their masks to the backs of their heads so that eye slots stared at you after they'd passed. Men who'd worked all night lined up at Marianni's sandwich shop for hoagies and steak sandwiches—hero rolls stuffed with meat, cheese, peppers, and onions, all of it dripping with oil. The men carried these sandwiches through the swinging door that led from the sandwich shop into the bar. There they gorged themselves and washed it down with beer.

The crew with which I was hired contained no welders, blacksmiths, or cranemen. We were high school students brought in to clear vacant lots of weeds and debris. The management kept us a mile upriver from the main yard, in Eddystone. We were forbidden to enter the yard, for fear that we'd be killed by swinging steel or run over by trucks. This was fine with me because the yard was frightening. Tales of death and dismemberment were common. A welder in my neighborhood once saw a man beheaded. The man came on at the start of his shift just as a piece of steel swung wildly out of control, shearing his head off at the shoulders. The body walked on, lunch pail in hand, twin geysers of blood arcing from the headless stump, rising and falling to the rhythms of his heart. The body walked for many seconds, then tilted and fell like a rundown toy. The yard was chaos. Overhead the cranes lifted enormous slabs and even hoisted superstructures onto the decks of ships. On the ground, trucks and forklifts streamed in every direction. Welders were at work everywhere, their tools spewing fountains of sparks.

I was a daydreamer. And daydreamers had no business in the yard. I was in danger even in the vacant fields of Eddystone. I often leaned on my scythe watching the cranes and imagining what the yard looked like from the craneman's point of view. Below him were hundreds of men in hard hats. I was daydreaming that way when the foreman backed into me with his van. The foreman must have seen me, but didn't apologize. He didn't even acknowledge that he'd hit me. Later his point became clear: He was telling me to stay awake, that daydreaming was dangerous in the yard.

My father eavesdropped on my phone calls. He greeted callers with obnoxious expressions like "Your dime, my time!" or "Hello, Grand Central Station!" then lingered to sample the conversation. It piqued his interest to hear his once timid son using lines and pitches, trying to get girls to come across. The call that found him out was from Chickie Mayo. I was talking to Chickie from the bedroom upstairs and speaking in my sexiest voice. I was supposed to be making time, but was bad-mouthing my father instead. "He couldn't be that bad," Chickie said. I responded, "Oh, no, you don't understand. My father is a veritable monster." My father let loose a howl of laughter. It was tinny laughter, the kind that covers hurt.

I crossed the line on my sixteenth birthday. That's what led to the fistfight. The subject was beds, which chronically went to splinters in our house. They collapsed from too many occupants. They also collapsed when younger children trampolined them to death. I was supervising the replacement brigade when my father appeared in the doorway and complained that we weren't working fast enough. His eyes were as red as fire from a day at the bar. He barked at me, "I thought I told you to put up these beds!" I barked back, "What's it look like we're doing? We're working as fast as we can!" The edge in my voice frightened even me. My father ate up the room in two quick strides and was on me. He snatched my glasses from my face and put them aside. "I guess you think you're a man now." I deflected the blows but was smart enough not to punch back. The blows hurt my arms but less so than if they'd landed on my body and head. I was pleased to be holding my own, so pleased that I smiled at him from behind my guard. This was a big mistake. He stopped punching and raised his hands above his head and smiled clownishly, baring his teeth. I let my guard drop, and then he sucker-punched me. The punch came in slow motion: the left hand snapping into a fist, his weight shifting to get behind the fist, the fist speeding toward my face, the ceiling falling away into blackness.

I woke up and stumbled to the bathroom to have a look at my face. The right eye was hideously swollen, the white of it red with blood. I was leaving the house that minute. I stalked back to my bedroom, gathered as many trousers, sports jackets, and shirts as I could carry, and stomped downstairs.

"Put the clothes back," my father snapped. "I paid for all of them."

"The hell you did! I paid for every stitch," I said and kept stomping.

My mother cried and persuaded me to stay. Then she got one of my older cousins to drive me around until I calmed down.

That night, as my brothers slept, I lay awake seething. I parted company with my family. Physically I remained with them, but mentally I was gone. I arranged to be out of the house at every possible minute. I prowled the city, banging against its limits.

I thought of moving back to The Hill and living with Larry or Mama Jordan. Larry's place was too small. Mama's was big enough, but Mama was slipping into senility. For years she'd greeted me with a smile, a pat on the cheek and surprise at how much I'd grown. Now when I passed through the house and saw her at the kitchen stove she kept her back to me. Not always but often enough. Mama left the big House and moved in with Larry. As the fog of senility thickened she no longer recognized me. Her face erupted in a scowl when she saw me. The scowl lifted when I spoke to her but only for a second or two. A woman who'd spoon-fed me as a baby had forgotten who I was.

Yvonne returned from "The Home." I was reminded again that she knew everyone in town. She introduced me to a man who ran the League of Women Voters office, a few blocks from our house. His name was Dumb-Dumb. He was a kindly, toothless old guy, with bad feet that he kept in bedroom slippers three sizes too big. I spent time after school at the office. Dumb-Dumb always had coffee and doughnuts and didn't mind if I took seconds. He wasn't pushy about conversation, either. Sometimes we talked. Sometimes I stared out the window into the rain. It was all the same to him.

The League of Women Voters was trying to increase voter registration as a way of shaking up the Republican machine. But Chester wasn't ready for reform. The machine rolled on and on.

Now and then a few diehards showed up to talk politics, but mainly the League office was empty when I arrived. Just Dumb-Dumb, shuffling around in boat-sized slippers.

The Friends Chester Project House was another good place to hang out. The project house had coffee, too, though rarely doughnuts, but was bigger, so that I could hang around and not get in anyone's way. The project house was a community organizing venture started by Quakers from Philadelphia. The staff included a Quaker man and his wife, a black social worker, and two black community organizers. I got to know the staff well. I rode with them around the city when they did their errands. The Quaker couple, Vint and Carol, were young and newly married. Later I would understand that they were something like missionaries posted in Chester, but back then I wasn't sure what they were. Vint was friendly but somber. When I asked him a question, he thought for a long time and searched around with his eyes before he answered. He seemed to be listening to a voice in his head.

Vint let me shift the gears of his Volkswagen while he worked the clutch. One day while we were driving somewhere, he asked what I planned to do when I graduated from high school. Reflexively, I said that I planned to join the air force. Nearsightedness would keep me out of the cockpit, but I could still load bombs and care for planes, which was almost as good as flying them. Vint paused for a long time, then asked me if I thought the war in Vietnam was just, in the moral sense. I was out of my depth. No one had ever asked my opinion about anything that mattered. It was still 1967. The antiwar movement was far away from me and from anybody I knew. I told Vint that I wouldn't be in the war, just tending planes on a distant airstrip. Vint said that distance from the war was beside the point. The question was whether or not the war was right. He didn't load the argument with images of burning babies, as I would later do. He urged me to think about what I was about to do, and left it at that.

The Project House arranged for a some kids from town to spend a week at Westtown, a Quaker boarding school near Westchester. I didn't know what a "retreat" was. But I was eager to go because it got me out of the house and out of the city.

Westtown was a bucolic scene with dormitories and a swimming pool that I didn't use because I couldn't swim. It had an outdoor theater, a woodsy coliseum dug into the ground, with stone steps as seats and trees and shrubs for the walls and ceiling. The retreat was a serious enterprise. In the mornings we met in seminars to discuss weighty moral problems of the day. Again, out of my depth, I listened and stole glimpses at people's watches, eager for the sessions to end. Out in the woods I tried to make time with the Quaker girls, but they were too reserved for my taste. They came from small towns I'd never heard of, towns that were even smaller than Chester.

We put on a play. The director was a young dairy farmer in white tennis shoes and khaki pants. His face was all teeth and horned-rimmed glasses. He bounced around, rubbed his hands together in a "Let's get to work" kind of way. It didn't seem plausible that he was a farmer. Farmers were weathered old men in overalls with weathered old wives. When we affected disbelief in his farm, the director took us to see it. "These are our cows," he said. "This is our bull." Then he showed us the silo-shaped tanks where they stored the milk. His parents were not quite weathered, but at least they were gray.

The farmer's play was like none I'd ever heard of. He chose poems from Whitman, Emerson, and others and had us recite them onstage in the open-air theater. I knew Whitman from my mother's copy of *Leaves of Grass*. I read around in it sometimes, but the thickness and the fact that my mother read it made it seem too much like a Bible, and that put me off it. The play consisted of us reciting poetry while playing games. Another boy and I recited Whitman while playing a game of catch. Others stooped onstage around a game of marbles. Still others recited while jumping rope. Whitman was cool read out loud. Especially, "I sing the body electric."

I knew that Quakers were a religious group, but not what kind. The dairy farmer took care of that. He arranged for us to perform before a Quaker meeting in Swarthmore. The meeting was held in an austere room with rough-hewn benches. No piano. No organ. These weren't needed because Quakers didn't sing. They scarcely even spoke. They sat in pews in silence. People got up and said things if they were moved to, but mainly the service was as quiet as a tomb. The dairy farmer nodded to us when it was time to begin. We got up, tossed our baseball, and recited our Whitman, then folded our gloves and went back to our seats. There was no applause, just more silence. The silence seemed eerie at first, but by the end I felt comfortable in it.

The Project House attracted people from all around. Among them were black students from Swarthmore College. I was drawn to a sunny woman with a Southern accent. Her name was Marilyn, and the accent was Florida. She seemed to be interested in me too, in a sisterly way. She invited me to a party at the college, and I went.

The town of Swarthmore was dramatically different from Chester and from everything. It began as a canopy of green ten minutes from the shipyard gates. There were generous houses surrounded by succulents and flowering shrubs. Every street was an avenue and nearly all of them were named for schools: Harvard Avenue, Yale Avenue, Princeton Avenue, Dartmouth Avenue.

The college announced itself with Parrish Hall, a ship of a

building with domes and curves and columns stationed at the top of a hill. Down this hill streamed a vast green lawn spotted with white Adirondack chairs. Down the center of the lawn ran a grand walkway more than a quarter of a mile long, canopied with oaks more than a century old. The campus had trees of every conceivable kind, all of them labeled in Latin and in English. A plaque at the top of the oak-lined walkway explained that the trees weren't just oaks, but live oaks.

The paths through campus were lamplit and calming to walk on at night. This was the most beautiful place I had ever seen.

The parties moved around. They were held in the cafeteria, in secluded lounges beneath hooded archways, and in stone outbuildings that reminded you of a medieval castle.

In Chester I avoided dances. You ended up in the wrong part of town late at night and got the shit kicked out of you. You stepped on someone's toe and got the shit kicked out of you. You asked the wrong girl to dance and found yourself facing some brute with murder in his eyes. Swarthmore College had no such dangers. Studying was the main activity. Even on Friday nights the dormitory windows framed lamplit faces hovering over books. That Marilyn and her friends were bookish and square was an added bonus. They didn't know hip from unhip, and thus I could claim greater hipness than I was entitled to. They looked to me for the latest dances and couldn't tell if I was dancing them well or badly. I danced as never before. I danced till I sweated through my shirts. I danced until my legs ached, and then danced some more.

I couldn't make time with Marilyn because she was already a senior. The underclass girls liked to dance well enough, but didn't go in for grinding on a dime in the corner. My lines and advances left them mute and unyielding. I was out of my depth on the make.

Swarthmore's black students were lonely and angry. They

were lonely because there were fewer than fifty of them in a white student body of a thousand, surrounded by a white town. They were angry because the school was bringing in fewer black freshmen each year. They were also angry because anger was the uniform of the time. All over the country campuses were in riot, with students taking over buildings and making demands. Television cameras had ceased to be interested in brown men in suits who talked about integration and peaceful change. The cameras were now interested in scowling Black Panthers who spoiled for gun battles and called for "offing the pigs." White people couldn't tell the difference between faux Panthers and the real thing. To adopt that Panther face as your own was to be changed in a miraculous way: You weren't just *like* them, you *were* them. The Black Panther fetishism was a simple inversion of what had gone before: Stepin Fetchit and Willie Best, the black actors of the 1940s and 1960s most noted for the shuffling, head scratching, and bulging eyeballs, were not men. They were a collection of bootlicking gestures. The Panthers were supranormal men, walking versions of the cities on fire, tumescence on two feet. They shouted "motherfucker" in mixed company.

Swarthmore's Afro-American Student Society was plotting its own Panther offensive. The group was led by a mild-mannered young man with the melodious name of Clinton Etheridge. But Clinton was only the titular head. Women, the Seven Sisters as they were called, ran things. Among them was Fania Davis, whose sister, Angela Davis, was soon to be charged with murder in connection with a courtroom shoot-out in California. But it wasn't the politics that drew me, or the parties.

I visited the campus even when there weren't any parties. Sometimes I walked a circuit around the lamplit pathways, returning just in time to catch the bus home. Sometimes I lingered long enough to take a milkshake at the snack bar and eavesdrop on conversations. The students were ferociously smart; the science they talked was way over my head. Once I overheard a long debate on a fine point of Old English. I loved the place, but I knew I could never cut it there. Bookkeeping and shorthand would not pass muster at Swarthmore. I ended the evening by descending the walkway in front of Parrish Hall. The oaks formed a cathedral overhead. The walk was like going to church.

At Chester High the way you looked was half the game. I worked hard during the summers and part-time during the school year and put every cent I earned into clothing fit for a star. I bought Italian shoes, Italian knit shirts; I bought blazers and expensive cardigan sweaters. I started down the woolen trousers route, then decided that sharkskin was my element. I bought sharkskin pants, then a silver-gray sharkskin suit with bone buttons. To this I added a black leather overcoat and black leather gloves. A black leather coat was fundamental to coolness. I carried the gloves in one hand and slapped them into the palm of the other.

I kept my clothes in a padlocked closet in the room I shared with my brothers. Now that Brad had come along, there were five of us in two beds. I slept with Brian and Bruce in the big bed. Blake and Brad shared the daybed across the room. Blake wanted to sleep with the big boys. This we resisted because Blake wet the bed. We were wary but not heartless. When we found him asleep in the big bed, we let him be and arranged ourselves around him. He lulled us to sleep with dry nights, but then he drenched us and we evicted him. Humiliated and back in the daybed, he cried himself to sleep. In our bed we turned and twisted, trying to avoid the icy lake in the sheets.

Bruce was still too young to be a wardrobe threat. Brian was another matter. He looked better in my clothes than I did, and took an acquisitive interest in them. One day after school I climbed the stairs and found him standing in the doorway of our room holding one of my Italian knit shirts. For weeks I'd smelled something alien in that shirt. Not stink, because Brian was immaculate, but something like another person. I'd dismissed the possibility because the closet was padlocked, and the only key was in my pocket. But Brian was a genius at burglary. Each day he took the door off its hinges, picked out some clothes, then returned them before I got home.

I let out a scream and vaulted down the hallway toward him. As I approached the doorway I leaped with fingers outstretched, intent on tackling him. Then came a dull crunch and things went black. I'd hit the top of the doorway and knocked myself out. I came to on the floor, a trickle of blood running down my forehead. Brian helped me downstairs, where my mother examined the wound and declared it minor, no stitches needed.

Brian was pretty and he knew it. His eyes were girlish, with short curly lashes, the eyebrows arched in permanent condescension. His features were sharper, more well-defined than mine. We were made of the same fingers, toes, the same high behinds, but Brian was a more harmonious version of these elements. The mechanic who assembled our bodies had less success with mine. Too many twists of the ratchet had collapsed my knees inward against each other, forced open my bite, and hiked up the right hip higher than the left one. Brian was symmetrical and handsomely proportioned. I looked at him with a wishful narcissism.

Brian was keen on self-display. He became a Black Muslim. While the rest of us walked around under billowing clouds of hair, the Muslims cut their hair so short that you could see their scalps. The look added to the sense of menace about them.

Black Muslims abhorred pork. The Swine, they said, put

your soul in mortal danger. We were a Virginia family on both sides, and therefore in double peril. Virginia means ham, pork chops, pig's feet, pig's ears, chitterlings. Pork was disappearing from the refrigerator. My mother suspected that Brian was throwing it out.

Black Muslims referred to white people as Devils. The Devils had ruled the earth long enough and now it was the black man's turn. The Muslim rant fit nicely with Brian's disposition. He was a screamer, and demonstrative besides. He stalked the room as he talked, gesturing broadly, palms up, as though feeling for rain.

I scanned the Black Muslim newspaper, *Muhammad Speaks*, which Brian subscribed to. Every issue seemed to carry the same cartoon: One panel showed a white woman, the other a black woman; both women were shapely in short, tight dresses; both captions read "The Filth," attacking exposure of flesh. But Brian loved naked women: girls his own age, women my mother's age. He was thrown out of school for what the *Daily Times* described as "causing a disturbance" in class and "threatening two teachers." Later Brian told me that a principal had walked in on him having sex with a teacher. My mother sued and Brian was readmitted. He lost interest in school and dropped out again.

The high school drama teacher asked me to try out for the senior play, Lorraine Hansberry's *Raisin in the Sun*. Mere high school plays were beneath me, I said. I had starred in the Chester Repertory Theatre's production of *The Death of Bessie Smith*, and in Edward Albee's *Happy Ending*, a scene from which I'd performed on local television. I would take the lead role in *Raisin*, but only if it was given to me without a tryout. The drama teacher was a pugnacious ex-priest who'd taught at a Catholic high school before coming to Chester High. His face reddened at what I'd said. There'd be none of that, he said. Tryouts would be held on such and such a day; I could come or not come; it was all the same to him. Of course I went. I had seen Sidney Poitier in the movie version of the play. I saw everything that Sidney Poitier did, right back to *The Defiant Ones* when he and Tony Curtis played escaped convicts chained together on the run. Black men in movies were mainly pimps and clowns, but Sidney Poitier was dignified. His diction was clean and crisp, almost British in its precision. He put that fat cracker sheriff in his place in *In the Heat of the Night*. He built a chapel for impoverished nuns in *Lilies of the Field*. He whipped those filthy-mouthed cockneys into shape in *To Sir With Love*. Yes, he had played the ne'er-do-well son, Walter Lee Younger, in *Raisin*, but that was one small stain on an oeuvre brimming with dignity.

I wanted that part badly. The repertory theater audiences were mainly adults, most of them from the suburbs. In *Raisin* I could play Sidney Poitier before an audience of my peers.

I arrived late at the tryouts to ensure a dramatic entrance. I swept into the room, my leather coat draped on my shoulders, flogging my palm with the leather gloves I never wore. "Make way! Make way!" I said. "Sidney's here. Sidney's here!" I made up a monologue on the spot, about a man who worked in a bottling factory. All day long he watched a machine put caps on bottles. "This would be his job for the rest of his life," I said. "Cap on bottle. Cap on bottle. Cap on bottle." The monologue sprang from a primal source. The man watching the bottles go by was me. This was my failure dream, the ritual of meaningless acts that was out there, waiting to claim me.

‖ Come the Revolution

I was standing at my locker, my books stacked at my feet, when a vast cloud of hair floated by me and stopped at a locker across the hall. The hair shimmered like graphite and was hyperreal in its size and roundness. It framed the lovely face of Josephine Hood, one of the first girls at school to wear her hair in an Afro.

Josephine cast a regal glance up and down the hallway, the cloud rotating slowly as she turned. She was letting herself be watched, and this was fine with me. I liked watching Josephine. I'd been watching her for a long time. Her legs were strong and beautifully shaped and moved sinuously beneath her as she stalked the hallways. The legs were widely set so that Josephine was more firmly planted on ground than most people. I ached to introduce myself, but didn't because she was magnificent. Also I was below her station: Josephine was preparing for college; I was doomed to the steno pool at IBM.

Josephine had a strong appetite for being at the center of things. She personified the anger of the time, and this won her a starring role in protests and agitations. She'd run for some office in student government and won. I had voted for her, twice.

Josephine's Afro was a symbol of courage. Girls who went "natural" got significantly more grief from their parents than boys. My own Afro had caused considerable friction with my father. He preferred the clean-cut look and had determined in advance that no "nappy headed niggers" would live in his house or eat at his table. I built the Afro surreptitiously, gradually increasing the loft, then holding it steady while he exhausted his anger. Then I let it out as far as it would go.

Girls had no such subterfuge. They washed their hair and, bang: the silky pageboy exploded into a bristling crown of kinks. Boys could be as outrageous as they wanted because most were only headed for the shipyard anyway. But girls had to work in offices; they had to find husbands. Parents worried that kinky hair meant unemployment and spinsterdom. Fathers raged. Mothers wept and pleaded. Girls gave in and fried their heads again. But Josephine had held out.

Josephine's locker banged shut. She hoisted her books onto her lovely hip and prepared to walk away. It was now or never. I went over the script in my head: "Hello, Josephine." No. "Hi, Josephine. I voted for you in the election. My name is Brent." (Extend your hand.) I planned to speak in a baritone, for maximum romantic effect.

I stepped over my books and crossed the hall to where she stood rattling the locker, trying to get it shut. Her face was turned downward, cast in shadow by her hair. I had no choice but to speak into the cloud itself. "Hi, Josephine. I voted . . ." Then the latch caught. She turned and glided away without even seeing me. She hadn't heard me either: My lips had moved, but the sexy baritone had died in my throat.

I put myself in places where Josephine was likely to appear. I cut study hall to sit in on the Black History class with the college-bound kids. Josephine was serious about radical politics, so seeing her meant joining the student group that thought of itself as radical. The group met all the time, at a community center, at the church annex, at the Project House, and at the League of Women Voters office. We converged on school board meetings and hectored the board about how it ran the system. We met for trips to Swarthmore College when the Afro-American Student Society put on cultural events.

The point of all the meetings was to Do Something. *Doing Something* was creating a commotion and challenging the powers that be. *Doing Something* was bringing the world around to the awful truth of racism. This mission sometimes took us into the suburbs. I appeared with Josephine on a panel at a community center in the town of Media. The center director wanted his white constituents to be educated about racism. The audience was sparse, mainly suburban housewives with purses on their laps. We gave angry speeches advising the racists to get their feet off our throats. Josephine was brilliantly angry, as usual. Her teeth flashed and she beat at the air as she talked. The women sat pensively, their purses still on their laps. After we finished, a hat was passed and the women put money into it.

There was a hard edge to Josephine. I was accustomed to coyness from girls. But Josephine was utterly unconvincing when she tried to be coy. Anger became her. But anger was the wrong music for making out in a parked car. I couldn't get started with her. I never even kissed her.

We decided to boycott the schools. The issues weren't compelling. The Board of Education had barred the wearing of African beads in lieu of ties but had rescinded the edict under pressure. We tried to make the case that not enough basketball players were getting college scholarships, but that was flimsy, too. There were, of course, not enough black teachers, not enough courses in black studies. But it was lame to think of Miss Riley and her colleagues as merely white. They were white in the narrow sense, but they were the mothers of the school, and devoted to us.

The rally to kick off the boycott was held in a church not far from the Project House. The turnout was encouraging, and a couple of basketball stars showed up, thus validating the event. Josephine and I took turns exhorting the audience. That the athletes were present hyped me up and pushed me to rhetorical excess.

The boycott failed miserably. A few of us held out for three, maybe four days, then gave up. By then we needed doctor's notes to get back into school. The doctor of choice refused to write the notes. Too many notes from him would cause suspicion in high places. Thus we journeyed to the suburbs and found a doctor there. We hoped that he'd write the notes for The Cause. He humiliated us by making us pay.

We weren't finished yet. We'd avenge ourselves by pulling a false alarm. This false alarm would carry more than the ordinary weight; we were nearing the anniversary of the fire that had destroyed half the school.

Swarthmore's black students had sent an angry Christmas greeting to their president, Courtney Smith. The greeting demanded increased black enrollment, a black dean of admissions, and a black counselor. "If you fail to issue a clear, unequivocal public acceptance of these nonnegotiable demands by noon, Tuesday, January 7, 1969, the black students . . . will be forced to do whatever is necessary to obtain acceptance of same." Two days after the deadline, the students padlocked the admissions office and began a sit-in. The sit-in was in its eighth day when Courtney Smith died of a heart attack. He was fifty-two years old, and worshiped by students and faculty alike. Appointed at the age of thirty-five, he had been one of the youngest college presidents in the country. He was a tall, free-striding figure, with long features and a baleful brow, the weight of high seriousness always upon him. His death was banner news locally, and resounded through the national press as well. *The New York Times* ran an obituary and castigated the black students in an editorial. An alumnus, writing in the *Washington Post*, described the death as a lynching. The press in general stopped just short of calling it murder.

But the stories were yet to be written on the morning of January 16. Courtney Smith's death would not be announced until 11 A.M. At that hour the band of radicals at Chester High was sequestered from the news, screwing up its courage for the false alarm. The alarm went off at the appointed time and had the desired effect: Students streamed into the halls and then out into the streets around the building. The panic was palpable.

Order was restored in time for English class. I had just taken my seat when Miss Riley planted her beefy fists on my desk and leaned in close.

"Don't you think I know who pulled that false alarm?" I felt a stab of panic. But she wasn't finished yet.

"And don't you think I know who killed my friend Courtney Smith?" Miss Riley looked steely. The steeliness welled up out of her eyes, moved down those chubby cheeks and into the deep, horizontal dimple in her chin. Then she stood up on her orthopedic heels and walked back to her desk. This was my first news that Courtney Smith had died. I was yet to find out how.

I had always wanted a dangerous reputation, but never would I have killed someone, or even wished him dead, to get it. Courtney Smith was actually and truly dead; Miss Riley was charging me and all of us with killing him. I sat there smiling dumbly, but inwardly I was numb. When the bell rang I bolted from school and hitched a ride to Swarthmore. The campus was consumed with grief. Students were sitting out on the great lawn, singly and in small groups, weeping. The blacks had ended the sit-in and left the campus. Before departing they had issued a statement that read, in part: "We sincerely believe that the death of any human being, whether he be the good President of a college or a black person trapped in our country's ghettos, is a tragedy." The statement was hard-assed and unsentimental. It bore no resemblance at all to what the students felt.

I caught up with them at the Fellowship House, a community center in the town of Media. I bounced into the house looking to talk trash with my party friends and get the lowdown on the sit-in. This was false joviality. Miss Riley's accusation had unnerved me. In the first-floor living room I ran into Bernie, a burly guy from Cleveland who had always been the life of the party. Bernie was slumped in a chair, paralyzed with grief and fatigue. "Hey, my man. What's up!" I said. He could hardly lift his head.

The rest of the students were in a similar condition: mute, wilted, paralyzed. I moved from one of them to another and tried to coax them into speaking. They weren't up to it. I asked where Marilyn was, and someone said, "Upstairs," but I lacked the heart to go up. This was not the posture of remorseless radicals. These were guilt-ridden people who thought they'd committed murder. The grief was crushing. I fled the house and waited for my ride outside.

I saw little of my Swarthmore friends after that. The parties dried up. The students retreated into corners and waited grimly for graduation. I continued to make the rounds of the campus, always at night. Occasionally I recognized a face through a dormitory window, but I never stopped in. After a circuit of the campus, I descended the walkway in front of Parrish Hall and caught the bus back to Chester.

Miss Riley's remark about Courtney Smith's death continued to trouble me. Twenty years later I found her in a retirement village and asked her about it. Had she said: "Don't you think I know who killed my friend, Courtney Smith," or, "Don't think I don't know who killed Courtney Smith, my friend."?

"I didn't know Courtney Smith, so it must have been the second, with the comma after Smith," she said. Miss Riley did not remember me.

Winter pressed on into spring. Diana, who had played my wife—that is, Walter Lee Younger's wife—in *Raisin in the Sun*, was accepted at Howard. Antone, one of the diehards of the high school radical group, was packing up his Volkswagen and heading off to Lincoln. Josephine was going to the University of Pennsylvania. It was rumored that she had blown away the SATs and won a full scholarship. When I asked about this, she smiled shyly and declined to answer.

I was going nowhere. I had not applied to college. Nor had I taken the SATs. I was walking all the time now, and Chester was growing smaller by the day.

One day after school Josephine and I ended up at the League of Women Voters office. Dumb-Dumb was shuffling around the office, setting out the coffee and doughnuts. He introduced us to a black guy named Eugene Sparrow and added that Sparrow taught sociology at PMC, the college at the east end of town. Sparrow wore a tweed jacket over a dark turtleneck shirt. His hair was short and wavy, brushed neatly backward and close to his head. He said "baby" when he talked: as in, "Listen to this, baby," and "Hear me out, baby," and this together with his turtleneck made him seem a beatnik. Later I found out that he was the college's only black professor.

We talked about politics. What other subject was there in 1969? We talked about the burning cities and the Vietnam War. Exhausting these, we turned to the copious graft and corruption of Chester's Republican machine. Sparrow didn't talk much, but drifted around in the room, listening. When the meeting broke up, he followed us outside and caught up with me at the corner. Josephine got in her car and drove away. Sparrow and I stood and talked.

"Have you ever thought of going to college?"

"No."

"Why?"

"Because my family has no money."

"What are you going to do?"

"Get a job."

"What kind?"

"I don't know. The Shipyard, maybe." (What a lie; the Shipyard scared me shitless.)

Sparrow took out his sunglasses and put them on.

"Maybe you ought to think about college," he said. "There is money out there these days." He explained that PMC was trying to increase its black enrollment from nil to something respectable.

I gave him more reasons why I couldn't go: It was almost April, too late in the year to apply. I was a secretarial student and I hadn't taken the SATs. As far as I knew, the last tests of the year had already been given.

Sparrow frowned and gestured at me with his cigarette.

"Come on, baby. Hear me out. Listen to me, man." The next words he underscored heavily: "*Never mind about the money.*"

By then I was clinging to every syllable.

"And never mind about the College Boards," he said. "You can take them in the fall."

He took out a notebook and scribbled the name and number of Vincent Lindsley, the director of admissions.

"Call him. Tell him I told you to call."

I did, from home, the next day.

I wanted this badly. The future that Sparrow had suggested was the only one that would do.

PMC I had learned was actually two colleges occupying the same campus: Pennsylvania Military College, which was founded before the Civil War, and Penn Morton College, a recently established civilian school. The two shared classrooms and some faculty but had separate dormitories.

The college was an undistinguished set of brick buildings, except for Old Main, which had Georgian columns and a white dome that lit up at night and hovered above that part of town. Out front were a stubby pair of mortars that dated back to the Civil War.

Vincent Lindsley was a stork of a man, all arms and legs, with a beak of a nose. He was bald on top, but his remaining hair went up in a birdlike flip at the back of his neck. He talked in rapid bursts, like a used-car salesman.

I was panic-stricken. I tried to be friendly and relaxed, as well as precise in everything I said. I held my own until he asked what *superfluous* meant. I didn't know. "This is how you figure it out," he said. "*Super* means 'extra.' *Fluous* means 'fluid.' " I nodded. "So you see, this is how you figure it out. *Super fluid*. More than you need. That's what it means, got it?" He went on like this for a long time.

During the next week I bit my fingernails badly, sure that *superfluous* had sunk me. Finally, a letter arrived. I'd been accepted as part of something called Project Prepare. I would spend the summer on campus in academic boot camp and would take the SATs in the fall.

‖ The Discovery
of Light

Project Prepare took in twenty-three guys, all of us black. Half were from Chester, half were from elsewhere on the eastern seaboard. A few were slated to become cadets, but most of us would enter the civilian college. The guys from Chester High had been on the academic track; I'd known them only as faces in the hallway. There were a few exceptions. One was Richard T. (Tea Bags) Bagley, with whom I had shared some classes. Tea Bags was quiet. He talked so little that anything he said seemed startling. His friend Lamont (Montesque) Givens was a sleepy-eyed guy who never seemed fully awake. In high school he'd been a clotheshorse. His wardrobe included lime-green and electric orange pants. Then there was Brion Harris. Brion's brother, Commodore, was a policeman who was said to be quick with the nightstick. Brion's father, Commodore senior, was well connected politically. When my mother sued to get Brian back in school, Commodore senior had showed up at our house to announce the city's surrender.

I'd met Brion under circumstances that I'd tried to forget. It happened when I ditched study hall to take a black history class with the academic students. The teacher was lecturing on slavery and had turned to the subject of overseers, the blacks who rode the fields on horseback inflicting cruelty on their brethren. I said, "Sounds a lot to me like Commodore Harris." Silence descended on the room. The teacher ignored the remark and went on. Then she read aloud a particularly lurid example of overseer cruelty. "Yep," I said, "that sounds like Commodore Harris." Silence again, but this time the teacher motioned with her eyes toward the back of the room. I turned and saw Brion sitting stiffly upright at his desk, his eyes wide with shock. I felt very small. I had no right to embarrass him like that. I wanted to apologize but lacked the courage.

Project Prepare had also recruited a couple of guys who had been out of high school for several years. One of them was my cousin George/Marty/Mohammed, the eldest son of my uncle Calvin. He was five years older than I and had spent time in the Job Corps and had changed religions, from Christian to Baha'i to Muslim. His given name was George, but he hated the name because he'd read somewhere that George meant "farmer." For most of his life he'd gone by the nickname Marty. That summer he jettisoned both Marty and George and became Mohammed Ahmed.

Mohammed, when he was still Marty, had the first Afro I'd ever seen in person. It was a grand cloud of hair, beautifully shaped, with the rakish version of the Staples widow's peak. The hairline veered inward above the temples, like the shorelines of twin lagoons, then came to a dramatic point in his forehead. That once grand Afro seemed scruffy now. Time had scrubbed away at that swooping widow's peak, leaving a series of tufts that grew thinner as they descended into the forehead. A speech impediment caused him to drop the first syllables of shorter words and to mangle the tail ends of longer ones. The mangling got worse when he was excited. It was also worse because Mohammed, now that he was a Muslim, preferred arcane African words that were difficult to pronounce in any case. I was disappointed in the way he clenched his pen in a fist, and drew his words laboriously across the page. Growing up, I had hardly noticed these defects. Now they were all that I could see. I resented him. His presence made a claim on me that I didn't wish to honor.

The project's director was a young history professor named Stephen Braverman. We called him Brahv, for short. He walked with a penguin aspect, reeling from side to side so that his tie swung in a pendulum motion. Ours was the first class of Project Prepare. Brahv caught hell when news got out that we were coming. He got threatening phone calls and his car was blizzarded with parking tickets. A few students withdrew from his class.

PMC was vastly more expensive than state schools. But parents who chose a military school that had only recently opened a civilian division knew what they were doing. A military school offered protection against the things that were worrisome about college at the time: riots, rampant sex and drugs, and especially against blacks, who were burning down cities and growing more menacing by the day.

The Philadelphia *Bulletin* said that Project Prepare would be "closely watched," and it was. Drivers slowed down to a crawl when they saw us sitting on the steps below Old Main. The school had gotten along for more than a century with only a smattering of blacks, most of them servants. Two dozen black faces at once must have been a jarring sight indeed.

Allan Rowe, the college basketball coach, taught math. He was an affable, roly-poly guy who owned a Dairy Queen and ate a lot of ice cream. His interest in us went beyond just math. Coach Rowe was clearly searching for basketball talent. He ran "basketball camps" where he tested our shooting, dribbling, and jumping skills. Brion and Lamont were the best talents. It was understood that the two of them would go out for the team in the fall.

The character of that summer was A. Christopher Cavin, the English teacher. Cav taught at a high school in Delaware but would join the PMC faculty in the fall. I was drawn to eccentrics, and Cav was surely one of them. He talked about literature while staring at the ceiling, his long, brown fingers stroking his goatee. He talked about Conrad and Faulkner and Hemingway and Hawthorne, and especially about Eugene O'Neill, whose play *The Emperor Jones* we were putting on at the end of the summer. He talked about the art of the essay: "Remember, people, compare and contrast, compare and contrast." Cav had grown up in a housing project in Chester and spoke often of his childhood. He seemed a pretender at first, but bit by bit I could see that he was real. He lived in words and stories, and he loved them. When he talked, he seemed to be reading from the ceiling.

Project Prepare was run like boot camp. We were rousted from bed at six, in class by eight. We worked part-time jobs in the afternoon, then hustled back for dinner and a long evening of homework. The writing assignments were endless and were collected before we went to bed. We slept in the dormitory, went to class in the dormitory, and were forbidden to leave it at night. The dictators of this regime were our dormitory counselors, Joel, Larry, and Cedric.

Joel and Larry were cadets. They were little, but wiry, with lots of fight in them. Joel practiced karate out in the open, white karate suit and all, to disabuse us of the notion that we could intimidate him. Larry showed us an enormous surgical scar on his shoulder, the result of a football injury.

Cedric was an ex-marine of enormous proportions, 6 feet 7 inches tall, and 240 pounds. He'd been brought along as muscle, in case we got out of hand. Cedric played center on the basketball team. His teammates dropped by over the summer to play pickup games at the gym. When Cedric grabbed rebounds, he roared, "Ball!" to let his teammates know he had it. The roar was startling until you got used to it. PMC's team was all white except for Cedric and one other guy. The whites weren't Joneses and Smiths, either. Their names were Zyla, Kulbok, Runo, Studzinski, Frau, and Brandenberger. When Zyla made a good play, Studzinski patted him on the butt and said, "Way ta go, Stash." I hadn't heard that since the Polish West End.

One night two guys went over the wall for hamburgers. Joel and Larry got wind of this, confiscated the burgers, and ordered us into our rooms. First they walked up and down the hall, taunting us. Then they threw the burgers into the hallway and watched us scramble after them like animals. We tore the burgers to pieces, leaving the hall littered with pickles and grease. Joel paced the hall, berating us. "Even the most dumbfuck platoon in the army would have chosen two guys to get the burgers and hand them out in an orderly fashion," he said. The point was that with discipline you could do anything. The point was that we were going to learn discipline if it killed us.

The astronauts landed on the moon. We watched the landing on a tiny television set in one of the counselors' rooms. The day had been scorching. The dormitories were out in the open with no trees to shade them. Heated by day, they baked us into the night. We crowded, sweating, into the small room and hunched over the screen. The voices from the moon crackled with static. Vaguely we made out the shadow of a man stepping down into the dust. The astronauts in their bulky suits bounded over the lunar landscape. My trip to college seemed just as miraculous. I was happy to get up at six in the morning, happy to accept boot camp discipline, happy even to bake at night in the dormitory. I would have walked on fire if they'd asked me to.

*   *   *

Tuition, room and board, and fees ran $3,200—not counting books, clothing, and incidentals. My father made $14,000 a year, a hefty sum in the eyes of financial aid officials. This put me beyond range of a full scholarship based on need. But my family could contribute nothing to my expenses. This meant I had to borrow heavily.

The loans required promissory notes, which both my parents were supposed to sign in front of a notary public. My mother signed both her name and my father's. I took this to mean that he'd refused to sign, thus adding one more brick to the wall between us. I went before the notary public and told him that my parents were too busy to come themselves. The notary didn't blink an eye. He sealed and signed the notes, took my four dollars and called out, "Next!"

The state scholarship forms were trickier. They required detailed income statements, including tax returns, which were not available, either because my father had lost them or because he'd not filed his taxes. I hadn't come all this way to be thwarted by forms. I hated legal documents; they all smelled like writs of eviction to me, and I took joy in faking them. All I needed was patience and a Xerox machine.

I was prepared to fake everything when my mother came up with a W-2 statement. I dug up the previous year's tax forms and tax tables and worked out a shadow tax return of my own. I thought about making my family dirt poor to ensure a full scholarship, but decided against it. What if I was caught? A bogus form with honest figures would be easy to defend. A doubly bogus form would have the slammer written all over it. In the end the shadow tax report looked just like a copy of an original.

Now that I was in college I felt compelled to become someone else. I put aside my sharkskin trousers and took up the look of the Black Panther Party. The model for this look was the famous poster of Huey P. Newton, the Panthers' "Minister of Defense." In the poster Huey P. was seated in a wicker chair whose back crested over his head like the hood of a cobra. He wore a black leather jacket and a black beret cocked to one side. He held a shotgun in his right hand and an African spear in the left. I copied the look, and added my own flourishes. I wore dark sunglasses and the black beret cocked to the side, barely keeping its grip on my Afro. It was too hot for the leather jacket, and so I wore a dashiki, a billowing African shirt that was paisley in emerald green. For the militaristic look, I wore tight-fitting jeans, their bottoms stuffed into my army-issue combat boots.

Thus was I dressed when I stepped from the car on the first day of school in September. I was prepared for white folks to look upon me and be afraid. But there were no white folks. I had arrived at the earliest possible moment; the campus was empty. Only later in the afternoon did it begin to fill up.

I was sitting on the top bunk looking surly, combat boots hanging down, when my white suburban roommate showed up with his mother. To affect further menace, I was cleaning my nails with a file that I hoped would be reminiscent of a knife. My roommate was a friendly, pear-shaped boy in crooked glasses and hush puppies. He'd gone to a prep school with an important-sounding name. I wanted the room to myself and set the goal of driving him out by semester's end.

In the first half-speed days before classes started, the Project guys stuck together. One night as we sat in front of the dormitory, we heard music. We traced it to the cafeteria. The room was darkened and decorated with balloons and crepe paper. A band was playing rock 'n' roll. Cadets and their dates were dancing away, the men in gray corsetlike uniforms, the women in party dresses. My friends and I lingered at the edge of the dance floor, tapping our feet. Then I couldn't contain myself.

I stepped between a cadet and a girl and was dancing in a fever when a pair of hands gripped me at the collar and at the waist, whirled me around, and threw me into the wall. I turned to face the cadet. He looked mad. His face was stern and pockmarked, red in its hollows from dancing. He stood feet apart, arms rigid at his sides, ready for a fight. All around him were young men in uniform, ready to fight, too. I took a step toward him, but my friends restrained me, just as I knew they would. We retreated to the dormitory to lick my wounds.

I couldn't see what I had done wrong. Cutting was a universal language. One dancer slid in between two others; the one who'd been cut slid in between two others, and so on. This was how you stepped up the dancing frenzy. The cadet's name was Jim Jette. Later when I confronted him he shrugged his shoulders and said, "What was I supposed to do, put my tail between my legs and run?" I struggled to explain, but there was no use; we were speaking different languages. These cadets were genuinely square.

PMC was college very much as it had been in the 1950s. Fraternity boys drank profusely and went on panty raids. Freshmen were expected to wear beanies so that upper classmen could haze them. When some of us declined to wear beanies, we were hauled before a dean who wondered why. It was all in good fun, he said, and part of a tradition.

The counterculture influence was small. A clutch of hippies lived in the dormitory just off the football field. They had state-of-the-art stereos and copious amounts of reefer, which they shared. But hairy, bearded people were a distinct minority.

The dearth of hipness among the white guys on my hallway was relieved only by Jeff and his roommate. Jeff was short, bowlegged, and turned in at the toes. His hair was longish, curly, and disobedient. All day long he rubbed his palms against the sides of his head, trying to make the hair lie down. Jeff said I should run for class president. Naturally, I was flattered, but I didn't understand why he thought this. "The time has come," Jeff said. For what? I thought. Who among these kids would vote for a black president? Jeff said that he and his roommate would run my campaign. They made up fliers and handed them out. I gave no speeches, posted no platform. On election eve I went to sleep as myself. I woke up the next morning President of the Class of 1973. There'd been a lot of write-in votes for cartoon characters and household pets. The school was rife with names from Eastern Europe. "Brent Staples" must have seemed a solid Anglo/Irish choice.

Flush with authority, I set out on my first initiative: to make the campus more hospitable to drinking and sex. The initiative met great support on Fraternity Row, and consisted of two proposals: that the administration lift its ban on drinking for students eighteen and over, and that men and women be allowed to spend the night in each other's rooms openly, instead of sneaking in and out as we were currently doing.

A faculty committee studied the proposals, and the committee report was broadcast live on campus radio. The room was jammed with students, many of them cross-legged on the floor. The committee chairman had already said no in several ways when I interrupted him: "The students are the college. Without us there is no school. We get what we want, what we are entitled to," or something to that effect. "Right on," said the room, "right on!" The students stirred around me, some murmured; electricity moved through the crowd. The committee chairman smiled sheepishly and put down his papers. He'd lost the day, and he knew it. I ended with the threat that we would get what we wanted "by any means necessary." This was the first time my constituents had heard me speak.

I walked back to the dormitory drunk on my performance. Jeff was stomping around the hall, in a pigeon-toed dance of rage. "How could you talk to professors that way? We oughta recall you from office." I was nonplussed. Raising hell was what I thought I'd been elected to do.

My supporters and I pressed ahead. Our plans for the demonstration were set: We would tap a keg of beer on the steps of Old Main, pass out cups to everyone who came, and dare the college to expel us. The fraternity boys balked at the last minute—surprising, given the way they drank. A meeting was called on Fraternity Row. The frat spokesman said that he was thinking of pulling out of the demonstration. "We could get kicked out of here for drinking," he said. "A lotta people are worried about that." He was a slender boy, with a pronounced Adam's apple in a swanish neck.

I promised protection. "If the college touches a hair of any-body's head," I said, "we'll get the brothers and sisters up from Chester and burn this motherfucker down." (Images danced in my head: the Georgian columns and the dome of Old Main going up in flames!) What a crock. No one in Chester would light a match for a frat boy, let alone burn down a building. But the frat boys didn't know this. The guy with the swanish neck smiled and seemed satisfied. The demonstration went on, with one change: we would tap a keg of cider along with the keg of beer so that no one would know who was drinking what.

The crowd assembled in front of Old Main. Even the cadets joined in, paper cups in hand. As we were about to tap the kegs, the dean of students walked down the steps of Old Main and came toward us. His name was Colonel Cottee. He was long retired, but could still summon the military swagger when he needed it. He parked a foot on the ice chest and intoned against the rashness of what we were about to do. I eased up beside him, cupped my hands, and yelled, "Tap the motherfucker, tap the motherfucker." Paper cups went up and were filled. The twin kegs of cider and beer were a stroke of genius. The administration couldn't prove a thing. We got what we wanted. The right to drink; the right to sex.

The coming of civilians had weakened military resolve. Cadets could now look out of their windows and see naked couples making love in rooms across the way. The dormitories were subdivided, with military and civilian life separated by a thin plywood door. The smell of marijuana wafted from our section into theirs. Reveille blared over the cadet public address system and bled back our way. But reveille was no match for Jimi Hendrix. We were converting them. One by one they defected to the civilian side.

The military academy was with us on borrowed time. The Vietnam War had made the military unpopular, and a rich trustee was looking to name the college for his family. The trustee was Fitz Eugene Dixon, Jr., heir of the Philadelphia Wideners and Harry Elkins Widener, who died on the *Titanic* and from whom the Widener Library at Harvard took its name. The military academy was done away with. In my junior year PMC became Widener College.

But that was yet to come when the board of trustees summoned me to dinner. The dinner was held at the home of Fairfax Leary, Jr., a lawyer who lived in Villanova, which was dripping with money and part of that string of communities known as The Main Line. I was driven to the dinner by Jack Pierpont, the college's director of development. Pierpont was taking this seriously. On the way out, he put a dollar figure to each of the men I would meet. This one was worth only a few million. That one was worth ten or twenty.

Still another one was worth more than a hundred. It was difficult to imagine that kind of money. At the moment I was worth maybe ten dollars, in addition to the suit on my back. And a fine suit it was: the gray sharkskin with the bone buttons. With it I'd worn a pink shirt and pale gray tie with matching hanky. My cuff links were mock diamonds three quarters of an inch in diameter. A sharp outfit and still new; I'd worn it only once before.

We rode on in the rain on Route 320, past a great lawn and the line of hundred-year-old oaks in front of Parrish Hall at Swarthmore, past Route 1 and Route 3. "We are in his driveway now," Pierpont said. I saw no house, only trees. We were "in the driveway" a long time before we came to the house.

The door opened onto a distinguished-looking man with glasses and sharp features. This was Fairfax Leary—Fax, they called him—and he was holding a glass of whiskey. He shook both my hand and Pierpont's and showed us in. We stepped into a room of white-haired men with reddish faces. Some had slick graying hair, some of it was thinning, one had hair the color and consistency of cotton. These were the men of millions. Fax showed us to the bar, and Pierpont went off to do business, leaving me there alone with the bourbon. The bottle had the name Dixon on labels that read "20-year-old bourbon." This was Fitz Eugene Dixon, chairman of the board. I filled a glass about a third of the way with bourbon, the rest with Coke, and stood there nervously, waiting. The editor of the school paper introduced himself, then disappeared. Surely some of these rich old codgers would come forward, shake my hand, harangue me, or say whatever I'd been brought there to hear.

Fitz Dixon was the only one among them with black hair. The hair was parted and swept back from a face that was very wide at the jaw. "Welcome, good of you to come," he said, speaking with his jaw locked. He was a horse man. He once visited us, the new blacks, in the dormitory, wearing riding clothes, boots and breeches, and smelling of horse. He smiled with that broad face and left me at the bar. No one else came forward.

The old men standing in couples and trios around the room seemed greatly affected by my suit. Theirs were all the same, deep blue, with pin stripes. My face was hot with the liquor and the nervousness. I was new to drinking and soon I was drunk. Why was I here? Surely they knew me. I had raised more hell in a year than most of them had seen in fifty. I stood there not far from the bar, close to several people, but none of them spoke to me.

Fax announced dinner. Pierpont showed me to our place cards. Mine was next to his, not far from the center of the table. Sitting across from me was Laurence Sharples. A street in Swarthmore was named for his family, as was the dining hall where the black students had held their dances. Sharples was old, very old. His skin was parchment, his hands long and slender, with veins and bones showing. He felt me staring and met my eyes. Years later I would see good humor and sympathy in that face. Back then I felt like a specimen.

There were others: Hannum, a name from the list of those who'd represented the colony at the Constitutional Convention; Pew, the owners of shipyards; Strawbridge, of Strawbridge & Clothier's, the department store; Kapelski, a tankish man in a wheelchair, who owned the ferry that connected Chester with New Jersey; Wetherill, the name of an elementary school. With the exception of Sharples, no one met my eyes. I sat heavily in my seat in my shimmering suit, fingering my cuff links.

Wine with dinner kicked up the volume around the table. The trustees were laughing now, talking loudly around me. Pierpont talked on, as though describing a museum exhibit: This one made his money this way, that one is worth so much. The kitchen door swung open, and through it came a black woman in servant's clothes, carrying on her shoulder a roast of beef. The beef was red. I remember the red because it made me queasy. The woman stopped dead when she saw me. I took this shock to say that mine was the first black face she'd seen at that table. She worked her way slowly around, eventually getting to me. I took a long time serving myself, as I was searching for beef that wasn't bloody.

The trustee at my left gave me his back throughout the dinner. These were people who ran cities, companies, whose families had come across with William Penn or soon after. I was nobody to them. *You are nobody*, they were saying to me. *You may think that you are hot shit, railing on in the local papers, drinking beer on the steps of Old Main, shooting off your mouth with the faculty, but you are nobody to us.* I got the point. I returned to the dormitory drunk and humiliated.

Brion, whose family I'd insulted in high school, did not hold a grudge. He, Lamont, Tea Bags, and I became friends. Brion and Lamont roomed together, and both of them made the basketball team. I signed on as a manager, but told the coach that I expected to be one of the most feared players in the league by the time I became a senior. I believed this utterly. This turn as manager would allow me to study the players' moves. And study them I did. I prowled the sidelines, plotting to overtake the weaker players one by one in my rise to stardom. I could hear the applause as my name was called at the start of the big game, visualize the press clippings of my best performances.

The evidence against this fantasy was heavy indeed, but I couldn't see it. Among these players were splendid athletes who'd played competitively for years. John Zyla soared effortlessly above the rim. Wally Rice, another player on the team, was later drafted by the Boston Celtics. I was slow afoot and couldn't dunk. Still I believed that there was a basketball star inside me. He just needed a year or two to get out. This miraculous leap to college had changed me. I no longer recognized even obvious limitations. I believed that through force of will I could become anything I wished.

The manager's job got old. It was fine for the road games, but was too demeaning at home where everyone knew me. Besides, I had little time to spare; I was running wild.

In high school I'd sipped thimbles full of wine. Now I got falling-down drunk and had to be hauled bodily back to my room. In high school I'd regarded reefer smokers as mental defectives. Now I went to class high and engaged the professors in loopy conversations. My high school girlfriend moved in with relatives closer to the school, presumably to spend more time with me. This claim I refused to honor. I cheated on her, then severed our relations.

In high school I always used condoms, and even then I was dogged by the prospect of causing a pregnancy. At college this fear had magically fallen away; the condom fell away with it. I didn't ask girls if they were on the pill because I didn't care. I behaved as though I were exempt from the rules of reproduction, which of course I wasn't. I was responsible for four pregnancies that I knew of. Each time I apologized to the panic-stricken girl and promised myself that I'd take precautions the next time. I never did. Two of the girls were sufficiently well off; their doctors performed abortions, even though abortions were illegal in Pennsylvania. Twice I raised money for abortion trips to New York City. The waiting rooms were filled with grim, speechless women, many of them on the verge of tears. They looked at me with accusing eyes.

I tortured my roommate. On weekends I hogged the room with girls and barked at him when he tried to come in. I chewed him out for leaving his underwear on the floor. I wolfed down food that his mother sent him. I ground him down until he moved out. I'd never had a bed of my own. Now I had two, a lower bunk and an upper bunk, and I slept in either as I chose. I spread out as I went to sleep, gripping the edges of the mattress with my fingers and toes. Across the room was my closet. My trash can. My two desks. My two windows.

Alone I was blissfully happy. I would never have gone home at all except that the dormitories closed over Christmas. I didn't yet know that the dean would give me permission to stay over.

My family had moved again, back toward the Polish West End, a block west of Andy's Musical Bar, in a house that faced the stone and wrought-iron fence around St. Mary's Ukrainian Orthodox Church. Retreating whites had surrendered yet another bar: The Ward Grille, a few doors from the new house. My parents had managed to buy this house despite years of bad debt. My mother had carried off this miracle, thinking that pride of ownership would make my father more responsible. It didn't. His drinking got worse. The atmosphere at home did too.

There was no longer room for me. My brothers and sisters had spread out, filling the space that I'd abdicated. I couldn't face being crushed into bed with my brothers again, and so I slept on the couch. The first floor was at sidewalk level. Heads, backlit by the streetlights, floated by the windows. Eventually one of the shadows would stop and stand reeling at the glass door. This was my father coming home drunk. The outline of him—tall and slender, struggling with his key—was unmistakable. I pretended to be asleep as he reeled by me and climbed the stairs, his key ring clinking with useless keys from houses past. I stayed the holiday, but fled back to campus at the first possible moment.

That summer I spent at Yvonne's. My mother was disappointed when I told her I wasn't coming home, but I couldn't bear moving in with the family again. A spasm of panic passed over my mother's face when I told her. For years afterward I wondered why.

Yvonne had taken a fourth-floor walk-up in a building opposite Andy's. I slept on the couch in the living room whose windows overlooked 3rd Street. One evening I saw Stephen's baby-blue Ford convertible parked across the street. The blue turned to violet under the sodium vapor streetlights. In the front seat two pairs of hands were passing a needle back and forth. One man put the needle in, then took it out, and passed it across the seat to the other man, who repeated the act. The hands behind the steering wheel looked like Stephen's. I slid down on the floor and caught my breath, then peered over the ledge again. Those were Stephen's wrists: slender and delicate, broken with a Balinese grace. Just then he grabbed the hilt of the needle and shook it, and plunged it into his arm. Stephen and a friend were sharing a syringe of heroin.

It was inconceivable that I would tell my uncle Paul what I'd seen. The Staples families didn't communicate that way; each kept its triumphs and tragedies to itself. Secretly I took a sordid pleasure in Stephen's fall: This kind of pleasure was not unique to me; it was the common way of being among my father and his brothers. Misfortune that visited someone else was misfortune that we ourselves might be spared. A flaw in a relative's character was evidence of one's own virtue. My feelings for Stephen carried my own peculiar twists. But the general sentiment was one that I'd come by honestly.

Stephen was still my barber. Once a month I walked down from the college to let him trim my Afro. Sometimes I waited for hours for him to arrive. Sometimes he didn't come at all. Sometimes he arrived, nodding on his feet, his nose running junkie snot. His life went to pieces. Mentally I pulled the shroud over his head. I expected at any time to hear that he was dead.

*   *   *

I was sitting in history class when the department secretary rushed into the room with a note. My mother had called. The note read: "Your brother is ill. He is asking for you. Come home." Home was less than three miles away, a brief ride on the city bus, but that day the bus seemed to take forever. I rode with my heart in my mouth, wondering what catastrophe awaited me.

Brian was tearing around the house yelling and throwing things, white teeth flashing. I noticed the needle tracks right away. They began on the back of his left hand and ran up the arm, twisting to follow the vein. He had hit that vein over and over again and left a solid line of punctures. He was babbling, incoherent.

My mother stood in the doorway between the kitchen and the dining room, watching us. She had one fist on her hip, as usual, and was wearing a print dress just like the ones I had always picked out when I shopped for her clothes. She expected me to do something, but what? Brian was far more worldly than I. What was I to do? Lecture him on something I knew almost nothing about? Tell him that he should stop or I would, I would, do what? Certainly not beat him up. Once I'd have bloodied his nose and shaken sense into him, but those times had passed. Brian was a man now, quick and strong. He was growing a mustache. Parked back on his head was a brown porkpie hat from the 1940s.

He calmed down when he saw me, though I can't say why. We talked, but about something off the point. The track marks frightened me, and so I said nothing about them. I wanted out. We talked more and he walked me to the bus stop. The sun was high. We stood on the westbound side of the street in the shade of an awning. We continued to talk about nothing. The eastbound bus came chugging out of the Polish West End. I crossed the street and caught it back to school.

*   *   *

From then on I lived at school year-round, over Thanksgiving, Christmas, semester break, and right through the summer. I spent the day of Easter, or the day of Christmas with my family, but that was it. That night I was back at the dormitory.

I grew accustomed to the dormitory emptying out. I lay in bed listening as the stairwells swallowed the last departing students. Then the building was an ocean liner, and I was its only passenger. The key-laden security guard came jingling up the stairwell, passed my door to the circuit breaker, and turned out the lights. The hallways were kept dark through the vacation, lit only by the faint red glow of the exit signs and by shafts of moonlight that fell through one window at either end.

Once dark, the hallways were mine as well. I prowled them, drinking in their space. I ate beer and hoagie dinners on the windowsill at my end of the hall. The window overlooked the parking lot behind the dormitory and Interstate 95 at the bottom of its manmade canyon. Beyond these the city poured downhill to the Sun shipyard and the Delaware River, a mile below. Bright yellow cranes bathed in arc light towered above the shipyard, prowling slowly on rails, like taxi-colored dinosaurs. The arc-welders' torches flashed in the night.

The bus that would eventually pass my family's street passed the dormitory every hour or so. It shot by so swiftly that the passengers looked like stills, painted on the windows. The brake lights lit up at the bottom of the hill, and the bus turned right, disappearing into town. I jumped ahead of the bus and watched it pass from different vantage points along its route. I looked down on it from the fourth-floor apartment above 3rd and Parker, where my tenth-grade girlfriend and I had wrestled feverishly, though quietly, because her mother was in the next room. I saw the bus through the chain-link fence of the Blue Line Transfer Company where my father's truck and those of my uncles were parked at the end of the day's run. Through the windows of the butcher shops and Laundromats and fish mongers along 3rd Street. As it shot past the corner where Sparrow had saved me, then past this alley leading to Gene's backstairs apartment. I saw the bus, wavy and distorted through the glass brick wall of Andy's Musical Bar where my father might well have been drinking at that moment. Then through the rose trellises and the wrought-iron fence of St. Mary's Ukrainian Orthodox Church on Ward Street, where my family then lived.

After dinner at the window I often went to the football stadium. There I smoked reefer and stared at the stars.

The campus guards came to know me well. They ceased to be startled when we encountered each other in the darkened hallways or in the stadium at night. They learned to trust me and gave me the keys to the gym so that I could amuse myself with basketball. When possible, I drafted another player to play full court, one-on-one. Sometimes a passerby saw the lights, heard the ball on the hard wood, and came in to join me. But often I played alone, against invisible adversaries. I practiced jump shots and lay-ups, and I pounded the backboard in mock rage. I made fantastic shots and spun around and fell down at center court, fists raised in triumph. That gym still comes to me in dreams.

I saw less and less of my family. My visits were brief, not longer than a few hours at a time. This was easiest in the summer, when I found my mother sitting on the step, and spent the visit without going into the house. On the sidewalk I kept tabs on the buses as they passed the foot of the street. My mother and I talked about school, about my father's drinking, and about the latest drama among my brothers and sisters. While we talked I timed the buses, planning my escape.

I tried to visit when my father was out of the house. It didn't do for us to meet. We paced the rooms, angling for the blow-up. The ritual of courtesy was thin. It came to an end in anger and flashing teeth.

It was clear that the distance between my family and me was not new, that I was just recognizing it newly. Now that I was absent from the day-to-day routine, changes in them seemed dramatically sudden, as though they'd come on overnight. One day I stepped off the bus to the sight of Sherri standing on the sidewalk enormously pregnant. My mother must have told me at some earlier point. But the fact didn't strike me until I saw Sherri leaning heavily against a tree, her belly floating out in front of her. She was fifteen years old. Sherri was the family's brightest student; there'd been talk of her following me to college. Pregnancy ended that hope, not just for her but for everyone else.

When vacation ended, I watched and listened as the campus filled up again. First a few cars turned into the parking lot, then a few more, then an endless stream. The first voices came bubbling up the stairwells. Then came the aimless half-speed pace of the days before classes. Then class, when everyone moved in deliberate lines from one building to the next.

I became a behavioral science major because the department was inviting. Sparrow and Brahv taught sociology. In the psychology department were three young professors who'd taken an interest in me. I worked at Freud and Weber and Marx, at statistics and experimental design, and studied German. Meanwhile, I made use of what I knew.

What I knew was Black Panther rhetoric. In Brahv's class I presented a defense of the Party's ten-point program: the call for a separate black nation, the release of all black men from prison, reparations from slavery, the whole deal. I put the program forward as though every right-thinking black person in America believed it as gospel. One of the cadets in class was an upperclassman and an officer with stripes. He fumed as I talked, but his stripes didn't scare me. I had stripes of my own, only I didn't choose to wear them. I'd told the most gullible cadets that I was a captain in the Panther Party, which meant Panthers everywhere would come to my aid in time of trouble. The burly cadet finally blurted out: "Who do you think you are? You don't speak for all black people." I shot something back, then there was shouting, and the class dissolved in chaos.

In the Panther paper I read a story about the internment of the Japanese Americans during World War II. This I incorporated into a speech I was writing for Professor Biddle's public speaking class. My thesis was that World War II was a racist enterprise. That we'd dropped the bomb on the Japanese and not the Germans and sent Japanese-Americans to prison camps was proof enough for me.

Professor Biddle sat in the rear of the auditorium, a few rows beyond the last student, his pencil in hand, his grade book open in front of him. He was a brittle and nervous man, the result of battle fatigue, other faculty members said. His reading glasses slid way down his nose, and he never looked at you. His eyes were searchlights sweeping steadily back and forth across the ceiling. When I spoke the words "prison camp," Professor Biddle sputtered and straggled to his feet. "My father! My father was against it! He was against it. How can you say . . ." His eyes went wild; I thought he was having some kind of attack. I kept an eye on him as I finished the speech. Later, I looked it up. His father was Francis Biddle, the United States attorney general under Franklin Roosevelt. Biddle was a liberal and didn't want to intern the Japanese. But Roosevelt buckled to public outcry and forced the issue. Professor Biddle had heard at his dinner table what I'd known only in snatches from the Panther newspaper.

Previously I'd thought of history as woven and packaged elsewhere; it came to you finished, like a sweater. This episode showed me that history had flesh and blood. The more distance I got on that moment, the more it seemed like the discovery of light. My speeches got better. Professor Biddle gave me an "A."

My cousin, Mohammed, was playing the Panther, too, but with Maoist flourishes. At his instigation we formed a Black Student Union and extorted a building from the college. They gave us the old chemistry lab adjacent to Old Main. The lab had expansive rooms and a sloping lecture hall and was a far too extravagant gift of a school that in the not so distant past had held classes in Quonset huts.

Mohammed seized leadership of the Black Student Union and assumed the title of Chairman, after Chairman Mao Tse-tung. A lame duck in my class office, I took the title of President. There were no elections to speak of; my cousin and I held leadership with noise and force of personality.

In April 1971 copies of stolen F.B.I. documents came to us in the mail. The documents showed that the Black Student Union had been under surveillance by Cointelpro, the F.B.I.'s program for monitoring "black hate groups." A "hate group" was any organization with the word "black" or "Afro" in its name. A group calling itself the Citizens Commission to Investigate the F.B.I. had broken into a bureau office in Media and stolen somewhere between 800 and 1,000 such documents. Now they were holed up with a Xerox machine copying the files and mailing them to the press, to Congress, and to people who'd been under surveillance. The files revealed wiretaps on the Black Panthers, surveillance of black student groups, and a network of several thousand "ghetto informants" who reported on racial matters. This was a public relations disaster for the F.B.I. and led Congress to curtail the agency's powers. The burglars were never caught.

The documents disheartened us. They described our Black Student Union as weak and "dormant." The documents contained an even bigger embarrassment for Mohammed and me: The F.B.I. had named the wrong students as leaders of the Black Student Union. Mohammed's name and mine were readily available from the pages of the *Delaware County Daily Times*. We mouthed off all the time, and some of it got into the papers. But reading the newspapers was too easy for the F.B.I. Instead, they interviewed a retired detective who worked for campus security. He named as leaders two students who were so scarcely active that it was almost a reach to call them members. He named them because they looked the part. The woman had a big cloud of hair, and, to the undiscerning eye, might well have resembled Angela Davis, with the case for similarity resting completely on her hair. The male student named was tall and broad-shouldered, with a brooding countenance and also a pretty big head of hair. The F.B.I. planned to open files and "develop informants" on these two. That they knew where the woman went to church was a fair indication that the spying had begun. This seemed excessive, given that we'd been judged to be toothless panthers and fakers before the world. The national press thought so, too. In a front-page story the *Washington Post* gave our case as evidence of the F.B.I.'s capriciousness and of what a danger to liberty the bureau had become.

Mohammed and I were fuming, not about dangers to liberty, but about the bad rap we'd gotten as revolutionaries and the way the spies had ignored us. We held a press conference where we harangued the F.B.I. and their campus informant. With the television camera in tow, we stormed into the president's office and demanded that the informant be fired. He wasn't.

Mohammed and I were natural rivals. The rivalry was good-natured at first but soon turned ugly. We argued often. His mangled pronunciation made it easy to outmaneuver him. The angrier he got, the more he did violence to his words, and the less he could defend himself. We were arguing, egged on by friends, when Mohammed jumped to his feet and stood over me. "Say another word and I'll punch you in the face." I opened my mouth, and he said, "I said one more word. One more word and I'll fuck you up." He had the advantage. I sat silently, my face burning. When Mohammed stepped back, I went into the next room, called him in, and closed the door. I told him that if he ever made good on that threat I'd do my best to kill him. I meant it as deeply as I'd ever meant anything. I saw in him every bully I'd ever faced. I was ready to be rid of them.

Mohammed was unmanned without an audience. He laughed a hollow laugh. "No," he said, "I'd be the one to take *you* out."

"Well," I said, "we'd see about that, wouldn't we?"

I felt it my duty to aggravate Sparrow. I was painfully aware that he'd saved my life. I kept hearing the gospel song "Amazing Grace": "I once was lost, but now I'm found." I hid my gratitude and played the hard-ass. Sparrow was a Unitarian minister and a conciliator by nature. The Panther routine sat badly with him. I knew this and so I poured it on. I wrote papers quoting Mao Tse-tung, elaborating on the notion that all change grew from the barrel of a gun. Sparrow bore up patiently under my ravings and made it his mission to nurse me away from them. This, in the end, was easy. Pantherism was something to cling to until I learned something else.

In my senior year I handed Sparrow a victory. I wrote a paper conceding that force of arms would not win the changes that black Americans needed. Sparrow read from the paper in class. He waved it in the air. "I gotcha now, baby," he said. "I have it right here in black and white."

Cavin was teaching humanities courses. During the summer of Project Prepare he'd taught Conrad and Crane and Faulkner and Hawthorne. Now he was teaching James Baldwin, Richard Wright, E. Franklin Frazier, and W.E.B. DuBois. And Plato. Cav had a bug up his ass about Plato. He returned again and again to the Myth of the Metals, the "noble lie" that Plato said was needed to establish the Good and Ideal state, ruled by the Philosopher Kings. "While all of you in the city are brothers, we will say in our tale, yet God in fashioning those of you who are fitted to hold rule mingled gold in their generation, for which reason they are the most precious —but in the helpers silver, and iron and brass in the farmers and other craftsmen." To this Plato added a second lie: "[T]here is an oracle that the state shall then be overthrown when the man of iron or brass is its guardian."

Cav had grown up in the Fair Grounds, a housing project near my first neighborhood on The Hill. He told us that the projects hadn't always been hovels, piled high with the poor. On his street had lived two teachers, a man who owned a restaurant, and a man who was foreman for the colored at the Sinclair Oil refinery. These people earned sufficient money to live elsewhere but were confined to the projects by birth, by the color of their skins. Cav stroked his beard and gazed slowly around the classroom. "Men of Gold. Men of Bronze. Of whom does Plato speak when he talks about men of 'baser' metals? Whom do you think that might be?" The answer was easy. Plato was talking about Cav and about me and about us. We were not the Philosopher Kings. Nor were we their golden children. We were men and women of bronze and copper, some so black as to be hewn from ebony. Plato was not to be trusted. The Myth of the Metals tainted everything he'd said.

Still I read more of him, especially the Symposium because friends had told me there was sex in it.

My excursions through Plato were an exception. Ordinarily I did not read for enjoyment or for ideas. I read for pungent phrases to pass off as my own. Shorthand had made me an excellent taker of notes. The notes were compendiums of my professor's pet phrases, phrases that I folded into papers and gave back to them at the end of the term. I was obsessed with grades. How could I be otherwise? I'd arrived at college with the word "risk" stamped on my forehead, and I wanted badly to wash it away. So and so: Black Risk Student. That's how the *Delaware County Times* and the *Philadelphia Bulletin* and the campus paper, *The Dome*, described us. Risk was a demeaning badge to wear. The truth was that most of the Project Prepare students would have done fine with no special handling at all. Brahv had taken few genuine risks, and I was one of them.

I piled up the "A" 's and doted on them like the greedy king in the counting house. At night I got out my grade reports and read them again, while others slept. The Dean's List wasn't good enough for me; I wanted the perfect semester, every grade an "A."

Most students waited for their grades to appear in their campus mailboxes. Not me. I paced up and down outside the computer room, watching the grade reports grow higher and higher in the basket at the computer's mouth. Then I watched the attendant bind the yellow pages into books. I waited for the Dean to fetch these books, then waylaid him and made him show me my grades then and there.

The perfect semester eluded me several times. When it came, it didn't change a thing. All it meant was that the risk had panned out.

The young faculty members in my department suggested that I go to graduate school. When I asked why, they said because I'd done well in statistics and in German, the two things that generally caused Ph.D. candidates to stumble. When I asked how this might be done, they said fellowships. I applied for two, one from Danforth and one from Ford, and won both. The Ford paid most lavishly. All expenses would be met. A generous stipend check would arrive by mail every month for the next five years. Five years seemed plenty of time to decide on who I wished to be. How little I knew.

The fellowships had required essays explaining why I wanted to teach college. The truth was that I'd never thought about teaching college. I'd only thought about escape. I wanted to escape my girlfriend. We were mismatched and lonely together. If I didn't get away, I'd marry her. I wanted to escape Chester. Twenty-one years old seemed old to me then, and in two decades of life I had been away from Chester for no more than a few weeks at a time.

I chose the University of Chicago with no greater care than I'd have taken hailing a taxi. My humanities teacher lit up when I told her. "Saul Bellow teaches there," she said. "You know. *Herzog. The Adventures of Augie March.*" I didn't know, and I could see the disappointment in her face. In my view Chicago's chief virtue was that I'd be nearly a thousand miles away. The only way I knew to change things was to leave them behind.

I visited Chicago in the spring. Lake Michigan was blue and endless, more an ocean than a lake. The university with its gargoyles and Gothic towers was more a medieval city than a school. The trip filled me with the images of leaving: the final walk up to the plane, the lift-off, Chester and Philadelphia falling away over my shoulder. Back in Chester, I suffered amnesia for the present. I drifted away during conversation. I lacked the concentration to read. Chicago was luminous with possibility. My mind had fled Chester and left the rest of me behind.

That summer I carried a rucksack slung across one shoulder everywhere I went. The rucksack contained a toothbrush, a clean shirt, and the precious papers that foretold the future. The papers were: the award letters from the fellowship foundations, the letter of acceptance from the University of Chicago, the story from the *Delaware County Daily Times* that explained who I was going to be. A reporter had interviewed me after I'd won the first fellowship. "I think that the college campus can be an exciting place for the exchange of ideas," I said. "I would like to be part of this in the future." The words seemed fraudulent. The reporter was the only living soul who'd ever heard me speak them. Fraudulent or no, words on paper solidified things. I read them over and over, breathing in the certainty they provided. By summer's end the papers were wilted from the sweat of my hands, and dirty along the folds from constant handling.

‖ Mr. Bellow's
Planet

I flew to Chicago holding the rucksack on my lap. At takeoff the stewardess had forced me to stow it under the seat, but I snatched it back as soon as she walked away. To let it out of my sight was to risk losing it, and that would be disastrous. The papers inside were proof of who I was.

I was certain that the University of Chicago had already forgotten me and that deans and registrars would greet me blank-faced, without a clue. The germ of this hysteria came from a Ford Foundation communiqué advising me to take along the award letter in case of a mix-up. That was one sentence in one letter in a ream of correspondence. I worried that sentence until it was a hundred pages long. To the cache of letters and newspaper clippings I had added my college transcript just to be on the safe side.

I was certain that my luggage would be sent to a distant city and not returned to me until who knew when. In the rucksack along with my documents I'd packed a shirt and toiletries so I could keep clean until my clothes turned up. All through the flight I worried about the can of spray starch in my duffle bag. It was an aerosol can; surely atmospheric pressure would cause it to explode. The can bore the likeness of an Indian maiden in a buckskin dress, standing beside an ear of corn as tall as she was. As the plane hurtled toward Chicago, I envisioned the can swelling toward explosion, the maiden and the corn growing larger and larger until, *Boom!*, the can blew up, making a jagged, flowering hole in the baggage compartment. When the plane hit a bump in the air, I assumed that the explosion had happened and pressed my nose to the window. There I saw my luggage as clear as day: my army duffel bag and my brown plaid suitcase falling down the sky.

I arrived in Chicago on Sunday, the twenty-third of September, a week before classes began. The streets of Hyde Park were drowsy with Sunday emptiness; the air was luminous with the reddish golden light of fall.

I'd taken a room at the Broadview Hotel, on Hyde Park Boulevard not far from Lake Michigan, and just opposite the Museum of Science and Industry. I dropped my luggage at the Broadview and went to find the quadrangles, which turned out to be more than a mile away. I walked west on 55th Street and was beginning to think I was lost until I came to Ellis Avenue, which I recognized from the university stationery. Walking south on Ellis, I encountered an enormous bronze sculpture seated between two tennis courts near 57th Street, next to the library. The sculpture looked like a skull and was roughly twice the height of a man, raised above the sidewalk on a granite mesa. This was Henry Moore's *Nuclear Reaction*. It marked the spot where Enrico Fermi and the Manhattan Project had created the first nuclear chain reaction, proving that The Bomb was possible. Elevated, set off in its own space, the sculpture seemed an object of worship.

I went up on the platform to inspect it. It was skull-like, all

right, but there were swirling contortions where the face should
have been, as though the artist had begun the barest foundation of
a face and then quit. I worked hard at conjuring up the eyes, nose,
and mouth, and let my hands glide in and out of the cool, smooth
curves. The sculpture made its claim on me. I returned to it often,
especially at night.

The main gateway to the quadrangles lay just across 57th
Street. It had been raining when I visited the campus that spring,
and I had hustled by the gate without looking up. Now I saw Cobb's
Gate—an ornate Gothic arch along whose shoulders crawled gargoyles and griffins, wings and talons in array. The buildings inside
the quad were made of the same gray stone, with towers and turrets
and cornices. There was filigree in the stone and medieval faces that
stared out at you from the past. I was bare chested in overalls and
sandals. The sun was buttery warm on my shoulders, but the
warmth was cool at the edges. The chill of winter was gathering
in the shade of the elms and in the lengthening shadows of the
buildings.

At the southern end of the quadrangle, a narrow, vaulted
archway let out onto The Midway, a swath of park three football
fields across. Down the center of The Midway ran two broad road-
ways separated by a strip of green and lined with the same gorgeous
elms as seen in the quads. The canopy of leaves reminded me of
Swarthmore. Across The Midway lay the law school, the school of
social service administration, and Bruno Bettelheim's Orthogenic
School.

From the far side of The Midway, the university seemed a
medieval fortress. A wall of gray stone ran for nearly a mile from the
university hospitals at the west end to the Main Quadrangles, to the
soaring tower of International House in the east. I walked east beneath the elms to Stony Island Avenue, then crossed Jackson Park

and Lake Shore Drive, and walked out onto The Point, a triangular spit of land that pushed out into Lake Michigan. The Loop glittered to the north. The Sears and Hancock towers were rivals, twin black obelisks that blinked fiercely at each other from the tips of their antennae, while lesser buildings huddled around their waists.

Lake Michigan would better have been named the Michigan Sea. It was the first lake I'd known whose opposite shore was not seeable with the naked eye. The view toward Michigan offered only water and sky. Later I saw that the lake changed its coat with the weather: slate gray, sea green, arctic blue. Some days it was as glutinous as Jell-O congealing. Some days it rammed its shoulder against the rocks and slammed fist after fist onto the jogging path and into the outermost lane of Lake Shore Drive. At the very tip of The Point were concrete breakers shaped like coffins. On nasty days the coffins were submerged in angry surf. In fair weather the lake lapped gently at the coffins while people lay upon them taking the sun. Guerrilla winter was evident along the water. On balmy days the wind would suddenly shift, bringing The Hawk in from Michigan to rake your bones.

I liked walking at night. During this first week I found the quadrangles tranquil and beautiful after dark, the turrets and towers lit by the autumn moon. On one of these nights, I was nearly given a heart attack when the lawn sprinklers burst into life. The Midway had a separate weather system. When the air on 57th was as still as death, The Midway, two blocks south, was alive with breezes. At night the quiet beauty was mine alone. If I had attended the official tours and lectures of orientation week, perhaps I'd have found out why. People were frightened of crime, and with good reason. Hyde Park was an island of prosperity in a sea of squalor. To the south, beyond the last university buildings, lay what Saul Bellow would later describe as "the edge of ratshit Woodlawn." To the north lay

Kenwood, a sliver of rambling Victorian houses, some of whose porches looked out onto the burned-out hovels of 47th Street. Across Washington Park to the west, the ghetto picked up again. Since I'd skipped the tours and lectures to wander on my own, I was ignorant of geography and danger. I had yet to notice the high-rise housing projects marching along the western horizon. My only certainties were that the lake was east and that everything was exhilarating, redolent with possibility. The newness excited me to the bone. I sang out loud, leaped and punched at the air. I was hopped up, manic, flying.

I was scanning the course listings when I spotted a talismanic name: Erika Fromm. With no justification at all, I assumed this Fromm to be the daughter of the famous psychiatrist Erich Fromm, who had been a student of Freud's and who, most importantly, had been psychoanalyzed by Freud, and a member of the inner circle. I'd admired Freud, for reasons that were corrupt. I admired him because he granted the analyst absolute power over the patient. In "discovering" the unconscious, Freud had placed the contents of the psyche beyond reach of the person who owned them. The psychoanalyst was part artist, part burglar, part scientist, but mainly a dictator who determined the meaning of every thought and action. People were books that could never understand themselves without us. I had yet to take my first graduate course, but already I thought of myself as a reader of minds.

If I had asked someone, I'd have found that Erika Fromm was not the daughter of Erich Fromm, and only a Fromm by marriage. That's if I'd asked someone, but I didn't. Fromm was a dramatic name. I took it for granted that dramatic facts came with it.

Erika Fromm was teaching "The Psychology of the Ego." Hers was the only course on the menu that required "an interview with the professor." For this interview I put on a shirt.

The woman who met me at the office door looked to be in her sixties, old enough to be venerable, old enough perhaps to have known Freud himself. She had a Valkyrie's high cheekbones and her hair was swept up and back from her face, in wings. As she turned and crossed the room, I could see that she had begun to stoop from the waist up. She took her place in the leather armchair and motioned me to sit in the plain wooden chair that faced it.

"You vish to study vis me ze psychology off de ego?"

I did.

"Do you know vat ego psychology iss?"

Yes, I said, I did. And I did. I tried to speak, but she cut me off, then lectured me about Anna Freud's breakthroughs in ego psychology. I was drunk on those apple-sized cheekbones, and especially on what I thought to be a Viennese accent, the way she said "zis, zees, zose, and zat."

"I vill admit you," she said.

Nothing could have prepared me for what she said next: "Vee haff been horrible to ze bleck people, ve heff treated zem so badly. Vee haff to mek it up. Vee must make it up. It may take you a little longa to get ze Ph.D., but you vill get it."

We must make it up. . . . It may take you longer to get your degree . . . but you will get it.

I was numb. It seemed Erika had told me that I was a dull child, to be treated with pity and patience, that I should accept condolences in advance for the difficulty I would have. The best I could do was nod until I got my senses back.

It came to me that a clever question might raise her opinion of me. Near the end of the interview, I recovered enough to form the question in my mind, along with the gestures I would use to deliver it. I smiled, leaned forward in my seat and asked it. My voice was hollow and foreign; it was coming not from me but at me, from somewhere across the room. I was still smiling and nodding as she showed me to the door. I vaulted by the students who were waiting in the hallway and rushed out into the quadrangle for air.

Back at the Broadview, I went over my documents yet again. The transcript said "Dean's List, Dean's List, Dean's List." It said Alpha Chi National Scholarship Honor Society. It said Cum Laude graduate, and I cursed myself for falling six one-hundredths of a percentage point short of Magna Cum Laude. I read again the wilted clipping from the Delaware County *Daily Times*—"Brent Staples, son of Mr. and Mrs. Melvin Staples, 316 Ward St., Chester, has won a Danforth Fellowship for advanced study for the Ph.D. degree, according to an announcement from The Danforth Foundation of St. Louis."—and I recalled the rush of happiness I felt when I read those words for the first time. "A frequent Dean's List student throughout the four years at college, he was elected President of his freshman class . . ." Nowhere did the story say that I was a foundling who'd gotten into college by accident. But it came close: ". . . Staples enrolled at Widener as one of 21 academic risks in the Project Prepare Program for educationally disadvantaged students." There it was again: "risk." I wondered if I'd ever be shed of it.

I needed a vote of confidence. I got it from one of the secretaries in the department, a bosomy, brown-skinned woman with a warming smile. Her name was Deloise. The first time we met, she mistook me for one of the construction workers who were jackhammering the sidewalk below her window. I appeared at her door shirtless, in overalls and sandals, a bandana hanging from my back pocket.

"The bathroom is right down the hall," she said.

"I know where the bathroom is," I said.

"Well, the water fountain is right there, next to the bathroom," she said.

"I know where the fountain is, too," I said.

A look of recognition crossed her face: This was the new black doctoral student, the one in those awful overalls.

I applied to Deloise for office space. She produced a ring of keys and told me to follow her. We got off the elevator on the second floor and stopped one door short of Erika Fromm's office. Deloise turned the key, threw open the door, and said, "This is it. You can have this one." The office was vast, the same size as Frau Dr. Fromm's. The window was framed in ivy and overlooked the green tranquillity of the social science quadrangle.

Mine was not the customary arrangement. Graduate students just down the hall were crammed three to an office: three desks, and three sets of books, three coffee cups, always one with fungus growing in it. I was alone in this lavish space, and also had heavy neighbors: Erika Fromm on one side, the department chairman on the other.

Deloise gave me a ruler, a stapler, and a dictionary. She apologized that the dictionary was used, and said that requisitioning a new one would take forever. Who needed a new dictionary? The used one was as good as gold. The gift of the office made me feel certified. To celebrate, I threw open the window, smoked the biggest reefer I could roll, and drank a very tall can of beer.

Deloise was brown-skinned Providence. Brown-skinned Providence smiled upon me from every corner of the campus. Secretaries seemed to beam when I came into the room. Administrative assistants cut corners in my favor. Tellers at the University Bank cashed checks that they shouldn't have because my account couldn't cover them. The university as white as it was depended heavily on black women's labor. These women were happy to meet black students and even happier to do them good. They greased the skids in a hundred ways. One of them took me aside and suggested with great tact that I would better represent my people if I ditched the overalls. I welcomed the concern, but overalls and jeans were the only clothes I owned.

I took an apartment across The Midway at the edge of Woodlawn, where nearness to the ghetto had driven down the rents. Five sunny rooms, with a sun porch and a walk-in pantry. I got the apartment illegally. The university had set aside this building and several others for married students and decreed that the single among us would languish in hotel rooms or in studios or in crowded shared apartments. I had not come a thousand miles to live in a shoe box. I needed *lebensraum*.

Brown-skinned Providence reigned at married student housing, too. I was clearly registered as single, but the angels who ran the office spared me the embarrassment of checking. They pointed out the best deals for the money. They cut me a break when the rent was late.

My building was a last outpost of university power. Under my windows middle-class Hyde Park ended and impoverished black Chicago began. The university police cruised east past my dining room and my bedroom, then turned north at my sun porch, back into Hyde Park.

The sun porch was my favorite room. Its windows looked east, along the dead-flat plane of 61st Street, and south on Ingleside

Avenue into Woodlawn. I studied there, I ate there and sometimes slept there. The days were punctuated by the screams of children at the elementary school just across 61st Street. At the start of recess they burst from the building as though from jail. First there was a trickle, then a rivulet, then eddies of boys and girls swirling around the school yard, coats and ribbons flying.

At night I let the house go dark so I could watch the street without being seen. The French windows were only eight feet above the ground, and when it was warm I threw them open and listened in on the conversations of passersby. When lovers paused below me I heard the wet sounds of their kissing and the breath coming out of their noses, the rustle of clothing as they rifled each other's bodies. I was invisible to them, but only an arm's length away in the dark.

On the school playground, basketball players carried on after dark. It was too dark to see the game from my porch, but I could hear the ball bouncing on the macadam court, banging off the metal blackboard. Eventually the game petered out. Traffic died down on 61st Street. The neighborhood went to sleep.

One morning before dawn I was startled awake by the voice of a man who sounded like he was in the room.

"You fucked them? You fucked them? They could kill me, you understand that? They could fuckin' kill me!"

Then I heard the muffled cries of a woman, the flat of his hand on her face and head. As I moved in a crouch to the window, I heard people in the apartment above me doing the same.

The woman stumbled backward into 61st Street, her forearm raised against the blows. The pimp was small but squarely built, an inverted triangle from the waist up, in a tight-fitting shirt and pants.

"Where's the money! Where's the money!" There wasn't any. They were detectives. She'd fucked the cops, and hadn't been paid. The pimp batted her around the intersection, then hauled her up Ingleside Avenue. Exit, shouting, stage south.

The pimp was a regular performer at my intersection. On another night I heard his voice. "I want my money! I want my money!" This time he was beating a man with a stick. The stick was big enough to cause pain, but too slight to bring the man down. The man retreated backward into 61st Street, warding off the board. Suddenly he raised his hands into the air and sank to his knees. The pimp dropped the plank and ran back into Woodlawn. The beaten man kneeled like a Muslim at prayer, his palms on the pavement, his bald pate glistening in the headlights of an approaching police car.

The pimp was also a seller of heroin. From my sun porch I watched the buyers who double-park in front of his building every evening beginning at dusk. The cars queued up on Ingleside Avenue with blinkers flashing, like planes awaiting takeoff at O'Hare. On my side of 61st Street the dealer would have been taken down in no time at all. On my side of 61st you couldn't sneeze without arousing suspicion.

On the other side and southward the crime was worse and so was the supermarket. At the Hyde Park Co-op the food was impeccable and fresh. At the 63rd Street market the meat was unfit for consumption. The produce stank of rot. The 63rd Street "shopping" strip was composed of vacant lots, burned-out buildings. This dismal scene was cast in shadow by the tracks of the Jackson Park el.

At night, I walked to the lakefront whenever the weather permitted. I was headed home from the lake when I took my first victim. It was late fall, and the wind was cutting. I was wearing my navy pea jacket, the collar turned up, my hands snug in the pockets. Dead leaves scuttled in shoals along the streets. I turned out of Blackstone Avenue and headed west on 57th Street, and there she was, a few yards ahead of me, dressed in business clothes and carrying a briefcase. She looked back at me once, then again, and picked up her pace. She looked back again and started to run. I stopped where I was and looked up at the surrounding windows. What did this look like to people peeking out through their blinds? I was out walking. But what if someone had thought they'd seen something they hadn't and called the police. I held back the urge to run. Instead, I walked south to The Midway, plunged into its darkness, and remained on The Midway until I reached the foot of my street.

I'd been a fool. I'd been walking the streets grinning good evening at people who were frightened to death of me. I did violence to them by just being. How had I missed this? I kept walking at night, but from then on I paid attention.

I became expert in the language of fear. Couples locked arms or reached for each other's hand when they saw me. Some crossed to the other side of the street. People who were carrying on conversations went mute and stared straight ahead, as though avoiding my eyes would save them. This reminded me of an old wives' tale: that rabid dogs didn't bite if you avoided their eyes. The determination to avoid my eyes made me invisible to classmates and professors whom I passed on the street.

It occurred to me for the first time that I was big. I was 6 feet 1½ inches tall, and my long hair made me look bigger. I weighed only 170 pounds. But the navy pea jacket that Brian had given me was broad at the shoulders, high at the collar, making me look bigger and more fearsome than I was.

I tried to be innocuous but didn't know how. The more I thought about how I moved, the less my body belonged to me; I became a false character riding along inside it. I began to avoid people. I turned out of my way into side streets to spare them the sense that they were being stalked. I let them clear the lobbies of buildings before I entered, so they wouldn't feel trapped. Out of nervousness I began to whistle and discovered I was good at it. My whistle was pure and sweet—and also in tune. On the street at night I whistled popular tunes from the Beatles and Vivaldi's *Four Seasons*. The tension drained from people's bodies when they heard me. A few even smiled as they passed me in the dark.

Then I changed. I don't know why, but I remember when. I was walking west on 57th Street, after dark, coming home from the lake. The man and the woman walking toward me were laughing and talking but clammed up when they saw me. The man touched the woman's elbow, guiding her toward the curb. Normally I'd have given way and begun to whistle, but not this time. This time I veered toward them and aimed myself so that they'd have to part to avoid walking into me. The man stiffened, threw back his head and assumed the stare: eyes dead ahead, mouth open. His face took on a bluish hue under the sodium vapor streetlamps. I suppressed the urge to scream into his face. Instead I glided between them, my shoulder nearly brushing his. A few steps beyond them I stopped and howled with laughter. I called this game Scatter the Pigeons.

Fifty-seventh Street was too well lit for the game to be much fun; people didn't feel quite vulnerable enough. Along The Midway were heart-stopping strips of dark sidewalk, but these were so frightening that few people traveled them. The stretch of Blackstone between 57th and 55th provided better hunting. The block was long and lined with young trees that blocked out the streetlight and obscured the heads of people coming toward you.

One night I stooped beneath the branches and came up on the other side, just as a couple was stepping from their car into their town house. The woman pulled her purse close with one hand and reached for her husband with the other. The two of them stood frozen as I bore down on them. I felt a surge of power: these people were mine; I could do with them as I wished. If I'd been younger, with less to lose, I'd have robbed them, and it would have been easy. All I'd have to do was stand silently before them until they surrendered their money. I thundered, "Good evening!" into their bleached-out faces and cruised away laughing.

I held a special contempt for people who cowered in their cars as they waited for the light to change at 57th and Woodlawn. The intersection was always deserted at night, except for a car or two stuck at the red. *Thunk! Thunk! Thunk!* They hammered down the door locks when I came into view. Once I had hustled across the street, head down, trying to seem harmless. Now I turned brazenly into the headlights and laughed. Once across, I paced the sidewalk, glaring until the light changed. They'd made me terrifying. Now I'd show them how terrifying I could be.

I played basketball nearly every day. I made several friends at the gym, one of them a Ph.D. student who'd played basketball for Princeton. He still owned his Princeton warm-up suit. It was a snazzy suit—black with bright orange trim, PRINCETON emblazoned across the back of the jacket. The pants had zippered splits below the knee; with the zippers open, bright orange panels flew stylishly in the air as he ran the court.

I admired this suit so much that my friend finally gave it to me. I wore it shamelessly, flaunting the implicit claim that I had played for Princeton. This claim was quickly seen through. Practicing alone at Widener had made me a reasonable shooter, but that was all. Invisible opponents had not taught me to drive through traffic to basket, or how to push and shove for rebounds. I was a poor defensive player too, but this had less to do with my physical skills than my mental habits. I fell victim to the spectacle. I watched the game when I should have been playing it. When an opposing player beat his man with a brilliant move, I stood rock still, awed by the strength and grace.

Still, I knew how to act the part. I chattered through the game—"great play," "pick left," "pick right"—and whacked players on the butt when they made spectacular plays. And when I made a shot, I trotted back to the other end of the court, stylishly repeating the shooting motion with my right hand. I was a ham. The Princeton warm-up suit was the finishing touch.

The gym was off-limits to people not associated with the university. But young black men from Woodlawn and elsewhere invariably got in, a few because they owned fake IDs. I got to know them and was invited to play in their recreational leagues. One of the leagues met at Fiske Elementary School, just across 61st Street from my apartment. One day I arrived early for a game and found the pimp horsing around on the court, still in street shoes and his fancy pimping clothes. He'd picked me out as a newcomer and a square. He offered to sell me sex, perhaps even from the girl I'd seen him beating. When I declined, he thrust a pair of dice at me.

"Want a game?" he said.

"Pardon me?"

"I said, 'Want a game?' " His face was uncommonly flat; his lips curled back chimpishly when he smiled.

"No, thank you," I said.

He laughed and walked away, mocking me: "Pardon me; no, thank you. Pardon me; no, thank you."

The recreational league tournament drew good-sized crowds. At the start of the playoffs we won a close game that we'd been expected to lose. After the crowd cleared out, we lingered by the court and talked until dark. As we crossed the school yard to leave, someone spotted the foil packets at courtside. The packets contained a tannish powder with chocolatelike flecks. It was heroin. Backtracking through the schoolyard, we found several more packets. It was decided that these had either fallen from a spectator's pocket or been dumped by someone running from the police. My teammates weren't surprised. A few of them divided the packets up among themselves and pocketed them.

I took one. How could I not? I was curious about heroin. I'd been curious about it ever since that night several years before when I'd watched Stephen shooting up. My curiosity had grown as I watched Stephen lose himself. In Chester no one had ever offered me heroin; I didn't even know what it looked like. In Chicago the streets of Woodlawn were paved with it.

Some of my teammates opened their packets and dabbed the heroin into their noses. I was curious, but not that curious. I saved my packet for later.

The team had won and we were happy. Someone ran up to 63rd Street for beer, which we drank while sitting on the front steps of the school. Across the street the drug customers began queuing up in front of the dealer's house, just as they did every evening at dusk. The cars double-parked on Ingleside Avenue, their taillights blinking, blinking, blinking.

I rationalized taking the heroin on the grounds that I was a scientist. The model for my drug experiment was Freud's *Cocaine Papers*, a new book that was making quite a stir at the university. It surprised me to find that Freud's first published papers were not about psychoanalysis but *über coca*. He didn't just praise it, he described it as the most important discovery since Prometheus stole fire from the gods. Cocaine, he said, was "a magical drug" that could be used to treat consumption, heroin addiction, depression, asthma, and could be used as an aphrodisiac. It was surprising to find that Freud hadn't been born a dour old man. *The Cocaine Papers* showed him young and vital, writing horny letters to his fiancée, Martha Bernays, promising to kiss her "quite red," and warning that he'd fall upon her like "a wild man."

The Cocaine Papers was thin rationalization for using heroin found on a basketball court in Woodlawn. In Chester I'd known a woman who had injected heroin poisoned with bathroom cleanser. She lived, but just barely. The chlorine in the cleanser damaged her bones and turned her teeth a grizzly greenish gray. I had a hundred years on Freud and was plenty old enough to know better. But I went ahead anyway.

At home I put the heroin on my shaving mirror. I rolled up a dollar bill, inserted the bill into my nose and blew a hefty portion of the heroin into the air as dust. This was the first lesson: breath in, never out. I snorted up two nostrils full and sat back to make my observations. Nothing happened, and so I did it again. I felt a little drowsy, but that was all. I woke up the next morning with the screaming shits. So did my teammates. I ran into one of them at a drugstore; we both bought diarrhea medicine.

Basketball took me deeper into black Chicago. The gyms were dank with the sweat of ages, so acid dank that no amount of airing could make them fresh. Black Chicago spoke, cheered, and heckled in a Southern accent, which was peculiar, given that many of the people had never been south of 95th Street. The Southern accent was the sound of segregation. Blacks had come north in The Great Migration and been locked into the ghettos of the South and West sides, with no hope of reprieve. Mayor Richard J. Daley had made sure the walls around those ghettos were impenetrable. I had once heard it said that your future depended on which side of the street you were born on. Nowhere was this truer than in Chicago.

At the university I was a passable player, but in the South Side leagues I sat on the bench, my legs crossed in my snazzy Princeton warm-ups. The games were rougher and faster, the players like cats to the basket. Some of them jumped and kept going up, up, and up. My teammates treated me well. Some kidded me about the Ph.D., one even called me Professor. They seemed proud that one of their own had made it to the university. They respected the achievement, even though many of them despised the university itself. This despisement was poisonous and mutual. It dated back to the 1930s and the first years after the great Robert Maynard Hutchins took over as president.

Within the university Hutchins was recalled as a demigod, cut from Socratic cloth. He championed liberal education, was devoted to the Great Books, and was credited with rousing the university to greatness. Historians of local race relations remembered him differently. Under Hutchins in the 1930s and 1940s the university subsidized property owners' associations that discriminated against blacks and it openly encouraged the practice. Hutchins defended racially restrictive covenants on the grounds that they were legal. Under his aegis the university established a fund to buy and control Hyde Park. To stimulate contributions, Hutchins organized a bus tour for trustees into the ghetto.

In the 1950s the university was seeking still greater leverage to hold back the ghetto when an opportunity presented itself: a burglary and abduction that sharply increased the local desire for security. In May 1952 a Hyde Park man and his wife woke up to an alarming sight at the foot of their bed. Years later Samuel Untermeyer described to me what he and his wife, Joan, had seen: "We sat up in bed and saw a little colored man with a yellowish complexion, holding a gun. He took some jewelry. Then he made my wife put on her coat, drove her away, and let her out in the middle of nowhere."

Samuel Untermyer was a nuclear engineer. Among his neighbors and colleagues were two of the Manhattan Project's brightest lights: Harold C. Urey, the inventor of heavy water, and Enrico Fermi, the father of The Bomb.

"Fermi heard me cry out and came running," Untermeyer told me. "I opened the door and there he was in his nightclothes, carrying a baseball bat. Fermi's conscience wouldn't allow him to own a gun, but the bat he thought of as fair. He'd wrapped the bat in sheets of lead so that he could hit very hard with it."

Picture it: the father of The Bomb brandishing a caveman's tool.

After the abduction Hyde Park ceded the university all the power it wanted. The university attacked crime and blight with what was first called "slum clearance," later "slum prevention." Vast tracts of land were cleared of buildings, housing went upscale, blacks were shuttled out of the neighborhood. Something like fifty bars and clubs were swept away. A neighborhood that had once played host to Charlie Parker, Miles Davis, and Earl "Fatha" Hines was devoid of music. By the time I arrived in Hyde Park not a single jazz club remained. The ghetto had been beaten back, but sterility was the cost. By day 57th Street was barren, by night utterly deserted.

What the university called "slum prevention" my teammates called "Negro Removal." One of them claimed to know blacks who had once been offered "bounties" to surrender their leases and leave the neighborhood.

Certainly "slum prevention" had its virtues. In Woodlawn derelict buildings became drug dens and firetraps. In Hyde Park such buildings were swept away, as though by the Hand of God.

The Hand of God hovered steadily above places where black men congregated.

Hyde Park basketball courts had remained stubbornly black as areas around them whitened and went upscale. In high summer the courts bristled with black men who had come to play and watch. These courts were Sunday schools compared to my heroin-strewn court in Woodlawn. No gangsters. No pimps. No drug customers queued up at the curb. But beer and reefer were sometimes consumed in copious amounts. The reefer was slipped discreetly from one cupped palm to the next. But the beer couldn't be hidden, especially when it was Gill's Beer from Gill's of 47th Street, which was sold in half-gallon jugs. Shady characters hung around at the edges of things, but where else to find pickpockets but in the town square?

The courts were also frequented by middle-class blacks—lawyers and artists and nine-to-five types from The Loop. Now and then a millionaire athlete stopped his Mercedes to reminisce. The players who most loved the courts had grown up on them, gone away to college, and returned to them once again. Basketball was a forum for their friendships, a binding ritual in their lives.

The courts were noisy. Spectators responded to great plays by howling, slapping each other five, and dancing up and down the sidelines. Pretty university students and professors' wives were greeted, as they passed, with wolf whistles and cries of "Hey, baby, ain't you fine." Howlers who got too specific were made to shut up. The courts were under suspicion and the older players knew it. But discretion was of no avail. The courts were being swept away.

The first to go was the most perfect court known to man. It was situated among the trees just off Lake Shore Drive, its eastern basket facing the lake. Gliding to that basket, with lake and sky beyond, gave you the illusion of flight. The second court to disappear was less beautiful but much loved by its players. It was farther inland, a simple stretch of macadam on the grounds of an elementary school. Shortly before the annual tournament, the backboards were taken down and carted away under cover of darkness. The third court was part of the YMCA on 53rd Street. The building fell on hard times and was razed with bewildering speed.

I began my doctoral studies just as psychology was losing legitimacy as a science. A hefty body of research had placed all psychology's tools under suspicion. Studies of psychotherapy had shown dismal results: a third of the patients got worse, a third got better, and a third stayed the same. Psychological tests had been shown to be hokum. A patient given three tests that purported to measure the same psychological trait—say, anxiety or aggressiveness—received three wildly different scores. Psychologists were equally unreliable. Therapists recalled not what and how patients behaved but what diagnostic manuals had told them to expect. The mind, once thought to be thoroughly figured out, was escaping like smoke through the bars of a cage. In the world at large, psychologists continued to thrive and be respected. Inside the university, the priesthood had been defrocked. The psychology department was dissolved and reformed around subdisciplines with stronger claims on science. We were the Behavioral Science Department now.

The shifting firmament provided a smorgasbord of the old and new. In the morning I studied Rorschach's Ink Blot test with an old German gentleman who believed that the test told all about the mind. In the afternoon I sat with a young statistician who treated the blots as meaningless toys to be used in statistical games. Erika Fromm held fast to psychoanalysis as the true and only gospel. The philosopher Paul Ricoeur taught that Freud's version of mind was one version among many. Ricoeur's book *Freud and Philosophy* dissected psychoanalysis to show how Freud had constructed it. Freud's psyche had begun as a map on which the conscious and unconscious were regions of light and dark with the Id, Ego, and Superego shared among them. Freud borrowed concepts from the physical sciences, and tried to build a machine that would run of itself. What a baroque machine this was, with "psychic energies" surging up from the Id and moving like steam through the valves and whistles of "psychic apparatuses." Freud was not "observing" the mind at all. He was interpreting it through a system of symbols that he himself had made.

Ricoeur was tough going, filled with references to philosophers I had not read. I began reading philosophy, first to keep up, and then because I enjoyed it. I lugged home the basic works of Plato and Aristotle, then continued more or less at random through Kant, Hume, Locke, Spinoza, Descartes, Husserl, Merleau-Ponty, Sartre, Scheler, Schopenhauer, and Wittgenstein. I didn't just read the books, I bought them. I preferred expensive hard-cover editions, and found their heft and permanence reassuring. I allowed myself nothing so frivolous as a novel. Homer and Dante were what I read at the beach.

The more difficult books required guidance. For this purpose I recruited a professor in the philosophy department who agreed to meet with me now and then to discuss my readings. His infirmities and equipment suggested that he had read mightily in his time. He sometimes wore a neck brace. And the top of his desk was an enormous easel that raised the book so he didn't have to bend his neck to read. He was generous with his time and tolerant of my ignorances. In time, those ignorances grew fewer.

I felt compelled to show off what I'd learned. My dissertation proposal began with a discussion of epistemology from Plato's time to the present. My research was appended almost as an afterthought. My dissertation chairman suggested with great tact that I dispense with Plato and the others. "We take it for granted that you know these things," he said. "You don't have to prove it to us."

I decided to write my Ph.D. thesis in the mathematics of decision making. Decision theorists had shown that equations predicted outcomes more accurately than people did. The theorist who first caught my attention did so in the most dramatic way. His name was Hillel Einhorn and he suffered from Hodgkin's disease. The disease was in remission when I met him, but several years earlier, while hospitalized with it, Einhorn had overheard doctors saying that he was going to die. He lived for many years afterward.

He designed a study to test how well doctors predicted survival in cases like his. He asked doctors to look at biopsies of Hodgkin's patients and predict how long those patients would live. (The patients were already dead; the time between when the slides were made and when they had died had been duly recorded.) The doctors didn't even come close. But a mathematical model of their thought processes did very well. The doctors looked for the right things in the biopsies but got mixed up in the processing. Equations didn't have bad days. The cool indifference of numbers appealed to me.

Jimmy's Woodlawn Tap was the student bar by default, as it was the only bar that remained along the stretch of 55th Street that had once been thick with them. The most lamented of these was The Compass Bar, which had been home to the Compass Players, who had counted among their members Mike Nichols and Elaine May. Jimmy's walls were painted a depressing brown to discourage dirt. The piss smell of the men's room could be overwhelming. The barroom was dank with spilled beer. Here I shared a table with Aaron

Rhodes and listened to his opinions on Thucydides and St. Augustine and Durkheim. Aaron was working on a Ph.D. at The Committee on Social Thought. Hutchins had created The Committee and dedicated it to the study of eternal ideas. Hutchins had despised bean counters and number crunchers and academic specialists of every kind. He viewed education as a Socratic affair, in which students read the great books, pondered the great questions, and listened to conversations among the great minds. TheCommittee's professors were a modern version of Plato's Philosopher Kings. The Committee's students were Philosopher-Kings-in-Training.

Aaron was true to the mold. He pitied students whose work consisted of statistics and surveys and other things that Hutchins had looked on as ephemeral. People who failed to heed the classics were "philistines," a word Aaron used with finality and with relish. "A philistine!" he'd say, dismissing the person with a flip of his wrist. Aaron wore a rumpled trench coat and walked toes out. He was still in his early twenties, but his bearing made him seem older, much older.

He'd have been middle-aged if not for his talents at mimicry. He was splendid at it, particularly around the mouth. As a child, he had mimicked a bear from a children's book so well that his teeth had been thrust permanently out of line. As Aaron explained it, his father had pried the teeth back into place with a dinner knife. This had been done in laborious sessions each night after the evening meal. Aaron specialized in sneers. He didn't have a sneer of his own, but could reproduce those of others. When he dismissed a philistine, he mimicked the set of the person's mouth for the occasion.

Aaron slept at my house when he stayed late at Jimmy's. There was no choice. He lived on the North Side; transportation in and out of Hyde Park was impossible after rush hour. The el stops

were in the ghetto, the buses slow boats to China. The next morning
he got up and trudged across The Midway to the office of the journal
where he worked. Passing through my living room, he admired the
glass bookcases overflowing with philosophy's greatest hits. Plato
through Husserl, Sartre, and Merleau-Ponty, chronologically arranged. It pleased him that I was "going about things the right way."
Aaron took an interest in my case.

Saul Bellow was The Committee's most public figure. His
novel, *Humboldt's Gift*, had just been published. The dust jacket
was screaming yellow, and copies were placed in every one of the
university bookstore's several windows. Inside, on the front-most
table, *Humboldt's Gift* rose in an enormous yellow pyramid. Bellow
signed copies by the gross. Even clerks who mainly read romances
sensed that something was up and got in line for autographs. A
signed copy was given to me as a gift. I still have it.

Humboldt's Gift generated endless gossip. Aaron's mentor,
the sociologist Edward Shils, had been kidnapped into the novel and
was said to be deeply angry. He and Bellow had known each other
forever. Apparently Shils had asked in advance that Bellow not include him.

Aaron spoke of Bellow as "Bellow," and Arendt "Arendt."
Edward Shils he referred to as "Mr." Mr. Shils wrote about tradition
and stability. The genius that Aaron saw in Shils's books eluded
me. His writings in the university *Record* were more accessible and
certainly more interesting. The *Record* contained his evaluation of a
popular young professor who'd been denied tenure, thus sparking a
takeover of the administration building. Shils was brutal:

> [Her] level of performance is at best unquali-
> fiedly mediocre." She has not a single relatively original,
> or even bold idea. She has not pursued a central theme

with rigor nor in depth . . . She lacks analytical skill. She is unimaginative. Such perspectives and theoretic framework as she possesses belong to the problematic clichés of the present day.

Aaron looked up this passage whenever he needed a hoot. It impressed me, too. How could it not? Professors didn't speak this way; they hemmed around, hid their disdain in euphemism. Shils was intellectual royalty with blue-collar tact. He came on like a boxer, aiming to break some ribs. The faculty accepted his assessment of the professor's work. The decision to deny the woman tenure was reaffirmed.

At other universities students took over buildings with little or no risk of reprisal. At Cornell students who laid siege to a building with guns endured not a single expulsion. Chicago was different. Faculty members walked among the demonstrators and identified them for disciplinary purposes. The sit-in ended without concessions. The participants were summoned to disciplinary hearings. Suspensions and expulsions followed. Shils had been the hub of power through it all. For this he was loved—and hated.

Aaron kept after me to attend one of Shils's seminars. Finally I gave in and went. The seminar met in a small oak-lined room not much bigger than the conference table it contained. Shils loomed at the table's head: a cannonball figure with beefy hands resting in front of him. The man radiated power. The space around him was his space; entering it placed you under his control. His eyes settled on me almost at once. He was probably just curious about who I was. The Committee had only one black student—a Caribbean character with dark glasses and a goatee—and clearly I wasn't he. Shils's gaze made me uneasy. His top lip curled upward and to one side, making him seem disdainful. Instead of merely curious he seemed to be sneering at me, objecting to me on principle. I tried to look away, but there was nowhere to look. The windows were well above eye level, quite near the ceiling. I stared into the wall and waited it out. I fled the seminar and never went back.

Mr. Shils had been kidnapped as Professor Richard Durnwald into *Humboldt's Gift*:

> Durnwald was reddish, elderly, but powerful, thickset and bald, a bachelor of cranky habits but a kind man. He had a peremptory blunt, butting, even bullying manner, but if he scolded me it was because he loved me—he wouldn't have bothered otherwise. A great scholar, one of the most learned people on the earth, he was a rationalist. Not narrowly rationalistic, by any means. Nevertheless, I couldn't talk to him about the powers of a spirit being separated from a body. He wouldn't hear of it.

It amused me that Bellow seemed frightened of Shils, too. The curl in Shils's lip Bellow had given to the character Mickey, a concessionaire in the Division Street Steam Baths:

> Mickey had a twisted lip. During the Depression he had to sleep in the parks and the cold ground gave him a partial paralysis of the cheek. This makes him seem to scoff and jeer. A misleading impression.

I scribbled "Shils!" in the margin. The theft didn't end with *Humboldt's Gift*. Shils was a thread that ran through several of Bellow's novels, a stolen essence that popped up everywhere.

Bellow's people leaped more vividly from the page than any

I'd encountered. Often he reduced them to a single bodily feature that carried their entire person in its wake: the set of the butt, the cleft of the upper lip, a gap in the teeth. He preferred a sexual organ if he could get it. At the Division Street baths he had waited vulturously for the steam room attendant to bend over so that he could record the squeaky-clean anus, juxtaposed with the "testicles swinging on a long sinew." If no sexual organ was available, anything would do. He sometimes snatched bodies whole, but mainly he cannibalized them, taking only the choicest parts. He stole from himself as well, giving characters his own enormous eyes and unflatteringly spaced teeth.

I lost the thread of his story when he paused to reflect on philosophy and metaphysics. The references were often oblique to the point of nonsense. Students from The Committee referred to them as Saul "Belching." This belching aside, the man was an alchemist. He could make the folds in a bald man's head seem like a window on the soul.

This was one of the first novels I'd read on my own. Most of the others had been assigned in college, and I'd ransacked them for facts to use in term papers and essays. Those novels had the added liability of being merely fictional: Their characters were elsewhere, living otherwise. *Humboldt's Gift* was local geography, people included.

The novel was cast as a farce. Its self-mocking star was Charlie Citrine, a middle-aged writer and Hyde Park egghead. Charlie is school smart but life dumb. Cannier types constantly exploit him. His fortune is being slowly extracted by a vindictive ex-wife and her lawyers. He hangs out with lowlifes who cheat him at cards. One of these lowlifes is a would-be mafiosi named Rinaldo. Charlie stops a check on Rinaldo. Rinaldo bludgeons Charlie's Mercedes with a baseball bat. When Charlie pays up, Rinaldo rips up the money and throws it away. Rinaldo wants humiliation. He drags Charlie into the shit stall and forces him to hold the toilet roll while he, Rinaldo, takes a dump.

The novel ceases to be a farce when a black man steps out of the shadows and, with no motive, slits a white woman's throat. Black people in the book were sinister characters. Rinaldo refers to them as "crazy buffaloes" and "pork chops." Crazy buffaloes populate the slums that surround Hyde Park. A pork chop chases Charlie down the middle of his street, presumably at night. These passages made me angry. it was the same anger I felt when white people cowered past me on the street.

Barbarousness in *Mr. Sammler's Planet* is a pickpocket who preys on the old and feeble as they ride the public bus in New York City. The pickpocket works in broad daylight. He manhandles bleary-eyed old men, rifles their pockets, and leaves them too terrified to speak. After spying this fellow at work, Mr. Sammler is chased down and cornered. The pickpocket says nothing, but shows Mr. Sammler his dick. What followed was the book's most vivid description:

It was displayed to Sammler with great oval testicles, a large tan-and-purple uncircumcised thing—a tube, a snake; metallic hairs bristled at the thick base and the tip curled beyond the supporting, demonstrating hand, suggesting the fleshy motility of an elephant's trunk, though the skin was somewhat iridescent rather than thick or rough. Over the forearm and fist that held him Sammler was required to gaze at this organ. No compulsion would have been necessary. He would in any case have looked.

Bellow wanted the dick remembered. He returned to it again and again as a symbol of spiritual decay, of the "sexual nigger-hood" that "millions of civilized people" had deluded themselves into wanting.

I expected more of a man who could see to the soul. I expected a portrait of myself, not as the beast I'd been made out to be, but as who I was at heart. I'd given up on this when Aaron lent me his dog-eared copy of *Dangling Man*, Bellow's first novel, written in 1944. "Read it," he said. "It speaks to our situation." The novel was written as a journal. The first page was an eloquent defense of the form:

> There was a time when people were in the habit of addressing themselves frequently and felt no shame at making a record of their inward transactions. But to keep a journal nowadays is considered a kind of self-indulgence, a weakness and in poor taste. For this is an era of hardboiled-dom. . . . Do you have feelings? There are correct and incorrect ways of indicating them. Do you have an inner life? It is nobody's business but your own. Do you have emotions? Strangle them. To a degree everybody obeys this code. And it does admit of a limited kind of candor, a closemouthed straightforwardness. But on the truest candor, it has an inhibitory effect. Most serious matters are closed to the hard-boiled. They are unpracticed in introspection and therefore badly equipped to deal with opponents whom they cannot shoot like big game or outdo in daring.

I sat up when I read this, and read it again. I was carrying a journal with me everywhere. *Humboldt's Gift* had given me the idea. I wrote on buses and on the Jackson Park el—though only at the stops to keep the writing legible. I traveled to distant neighborhoods, sat on their curbs, and sketched what I saw in words. Thursdays meant free admission at the Art Institute. All day I attributed motives to people in paintings, especially people in Rembrandts. At closing time I went to a nightclub in The Loop and spied on the patrons, copied their conversations and speculated about their lives. The journal was more than "a record of my inner transactions." It was a collection of stolen souls from which I would one day construct a book. Bellow had made it seem easy enough: Kidnap people onto the page, stir in stories from the papers and from your life, and *voila!* you had it made.

A journal of Chicago is a journal of weather. Winter lasts forever there. Dirty gray ice hangs on in the gutters through Easter. June suckers you outside in shirtsleeves, then shifts its winds, bringing January to rake your bones. Warm weather smells of an ambush until August. Then the lake heats up, the breeze stops, and it's too hot to breathe.

In deepest winter, arctic winds dipped down from Canada and froze every bit of moisture from the air. Indoors the air was so dry that it split your lips and gave you nosebleeds. The cold slipped its knife through the bathroom window and cut you as you showered. Outside, the storm drains along the street vented steam, as though boiling. As you walked to the corner store, steam flared from your tearducts and from the surface of the eye itself.

The beauty of the nights compensated for this cruelty. The wind that punished had also swept the sky clean and left it breathtakingly clear.

In the fiercest cold the lakefront fell exclusively to the runners. Trotting through the arctic waste by the lake, I imagined myself an explorer, racing to the Pole. Occasionally another runner appeared in the distance, steamy breath curling around his head. As we drew closer to one another we could see the sweat frozen into icicles hanging from our woolen caps and from our beards. We smiled at one another through ice-coated whiskers, then steamed on. Back at my apartment, I lazed in a hot bath, then wrapped myself in Miles Davis. "Miles Smiles." "In a Silent Way." "Kind of Blue." "Live in Stockholm." Then I turned to writing in the journal.

I suffered lung burn from running in subzero weather. The lung tissue was frozen and scarred and could no longer transfer oxygen. I lay in bed for days, too weak to sit up. My face was ashen, as pale as death. The doctor said the condition was temporary, but it still had scared me. It taught me respect for the cold.

The winter of 1977 was one of the cruelest on record. The temperature stayed below freezing for the entire month of January, with several consecutive days well below zero. Sunday, January fifteenth, started out at 19 below zero, far too cold to run, too cold even for a walk around the block. An icy frost was covering the sunporch windows faster than I could scrape it away. Finally, I gave up and let it wall me in.

By nightfall I was crazed with cabin fever. I decided to go to the movies. This meant taking the el to the North Side, to the Biograph Theatre. The trip was punishing, especially with the Jackson Park el on its Sunday schedule. A wait of forty minutes was not uncommon. Some el platforms offered the mercy of enclosed waiting areas. But mainly you stood in the open while the guillotine winds cut you to pieces.

I set out for the el stop at 63rd Street and had just crossed 62nd when the northbound train roared across the horizon and disappeared into the night. This had happened many times. Ordinarily

I beat it back to my apartment, waited twenty minutes, then started out again. This time I pressed on to a diner under the el tracks. I ordered tea and a Danish and filled the time writing.

The journal notes that the tea was served in a disposable cup and that the restaurant was dimly lit and nearly empty. The waitress behind the counter stared out at the night and hugged herself against the chill. There were two other people in the place: a man using the phone in the foyer and a woman sitting at the counter. The woman wore a strawberry-blond Afro wig. It was an enormous wig, its curls obscuring her face. Her coat, draped across her lap, was thin and trimmed in fake fur. I wrote first about the man at the phone:

> There's a reason for placing a phone in the foyer of a restaurant; in a place like Chicago there's a better than even chance that the patron won't spend hours out there pleading his case. This joker in the foyer is probably explaining to his wife why he's late, telling her he's in a phone booth. It's so cold that the call doesn't take long.
>
> I sit down to order my tea and Danish, really to get the change for the train because the CTA doesn't take twenties. I look right and see her: the archetypal underdressed party girl: Her strawberry-blond wig is about the size of a basketball and droops around her taffy-colored cheeks. The wig is too big, slides way down around the outlines of her face. She wears one of those bare-shouldered Jane Russell blouses, spanning the skin from shoulder to shoulder (including the bruises bitten into her by some passionate lover). Her coat! Cheap. Super-thin. Fake to the Chicago wind, trimmed in fake fur.
>
> He comes in from the phone. Wrinkled and

kinky from a weekend out in the same clothes (it's Sunday), and sits down with the lady who is by now ravenously biting into her cheeseburger deluxe.

"How's the food?" he says.

"OK," she says.

"You know what happens after this?"

"Mmmm." Mouth full of burger.

"You know what happens next?"

Inaudible response.

"We goin' to the crib, right?"

She sees me looking at her, peeks around the edges of her wig. (I wonder if she suspects that I'm writing this down.)

He's loud. He bought the pussy for a cheeseburger deluxe and hasn't the decency to keep quiet about it. I feel myself hating him.

"We goin' to the crib, . . ." she says.

"Then what's gonna happen?"

Inaudible.

"Yeah!" he says.

Then he gets off his stool and walks back to the pisshole. By this time I've finished my stuff. I slip my journal and pen into my rucksack and wrap up to split. At the door I do my classic full turn before moving off-stage. Her eyes catch mine. They admit humiliation, desperation, and unhappiness . . . I pay my fare, and up the stairs to wait for the train. God, it's cold out tonight.

The tale of the prostitute and the burger deluxe typifies the journals in winter. The stories are gray and sad, like the weather. In Chicago I learned that weather made me who I was. Successive gray days left me on the verge of tears. The mood was impenetrable. I didn't know it was a mood until the sun came shining to the rescue. The lesson was new each time.

The journal writer in *Dangling Man* is Joseph, a young Hyde Parker who waits a year to be inducted into the army. Red tape delays him. Meanwhile he quits a job that he can't get back and holes up in a rooming house with his wife, Iva, waiting out the grim Chicago winter. Iva as Bellow presents her is no more alive than a piece of furniture. Her purpose is to bring Joseph books and punctuate the long days of solitude during which he writes in his journal and watches ice forming on the windows. Aaron was right. The book spoke to our situation: Like Joseph, we were in our twenties, trapped in Hyde Park, wondering who we would be.

Joseph suffers from "a feeling of strangeness, of not quite belonging to the world, of lying under cloud and looking up at it." He changes restaurants so waitresses won't get to know him. He feels unfit for company, especially on holidays. On December 20 he writes: "We have two invitations for Christmas dinner, one from the Almstadts and another from my brother Amos. I am for refusing both." I appreciated the impulse. Christmas had been among the grimmest days of my family's life. Christmas carols left me leaden and depressed. The forced mirth of the holiday highlighted how close to the edge we lived and how unhappy we were.

I'd promised myself that I would never spend another Christmas under my father's roof. Then my mother left him and fled to Roanoke with my brothers and sisters in tow. Now I was obligated to visit them, if only at Christmas. But nothing had changed. The holidays were as grim as they'd always been. I spent the days pacing the city, hanging out in libraries and restaurants. Finally I struck a compromise: I would spend one Christmas with my family and take the next one for myself. I announced the compromise by acting on it.

It was easy to remain alone during minor holidays—Easter, the Fourth of July, and Labor Day. Thanksgiving was trickier. People you hardly knew tried to draft you into ad hoc families. Unmarried out-of-towners were sought out as though we were infirm. Mainly I turned the invitations down. The few that I accepted gave me the same sense of imprisonment that I felt with my family. Holidays were a form of tyranny; it was best to face and fight them alone.

Spending Christmas and New Year's alone required a conscientious system of lies. These lies I began to tell in mid-November, when the crimp on the half-and-half carton said: "Sell before December 24." I wrote my mother that I was tied up with my dissertation or too broke to travel. I assured people in Chicago that I was "going home" for the holidays. Lovers went home to their families; I led them to believe that I was going home to mine.

As Christmas closed in, I laid in food, wine, and books so that I could stay out of sight. I slept late on Christmas morning, ate a big breakfast, and read until it was digested. Then I went for a run along Lake Michigan. The streets had a distinctive holiday emptiness. The city had been left to the mad and the homeless, all of whom were more crazed than usual. Traffic was almost nil. Such cars as there were contained well-dressed families plying the path from home to Grandma's and back again. Back in my apartment, I took a long hot bath, then lounged in the sun porch, drinking tea and writing in my journal. I napped at will. The children who lived above me had taken their thundering hooves to Grandma's house.

Some years I knocked down the whole of the holiday this way, from Christmas Eve through New Year's Day, without seeing a soul. The run of New Year's Day was always especially rewarding, the runners especially pleased with themselves. We the runners were superior beings. The rest of the world was hung over in bed, its head throbbing from drunkenness.

After the holidays I felt I had lived time that other people hadn't. Faces and voices had a stark clarity about them. The world stood out in sharper relief.

Dangling Man captured it all. The chrysalis character of graduate school. The idleness and sterility of Hyde Park. The vast emptiness of the wintertime streets. The ice clinging to the gutters into spring, and the desperate longing for warmth. This novel was the ground beneath my feet.

I felt for Bellow what the young Charlie Citrine had felt for Von Humboldt Fleisher: I envied his luck, his talent, and his fame. I wanted to be near him—but not too near. His sentiments about black men made me wary. So did the way he dissected people with his eyes. You had to protect yourself in Bellow's presence. He went over you like you were some kind of phenomenon.

Bellow lived in an apartment tower just off The Midway on Dorchester Avenue, next door to International House. I knew from the novels that his apartment faced the lake and that it therefore overlooked my running route at the eastern end of The Midway. When passing that spot, I concentrated on the upper windows of the tower. I envisioned him staring down at the lone runner trudging along The Midway. I raised my arm and waved.

I added the tower to my evening walks. The intersection at 59th and Dorchester was the dark stretch of sidewalk where I had played the cruelest innings of Scatter the Pigeons. The night walkers there were either students scurrying toward International House or gray-haired couples rushing from their cars into Bellow's tower or into the Cloisters, an apartment building just north of it.

Now and then I bounded up the tower stairs to make sure Bellow's name was still on the bell. A security gate cut you off from the base of the tower itself, which was too bad, because there were shadows there to linger in. His neighbors suffered mightily from my visits, especially when they encountered me descending the stairs in the dark.

What would I do when I caught him? Perhaps I'd lift him bodily and pin him against a wall. Perhaps I'd corner him on the stairs and take up questions about "pork chops" and "crazy buffaloes" and barbarous black pickpockets. I wanted to trophy his fear.

I stalked Dorchester Avenue for months before I caught him out. The night it happened I had almost given up hope. I turned out of 58th Street and was passing in front of the Cloisters when I saw him: a little man in an overcoat, hurrying along the sidewalk about twenty yards ahead of me. I cursed my timing. Ten seconds earlier would have put me right on his heels. I could easily have run him down, but that wasn't the game. The game was to wait for chance to place me squarely between the tower and him. That way he'd have to face me in the dark. This was not to be the night. He threw back a glance, wisps of white hair flying, then picked up his pace. He showed surprising bounce getting up the stairs. When I reached the tower, I saw only his shoe disappearing through the gate.

I finally got the advantage of him in broad daylight, in an afternoon crowd in front of the Hyde Park Bank. The crowd wasn't as good as darkness, but it provided camouflage. I could watch him without being seen. He was walking toward me, his khaki cap pulled low to protect his eyes from the sun. Even squinting, the eyes seemed saucerous, huge, the skin around them slack from heavy use. Spider-legged squint lines radiated from the corners of his eyes, upward into the temple and downward into the jaw. The skin over these squint lines was translucent, like the membrane of an egg, so luminous in the sunlight that I nearly reached out to touch it. He moved through the crowd looking downward, hungrily scanning asses, hips, and crotches. This was how he did it. The rest of us were a junkyard where he foraged for parts. I wanted something from him. The longing was deep, but I couldn't place it then. It would take years for me to realize what it was. I wanted to steal the essence of him, to absorb it right into my bones. After I passed him, I felt faint and reached out for a wall. That's when I realized that I'd been holding my breath.

I took a summer job teaching at my old college. The idea of returning to Chester disturbed me. Chester was the past. In this case, the past was a dying city peopled by ghosts from my childhood. I was relieved to find that the session was only five weeks long.

Few of my old professors were happy to see me. Four summers earlier I had left them as a student. My return as faculty was a reminder that time was ticking by. I kissed one of my humanities teachers and was about to way, "You look great," but before I got to the "great," she said: "I look old. Old is what I am." She was thin, a wisp of a woman with gray hair, boyishly cut. The years had done their work, creases fanning out from her eyes, pouches under them. Her tone was weary and accusing.

After the first morning of classes I strode boldly into the faculty dining room and could find nowhere to sit. The tables, each of which seated a half-dozen people, were filled. I stood by the door waiting for someone to invite me; no one did. Instead they hunched over their plates, averting their eyes. Mercifully, one of the deans waved me over. His companions made room and pulled up an extra chair. The conversation was strained. I ordered an iced tea, gulped it down, and fled. For the rest of the term I ate lunch in my office.

My father was living alone in the house where the family had left him, across from St. Mary's Ukrainian Orthodox Church, at the edge of the Polish West End. I arrived after dark and stood on the sidewalk looking in through the window. My father was asleep in a chair, with a rifle across his lap, one hand on the stock, the other on the barrel. His mouth was open and he was snoring. His clothes were the same as they had always been: the drab green work pants with the matching shirt. The black motorcycle boots. His cap, festooned with Teamsters buttons, had slipped from his head and was lying on the floor behind the chair. The floor, once covered with rugs, was now bare boards. The room had been stripped of furniture, except for the chair where he slept. On the floor next to his chair was a small lamp with a ghastly orange shade.

The rifle was the bolt-action Springfield that I had played with as a boy. *Chick-chack* was the sound of the bolt being turned and rammed into the breech. I often placed the bullet into the breech, but never had the nerve to ram it home. Once that was done the only way out would be to fire.

I was afraid to knock for fear that my father would wake up shooting. I moved to the right of the door to put the brick wall between us, then I reached out and rapped on the glass.

"Who is it?" he asked.

"It's Brent," I said.

He got up, stood the rifle in a corner, and opened the door. Neither of us showed surprise. But I must have seemed as much an apparition to him as he seemed to me. We hadn't spoken in four years.

He slept with the rifle because he was plagued by burglars, one of whom had recently hit him across the head. An egg-shaped lump had risen on his forehead. "I almost got him!" my father said, grinning. "I almost shot his ass off." In support of this claim, he pointed to a bullet hole in the wall. It was clear to me that he had fired after the fact, as a bragging point, as proof to the rest of us that he could protect himself.

I needed a glass of water. We walked through the empty dining room, into the empty kitchen. The kitchen was overrun with Colonel Sanders' Fried Chicken cartons. The red-and-white-striped cartons repeated and repeated across the sink and the stove, onto the windowsills. I drank the water and followed my father back to the living room. The orange light was hideous; despite its emptiness, the room in that light seemed tight, claustrophobic. I kept up the pretense that this was normal. Sleeping upright in a chair with a rifle on your lap. The sad train of fried chicken boxes stretching around the kitchen. We talked about the weather in Chicago. Yes, the winters were wicked, the snow deep. I managed half an hour of this, then hurried out to my car. Nine years would pass before I saw my father again.

That night was only the beginning of my father's decline. Later he locked himself out of the house and received a horrible gash in the leg when he kicked in the plate-glass door. Later still he fell and broke his hip. Eventually the trucking company fired him for driving drunk. For a time he ceased to come home at all, but slept on the pool table at the bar. When my uncle Calvin rescued him, he was living in an abandoned garage.

Chester was smaller and darker than I remembered. I spent most of the term in the suburbs and in Ridley Creek State Park. In college the drive to Ridley had been a mystical trip. My friends and I were packed into the car, rock 'n' roll blasting, the air thick with reefer smoke. The shipyard, the oil refineries, and the paper mill fell away behind us and seemed no longer to exist. At the park we trekked into the brush, past the old stone millhouse that dated back to Colonial times, to our favorite spot along a creek where the dragonflies lived. We lowered our six-packs into the water to keep them cold, and sat down to watch the dragonflies mate on the way. This time the path to the creek had been closed for restoration of the millhouse. A walk in the woods would have to do.

At night I went home to Brian and his wife, Faith. I was staying with them at Brian's insistence. Brian had neglected to tell me that Blake was visiting from Roanoke and had claimed the spare room for himself. Blake complained bitterly when I evicted him to the couch.

Blake had fallen behind in school and had either dropped out or was just about to. I knew better than to lecture him. My plan was to shoot the breeze for a while, then work my way around to how he was living. I convinced him to take a ride with me to the park. We drove with the radio cranked up, the highway smooth beneath us. Blake was fifteen. I was twenty-six. The age difference seemed less vast than when I'd left home for college. He was still small next to me on the seat, the head still a little too large for the body, the eyes big and mournful. He lit a joint, pronounced it great stuff and passed it to me. It was horrible. It ravaged my throat and threw a lead blanket over my spirit. The taste told me that it had been treated with something. I soothed my throat from a beer that I'd stashed under the seat.

The evergreens sprang up on either side of the road and we were there. I was headed into the woods when I noticed that Blake wasn't following me. Back at the car I found him with the windows rolled up and the air-conditioner going. When I motioned to him to come on, he shook his head no. The woods held no interest for him. He was content to view them through glass. I left him and headed down the trail.

Brian and Faith were re-creating the life that Brian and I had grown up with. They fought while their children cowered in corners. I came home one evening to find Faith badly beaten up, her face a mass of lumps and bruises. Brian was cooling it in jail. I left him there for two days, then called my cousin Mohammad. Mohammad ran a social service agency that coped with sundry community problems, one of which was arranging bail for the poor. The two of us drove to the prison and fetched Brian home. Brian had just set foot in his house when he began to scream at me for not getting him out sooner. "Where the hell you been, man! Man, I got all these warrants hangin' over me! What if one of them dipsies hadda caught up with me, man! Any of them coulda caught up with me!" This was vintage Brian, the adult version of the toddler whose shrieking could wake the dead. The teeth flashed; the girlish eyes scorned me. He saw that I was stunned and darted in close, his nose almost touching mine. "That's right! I'm talkin' to you!"

One day I came home from school to find Brian storming around in a rage. A man we knew had burst into the house and put a gun to his head. "In front of my family!" he said. "In front of my wife and children!" Brian was vague about what had prompted the episode; the full story was none of my business. The next morning he got up early and went out on a mission of revenge. I fled to Chicago.

While I was away, Hyde Park had experienced the murder that would form the heart of Saul Bellow's next novel, *The Dean's December*.

The first reports came straight from the Hyde Park stock of horrors: a white student sits at home studying when black house-breakers surge in and cause him to fall from a window to his death. This story soon proved false. The student had been making the rounds of the bars, one of which he'd been kicked out of at 2 A.M., drunk. This was not Jimmy's, the student bar, but a racier place in a part of East Hyde Park where sex was for sale. The student had invited his assailants back to his apartment to "party."

The university offered a reward through its community affairs arm, the Southeast Chicago Commission. A man and woman, both black, were arrested and charged with murder. Friends of the deceased said the drunken carouser depicted in the press bore no resemblance to the man they knew. A campus chaplain described him as "a faith-filled person who participated in Mass everyday." Supporters of the black defendants implied that the deceased was a whoremonger who'd courted disaster and met it. That the female defendant was described in the press as a prostitute reinforced this thinking.

I had no idea which view was accurate. But perhaps both were. The student could easily have courted whores at night and gone to mass the next morning and could have gone on doing so but for this fateful error in judgment.

I remember the tenseness of the night, the air as tight as a drum. Hyde Parkers came forth with whistles on their key chains or hanging from strings around their necks. The whistles were part of a crime-prevention program. People blew them when they heard a shriek, or when they saw someone bounding down the street with a stolen purse, or when they heard another whistle. Ideally the whis-tling would pinpoint the criminal so that the police could close in.

I was walking home from the lake after dark when whistles began to blossom in my direction. I reversed field and headed back to the lakefront. The suspect was always black and in his early twenties. Meeting the police inside the whistling radius could be dicey indeed. I stayed at the lake for an hour before starting home again.

In my view the graduate student's death had resulted from a series of random events, the first of which had driven him to leave the student bar for the racier place in East Hyde Park. As luck would have it, the pair of criminals he invited home lacked what it took to subdue a mild-mannered English student and his terrified wife. By chance the male assailant had a broken jaw, which doubtless diminished his efficiency. A stronger, more practiced criminal would have pressed the student to the wall and breathed terror into him, while his partner cleaned the place out. Instead, the two of them staggered like drunken dancers around the room until the student fell through the window into the night.

The Dean's December was faithful to the facts. But Bellow admitted nothing so pedestrian as chance. In his view the dead student had been overtaken by Evil, in the classical sense of the word. Plato's Myth of the Metals was the novel's key metaphor. Bellow could tell from the set of the corpse's lips that this had been a virtuous man in whom carousing would one day have run its course. Plato's lesser men, those of bronze and copper, didn't enter the discussion. As Bellow saw it, this golden child had been slain by men of lead, the basest element of all. This was the world through Plato's eyes: Game, set, and match to the Philosopher Kings.

I moved from the three-story walk-up at the edge of Woodlawn to a fifteen-story building in the heart of Hyde Park. The new building provided a wealth of people and incidents for the essays and reminiscences that I had begun to publish in the *Reader*. The *Reader* was a fat and sassy weekly, hungry for stories. Mine were mainly first-person essays, most of which paid $110 each. The paper paid up to five or six times as much for reporting pieces, but reporting didn't interest me. Lived experience was more compelling than politics. After a dozen first-person essays, the managing editor said he'd had enough. "If we wanted Anais Nin, we'd go out and hire her!" But things were happening to me. I didn't want to miss them.

I stole from the writer I knew best. I mimicked his phrasing and his body-snatching eye and the way he wrote "this" where other writers wrote "that." One of the first pseudonyms I used in a story was lifted from Demmie Vonghel, one of Charlie Citrine's lovers in *Humboldt's Gift*.

My new building had a resident pimp, one who was far more discreet than the one who'd brawled beneath my windows on 61st Street. I said hello to him in the elevator for nearly a year before I found him out. He was a slender man, with sea-green eyes that stared balefully out at you from the shadow of his baseball cap. There was always a woman with him, sometimes two. The women were a bit on the prancy side but not so prancy as to arouse suspicion. In the elevator, they minced lightly and the pimp stood quietly behind them, as solemn as a priest. One night in the elevator he gave me his pitch.

"Wanna buy some pussy?"

"Pardon me?"

"I said, wanna buy some pussy? She's up in my apartment right now." The sea-green eyes rolled slowly heavenward, toward the upper floors.

That's when it all came clear: The mincing women. Him staring at me in the laundry room. He'd made up his mind that I was a poor example of the species who needed a broker to get his sex. This judgment was wounding to me, coming as it did from a professional. "No, thank you," I said, and pinned my nose to the elevator door.

A trip on the elevator meant passing through the cloud of garlic and cabbage that had permanently engulfed the second floor. The smell came from the janitor and his wife. They consumed garlic by the ton, all of it in boiling things. You knew blindfolded when you were passing their floor. When I locked myself out, I went to them for the spare keys. When their door swung open, a warm, garlicky fog rushed out to greet me.

The janitor traveled in a cloud that was uniquely his own and that stayed behind in the elevator long after he departed. His cloud was made of the garlicky food, but also of sex and sweat. He fished my discarded running shoes out of the trash and wore them. The shoes were at least two sizes too big, and I supposed that he'd stuffed them with paper to make them fit. I never let on that they were mine. I took a secret pleasure in watching my feet walk along beneath this foreign body.

My next-door neighbors were a stern, no-nonsense woman in her late forties and her husband, who was probably a decade younger. He was pretty, in that Elvis Presley way, even though he was pudgy from drink. He was short but wore his raven-black hair piled high to give the illusion of height. He often came home drunk. When I helped him from the elevator, I found him astonishingly heavy for his size. He spoke in a boozy voice even when sober. But this was clearly a scam. His eyes were hard and clear and cunning. Behind the booziness he was sizing you up for the take.

He was the first of my neighbors to appear in one of my essays, and the only one to appear in two of them. The first essay was about brutish lovers who refused to go away when women asked them to. The second essay was about the night his wife stabbed him to death.

I had just put my key into the door when I heard him cry out in pain. Then she said: "I told you! You keep messin' with me and I'll gash you to death." The next time I helped him from the elevator, drunk, one of his hands was wrapped in a bandage.

Soon afterward she kicked him out. He refused to stay away. First he kicked the door in. Then he paid the visit during which he provoked her to kill him. This happened on December 30, 1981, at approximately 5:50 P.M. I arrived in the lobby to find the floor awash in blood. The janitor had tried to clean up, but the detectives had apparently stopped him. Ragged wads of paper towel mimicked blood clots on the tiles.

This I was seeing through stalks of broccoli and the other items that were jutting up out of the grocery bag I was clutching. These were my supplies for the siege of New Year's Eve and New Year's Day.

The passenger elevator was also awash with blood. His wife had stabbed him on the tenth floor, and he'd bled to death on the way down. I took the freight elevator up to ten, dropped off the groceries, and came back down. The body had been dragged from the passenger elevator into the gangway behind the building. There he lay, his head resting in the crook of his arm, his jet-black curls in a sleeper's disarray. His blue jeans had turned burgundy with blood. To get at the wound, the police had pulled the jeans partway down, exposing his underwear. It was fancy underwear, with a sexy cut.

The crime lab boys came, blasting the blood and body with their cameras. The janitor stood by waiting to clean up. He was nervous and needed to talk.

"Is good you never marry, eh."

I nodded.

"Is why my wife, she have something to say, I *bop-bop*."

With this he made slapping motions in the air. "I am boss. Is what you must do."

I thought to myself, Right. What laid out my neighbor can lay you out too.

I went back to my apartment and began to write. After two hours I went back down to have another view of the scene. The black-and-white tiles of the first floor were cleaner than I had ever seen them. The air was singing with pine oil. This shocked me because the janitor wasn't known for thoroughness. I made note of this and continued on to the body. The corpse had moved. The muscles and tendons had contracted in the cold, causing the body to turn from its stomach onto its back. The right arm was now extended toward the sky, the fingers spread as though reaching for something. The eyes were wide open; the milky film of death had formed over the pupils.

The story kept me occupied through New Year's Eve and into New Year's Day. I wrote obsessively, summoning every detail I knew. Most reporters found their first bodies in distant neighborhoods and had to scrounge for details. This death had come on familiar terrain under circumstances that I knew well. The Chicago *Sun-Times* ran only a paragraph about the death. My essay in the *Reader* was long and involved, complete with dialogue from the janitor and the police. I included the janitor's statements about beating his wife. I also wrote that bloody newspapers were still littering my hallway on the morning after.

The janitor didn't mind the part about beating his wife but was livid at what I'd said about his cleaning.

"You should no write about the clean! No, sir! No, sir!"

For writing about the clean, I would never be forgiven.

*   *   *

My fellowships had run their course, and essays for the *Reader* did not pay the rent. For that I worked part-time as a psychologist for a social service firm in The Loop. I also worked as a teacher, to build my résumé.

I had dreamed of becoming an Ivy League professor in tweeds. But Princeton didn't call me. Neither did Harvard or Yale. The market was glutted. New Ph.D's were taking jobs at tiny out-of-the-way colleges I'd never heard of. Some became academic bedouins roving from one temporary post to the next, trailing change-of-address cards behind them.

I woke up from my Ivy League dream at Roosevelt University in The Loop, in a classroom whose windows overlooked the el tracks. My class met at the start of the evening rush hour, and every few minutes the scream and slam of trains drowned out the lecture. I was an adjunct, a slave of the academic world. The pay was nothing, and there were no benefits. I was called in at the last minute and forced to prepare at breakneck speed. I was teaching Statistics 101, which some people called *Sadistics* 101. A few of my students were pale and studious types who were bound for graduate school. But most were part-time secretaries, court stenographers, and social workers who came to class surly and beat from a hard day's work. Equations inspired no euphoria in them. Sadistics 101 was a crown of thorns.

My windows stayed open to the screaming trains because there wasn't any air-conditioning. The hottest days I survived by wearing a singlet and running shorts. The younger students found comfort in the informality, but many of the older ones were put off. It was somehow harder for them that the professor looked eighteen and kept his gams out all the time. The shock was especially evident in rich North Shore matrons who'd only dealt with blacks as servants.

By the second term I'd begin the class by sitting among them as a student. When the room was full I walked to the board and started the lecture. The first time I did this, a woman to whom I'd been talking in the interim nearly had a heart attack. She was elegantly dressed, in her sixties, with North Shore affluence written all over her. The shocked expression faded as the weeks wore on, but never fully left her. It returned in full when she got a "D" on the first exam. The fact that it was a take-home exam made the "D" particularly scalding. "Excuse me," she said, "but this grade couldn't possibly be right." An executive friend had helped her, she said; he was famous in business and couldn't possibly be wrong. Oh, but he was, I said, and very wrong, too. She stalked from the room, letting drop that my department head would hear from her. The threat made me laugh. Adjuncts didn't get fired; they escaped.

The news from Chester was grim. Sun Ship had cut back to a skeleton crew and was no longer building ships. The city was looking ravaged and war-torn, in the final stages of decline. The drug trade rushed in to take center stage. One of its first casualties was Stephen Dale, a friend from junior high school. Stephen was found dead, shot four times in the head and face. In the pocket of his overcoat were $100 in cash and seven glassine packets of heroin. The two of us were the same age, twenty-nine, and born five months apart.

His body was discovered near the intersection where my cousin Wesley had been shot to death fifteen years earlier. The coincidence opened the door onto that strip of 3rd Street near Andy's Musical Bar where my family had lived in the early sixties. Memories came flooding back. I remembered William Butcher and the bloody cast he wore after taking a shotgun blast to the shoulder. I remembered his older brother Leonard, the vulturish bend in his neck and the black patch he donned after his eye was beaten out. I remembered Davy and the cool guys singing doo-wop songs under the streetlights on quiet Sunday nights. And I remembered Stephen Dale when he was a cricket-faced boy, number 14 on our football team. All this I recalled in an essay for the *Reader*. The essay was grisly. I imagined Stephen's brains like "an alien custard" on the sidewalk. I imagined myself shot, a victim of similar violence.

‖ A Letter from Blake

Brent

I had to leave Roanoke because things is getting hot there. This boy robbed me over some coke not long ago. They found him in an alley, shot three times. The boy is paralyze [*sic*] from the waist down! I had to get out of town. They think I did it, Brent. Dad won't give me no money or no place to stay, nobody will. I'm asking you for help, Brent. Because if I don't get no help, one of these banks is going to be my next move.

Your Brother,
Blake

This letter arrived in July 1982. It was Blake's first letter to me and would also be his last. The announcement that someone had robbed him "over some coke" was my first notice that he was dealing drugs. The threat of bank robbery I recognized as dramatic effect. The plea of innocence was clearly a lie. The letter as I read it said that Blake had ambushed and shot someone, and that cocaine was the motive.

But Blake had taken greater liberties than I knew. The victim had not been ambushed in an alley but on the dance floor of a disco. Blake's claim that my father had abandoned him was also a lie. My father had gotten Blake a job with a trash collector who serviced the suburbs of Jersey City, and arranged for him to eat on the tab at the local diner until his first paycheck. But Blake was too much the dandy for hauling trash. My father arrived in Jersey City to find that Blake had quit the job and left an enormous bill at the restaurant, courtesy of a feed for his work mates. Blake went back to Roanoke and the cocaine trade.

I knew that the shooting would be avenged, and that Blake could well be killed. The bogus scenario in the letter provided the images through which I prepared myself for what was to come. The alley I envisioned as running between two of the weather-beaten houses I'd so often seen in Roanoke. I saw the ambulance screaming up to the scene, and the paramedics carrying someone away on a stretcher. When I looked down at the stretcher, I saw Blake's face instead of his victim's.

Blake and Stephen Dale were but two elements of the drug news from home. Yvonne was doing time in Leavenworth. I hadn't spoken to Yvonne in years. Then I picked up the phone and there she was. "Brent, this is Vonnie. Come home." When I asked what was the matter, she repeated, "Come home," and put my mother on the line. My mother said that Yvonne was "in trouble." This was an understatement given that Yvonne was on trial in federal court, charged with conspiracy and distribution of methamphetamine, a controlled substance. She'd drawn the meanest judge in the district, a bitter old man who bullied people to tears, then berated them for sobbing. Defendants were hauled into his chambers and promised hellish consequences if they didn't turn government's evidence. The judge's name was familiar. He'd been a trustee at Widener and was probably among the group that had snubbed me at the trustees' dinner when I was a freshman.

Yvonne's was a penny-ante case. But the government was squeezing her for a bigger fish whom it wanted badly. Perhaps she had that fish, perhaps she didn't. If she did, she'd have been a fool to give him up. Her life would have been worthless afterward.

But these facts I learned elsewhere. During the phone call my mother told me almost nothing. She chose her words carefully. Too carefully. From this I gathered that the phone was tapped. I could sense Yvonne in the background pacing the room and gnawing her nails. Finally she exploded: "That's enough! Tell him to come home, and hang up the phone!" Perhaps my sister wanted a family portrait in court, an image of normalcy that might sway the jury to mercy. It was easy to imagine the scene. The white-haired judge, glaring down from the bench. The U.S. Attorney grilling my sister on the stand. The drug dealer keeping an eye on his interests. My mother on the verge of panic. In this I wanted no part. I was elsewhere, living otherwise, and determined to stay that way.

I was angry with Yvonne, but never was I afraid for her safety. Yvonne was cunning and tough. Blake was a child, in over his head.

Blake's letter did not include a return address. This was just as well; I couldn't have sent a dime. The psychological services firm had gone bankrupt. I was also being evicted. The envelope that should have contained the next year's lease had held a letter ordering me out. The reason—that I'd been too often late with the rent. The janitor was beside himself with glee. In the elevator he smiled archly and said: "I told you. No write about the clean! Not about the clean! No, sir!" He was wearing my discarded running shoes at the time, the gray ones with the racy stripes. Betrayed by my own feet.

I walked around in a panic, woke up at night in cold sweats. Once again I was a boy on The Hill watching the sheriff set our furniture on the sidewalk. The panic ceased when I recognized the opportunity I'd been given: This was my chance to make myself a writer. The Ph.D. was finished, nicely framed and hanging on the wall. The bankrupt firm had bequeathed me four months of unemployment compensation. With nothing to distract me, I could write to my heart's content, perhaps even write my way into a staff job and a cushy retainer at the *Reader*.

I abandoned most of my belongings where they stood and sublet a furnished apartment. *Chicago* magazine gave me a contract to chronicle the restoration of a painting at the Art Institute of Chicago. At the same time, I undertook an epic history of the American Nazi movement in Chicago as told through the three kooky characters who'd inherited the Nazi mantle in the city. Between restoration and the Nazis I wrote about books, politics, agriculture, anything to make money and to keep my name in print. Eviction was a tonic. I was writing for my life.

The unemployment ran out. My editor at *Chicago* magazine took pity on a homeless writer-to-be and found an apartment-sitting job that let me live rent-free for several months. The *Reader* ran the Nazi story on the cover but did not put me on staff. The editors were probably worried that I'd turn back into Anaïs Nin. The house-sitting job was coming to a close when a letter arrived from the Chicago *Sun-Times*. An editor there had been reading my work. She wanted to talk to me about joining the paper as a reporter. I didn't think of myself as daily newspaper material. The *Reader* paid a miserly wage but let me write at length on any subject I chose. Daily newspaper stories were short, the subject matter conventional, the writing formulaic. First-person essays were out of the question. But what choice did I have? I was broke and jobless, with nowhere to live. A reporter's starting salary was $463.90 a week, more than I could earn at the *Reader* in a month.

I showed up at the *Sun-Times* in a tweed jacket I'd worn to an ill-fated interview at Lake Forest College. Tweed at the *Sun-Times* was a mistake. The Ph.D. had already put me under suspicion. The job required newshounds, not eggheads. Newshounds were gritty, rumpled characters who smoked cigars and talked with Chicawgo accents. The city editor smoked the biggest, stinkiest cigar of all. He plucked it from his teeth and said: "You dress like a goddamn college professor." Things went downhill from there. The *Sun-Times* was wary of my pedigree and declined to hire me outright. The paper offered a six-month tryout and of course I accepted.

I was writing one of my first stories when an assistant city editor trotted by my desk, barking instructions as she went: "Four hundred and fifty words!" she said. "And don't start until I come back and tell you what I want the story to say." I called her back and asked if she'd read my clips. She looked perplexed and I asked again. "Have you read my stories? I get four hundred fifty words when I blow my nose." I said this because I was full of myself, but also because it was true. The Nazi story had run at nearly 10,000 words and left 5,000 words of outtakes. I'd written it with no consultation from anyone. The editors had fixed the misspellings and unkinked some sentences, but that was all. Daily newspapers were a different game. The editors decided what would be written about and often dictated the first paragraph.

That I was on a tryout was only the first reason to keep my

mouth shut. The second reason was that the *Sun-Times* already had its Black Man with an Attitude and didn't want another one. I had yet to meet the Attitude Man, but his volcanic temper was common knowledge in the newsroom. The bit about blowing my nose was pale in comparison, but even a pale resemblance was enough to sink me.

The city editor summoned me to his cigar-stinking office and tortured me over his own special coals. There was no fucking room on his staff for an arrogant goddamn college professor, he said. I left the office shaken and relieved to have a job. In point of fact I didn't. The decision had been made to fire me at the end of the tryout. At the moment of truth the editors made a crucial mistake. They said they were letting me go because I wasn't good enough. This I refused to accept because it wasn't true. In my considered and arrogant fucking opinion I was as good a writer as any on the staff and better than many of them.

I had compensated for my blowup by working my ass off, even on weekends for no extra pay, and by writing book reviews in my spare time. Still the senior managers had not forgiven me. To them I was a son of a bitch who would be a pain in the ass for life once he got into the union. Had they presented me with this truth, I'd probably have cleaned out my desk and gone home. That they had demeaned my work instead made me determined to stick. I drummed up support on the staff. They argued my case until the decision to send me packing was rescinded.

I touched down in Roanoke two days before Christmas, 1983, my first visit in three years. The family had gone on like nomads and had moved yet again. Their pages in my address book were a mess of crossed-out addresses and phone numbers that no longer worked.

My youngest brother, Brad, was fifteen and the last of my brothers and sisters who still lived at home. My mother had kicked Blake out when she discovered the drug dealing.

She had noticed two men in a car watching the house. Somehow she had found that the two men were rival drug dealers or suppliers and that they had come to take Blake's life. Then there was the story of the gun. She was going about her business in the house when she heard Blake calling out to her: "Mom! Mom!" She went to his room in the basement and found him holding Brian at gunpoint.

"I said, 'Why are you holding a gun on your brother!?'

"Blake said, 'Get Brian out of here, Mom, before I have to hurt him.' " But Blake had called for his own sake, not for Brian's. Brian had this steely, mongoose patience. He would have chopped down Blake's resolve, inched up to him, and taken the gun right out of his hand.

Brian had faced men with guns before. He'd told me about the time he walked into a bar and saw a woman he knew being beaten up. Brian slapped the man around and led the woman into the street. The man came out after them shooting. Brian mimicked the gun with his hands clasped, the index fingers pointed at me. "*Wump! Wump!* Every time he shot that goddamn 9 millimeter, the damn thing jumped up. *Wump! Wump!* I threw the bitch under a car so she wouldn't get shot and waited till the motherfucker shot the whole clip. Then did I commence to beatin' his ass? Don't you know that bitch flew all over me—'Stop hittin' him! Stop hittin' him!' If that don't beat all! The motherfucker tries to shoot me with a 9 millimeter, and the bitch is pulling me off him." Brian's stories held a deep claim on me. He was a strong, confident narrator, certain to be around at story's end. Blake's bravado was tremulous and unconvincing.

*   *   *

Blake had once been obsessively clean. My mother said that, before she threw him out, he'd begun to go unbathed and filthy. Blake was snorting up his inventory, so strung out on coke that he failed to smell himself stinking. My mother brooked no filth. ("If you live in rags, live in clean rags," she used to say.) She hauled him to the shower and threw him in. Then she washed his clothes and hung them out to dry.

My last sight of Blake came on Christmas Eve. Yvette took me to him, in a dismal housing project in Roanoke. The room I stepped into was crowded and half in darkness, lit by a tiny Christmas tree in the corner and a shaft of light from the next room. People milled around in the shadows, most of them drinking, a few stumbling drunk. Blake was standing across the room, near the stairwell, with his back to the door. He was dressed in black and wearing sunglasses despite the darkness.

I had just closed the door when it opened again and another man stepped in. Blake didn't notice either of us, didn't even glance in our direction. He'd have been dead if one of us had come to kill him.

One of the men Blake was talking with had just snorted cocaine: he was pinching his nose and grimacing; he clapped Blake on the back and said, "Good stuff, man! Good stuff!" I had crossed the room to Blake and was right on top of him before he turned to face me. He lifted his shades and stared for a long second before he recognized me. He was the same as ever: the heart-shaped face, the steep widow's peak, the big, dark glittering eyes. The door opened again while we were embracing; I turned him so I could see who'd come in. Where drugs were sold, people came through doors shooting.

A drunk reeled into me, and I threw a quick shoulder into him. I was keyed up and jumpy. But Blake was perfectly relaxed. The business was going well, he said, except for a recent bust at his apartment. "They had to get a tow truck to pull my door off," he said. "While they were trying to get in I flushed three ounces of pure coke down the toilet. Pure coke, man! Damn!"

One of us told a joke and we slapped each other five. Blake screamed, gripped the wrist of his left hand, and ran up and down the stairs, groaning in pain. He showed me the hand. The webbing between the thumb and index finger had been cut almost to the hilt and stitched up. "I was shootin' a shotgun," he said. "The thing kicked back, jammed the trigger all the way up to here."

I told him that everybody knew what he was up to and that it would be better if he left Roanoke for a while.

"How much money do you have?"

"Twenty thousand," he said, "in a shoe box at my old lady's house."

"You could put that in the bank. I could invest it for you. And you could get a job. You could get killed doing this. I can see that, and I've only been here two days. You could get killed right here in this room. Let's go downtown tomorrow and buy a plane ticket, to anywhere. You need to get away from here."

"Oh, I can come and stay with you, hunh?" He asked this defiantly, with a look to match: I won't stop this unless you take me by the hand and perhaps not even then.

Coming with me to Chicago was out of the question. The drug trade there was brutal and graphic. Corpses were found with their balls in their mouths. I'd come home from work one day and find my apartment shot up and Blake dead. No, he wasn't coming with me. If he insisted on killing himself, he'd do it without my help.

Surely there were places other than Chicago that he wished to see. Puerto Rico. Jamaica. Mexico. He could look at the map and choose any one of them. With twenty thousand dollars in the kitty he could go where he pleased.

"Let's go downtown," I said. "This weekend we'll do it. We'll buy a plane ticket to anywhere you'd like to go. Just get yourself out of town for a while. Bruce is having a party tomorrow night. Meet me there and we'll talk about it."

"I'll be there," he said. He was lying; I could hear it in his voice. We embraced again, and I left him there.

The next night at Bruce's we waited for him until well after midnight. Brian, Bruce, Brad, and I posed for a brothers' picture without him. The next morning I flew back to Chicago.

I had settled on the North Side, not far from the Biograph Theatre. I'd taken the top floor of a drafty frame house on Wrightwood Avenue. The place was a sieve to the cold. But the back porch offered a stunning view of The Loop. My lover and I were having dinner when the telephone rang with the news. I had taken a fork full of food and was staring past my lover's face at the Sears and Hancock towers blinking. The night was brutally cold, the sky velvet clear and inscribed with stars. The table was mat black. The plates, pale blue. The meal, barbecued chicken, purple cabbage salad, and baked sweet potatoes split open and steaming. My lover's face was pale and winter-white. Beyond the ivory disk of her face, the twin black obelisks were blinking in a sky that was clear beyond imagining.

The ring of the telephone was explosive. I knew before I picked it up that something was wrong. It was Bruce.

"How you doin', Brent?"

"O.K.," I said, waiting.

"Brent, Blake's dead. A guy pulled up and emptied out on him with a magnum. He's dead."

Blake had been gunned down in front of a nightclub called the Playpen. The killer was Mark Stephen McGeorge, the cocaine customer whom Blake had ambushed and shot at a disco eight months earlier.

There were three versions of how Blake met his death. In the first, Blake and Mark both go for their guns and Blake is outdrawn. In the second the two of them argue, Blake throws a punch, Mark pulls a gun and fires. The third and most plausible version is the ambush in which Mark jumps from a car and shoots Blake six times, three of them in the back.

People scatter into the night, running from the flash and bark of the .44. Blake crawls backward on the ground, begging for his life. "Please don't shoot me no more! I don't want to die!" Finally he pulls himself partway under a car to hide from the fire. Mark bears down on him, empties the gun, and flees.

Not far away, Yvette is sleeping when the phone rings with the news that Blake has been shot. Yvette and one of my nieces arrive at the Playpen ahead of the police and find Blake still lodged partly under the car. Bystanders help them pull him into the open. Delirious from blood loss, Blake says over and over again: "I'm not gonna make it this time, 'cause I don't have no drugs in my body. I'm not gonna make it this time . . ." At some point he says to another woman: "I am dying. Get me to the hospital because I don't want to die out here in front of the Playpen." The woman runs off to get her car.

A policeman arrives and finds what he later describes as a black male lying on the ground with large wounds, bleeding profusely. The policeman asks Blake three times: "Who shot you?" Each time he answers "Timmy," which was Mark's nickname. "Had there been an argument?" No. "Had there been a drug transaction?" No. The ambulance screams up the avenue. The paramedic cuts away Blake's jeans to get at the wounds. Then she slips him into rubber shock pants, which she inflates to keep up his blood pressure. Blake says to the paramedic, "I'm scared," then passes out. He dies on the operating table.

I hung up the phone and went back to the dinner table. I told my lover that Blake had been murdered, and continued eating. Twice I stopped and struck the mat-black table with my fist, but mainly I kept eating, because continuing to eat seemed a vital thing to do. My lover said something I couldn't hear. Her lips moved, but the words were far away. We finished dinner, and I sent her home. For a long time afterward I watched the towers in the black velvet sky. I was determined not to go to the funeral. I mourned Blake and buried him months before he died. I would not suffer his death a second time.

That night I dreamed that I was chasing Blake across a barren landscape, holding out a parchment scroll that I wanted him to read. By reading the scroll he could protect himself from what in waking life had already happened. Blake laughed and dodged away from me. When I reached for him, I caught only the place where he had been.

*　　　*　　　*

The next morning I went to work as usual. I said nothing to my colleagues about Blake's death. I could do without flowers from the Newspaper Guild and reporters filing by my desk in postures of sympathy. What did I need sympathy for? I'd done my mourning in advance. But this was self-deception on a monstrous scale. The rituals of grief and burial bear the dead away. Cheat those rituals and you risk keeping the dead with you always in forms that you mightn't like. Choose carefully the funerals you miss.

I lacked a way to talk about Blake's death. I tried writing but failed. After two or three paragraphs a smothering heat boiled up from my chest and into my head. My thoughts became tangled and useless.

Then the writer Calvin Trillin appeared on my schedule of stories. Trillin was touring in support of his new book *Killings*, a collection of pieces from *The New Yorker* about people who'd died violently and those who had killed them: two families in a California barrio, locked into a cycle of murder, revenge, and murder; a movie producer who is shot when he gets too close to his subjects, the hill folk of Kentucky; a Russian defector turned evangelist, found dead in a hotel with a seventeen-year-old girl. My editor said that she could take the story or leave it because the *Sun-Times* "did Trillin" every time he came through town. But meeting Trillin and writing about him held a morbid fascination for me. I pressed through the editor's objections and scheduled the interview.

We met at the Ritz Carlton Hotel in Water Tower Place. I was standing in the lobby when he stepped from the elevator. His face—mordant and long, receding chin, deep, humorous folds in the forehead—looked exactly as it did in caricatures. We shook hands and crossed the lobby to the restaurant. He ordered a fruit cup (it is so easy to gain weight during book tours, he explained) and I had two eggs, scrambled, with wheat toast.

I started the tape recorder, and Trillin mouthed the words he'd spoken to reporters at a dozen breakfasts like this: How he finds these deaths in the out-of-town papers at Hotalings, the newsstand just off Times Square. How "the killings themselves are little more than what Alfred Hitchcock used to call the MacGuffins—you know, that thing that makes the story move. They are in a way an excuse for me to be there. Somebody's getting killed makes it easier to find out about their lives because when ordinary people's lives end suddenly, a kind of noise is made, and there is a kind of drama that their lives may not have otherwise." He smiled, contented with the recitation, and dipped into his fruit cup. Later, when I played back the tape, I could hear the clink of silver on plates and my own disembodied voice saying, "I had a brother who was murdered not long ago." I couldn't help myself; it was what I'd come there to say. The words seize him by the throat. His mouth falls open; he puts down his spoon. "My God, man!" he says. Rewind, repeat: "I had a brother who was murdered not long ago." "My God, man!" Furrows deepen in his brow. His spoon rests in the cup of fruit, synthetic cherries among melon and citrus. Rewind, repeat: "My God, man!" Rewind, repeat: "My God, man!" This was my grief, from the mouth of a stranger.

The Chicago *Sun-Times* was sold to the Australian press baron Rupert Murdoch. The reporters and editors were herded together to hear the announcement. Murdoch marched in with a retinue, four or five pale young men in impeccable suits, carrying calfskin briefcases. We crowded around, some of us standing on desks. Murdoch stepped forward and said in his Australian accent: "We just bought your paper for ninety million dollars, cash." The first words out of his mouth: "We just boot yoah paypa for noinny millyun dullahs, cash." Translation: I own you and you and you and you.

The *Sun-Times* was a serious newspaper. What Murdoch might do to it was unclear, but there were clues. He owned the staid and stately *Times* of London. But he also owned the New York *Post* ("HEADLESS BODY FOUND IN TOPLESS BAR!" "MOM SUCKS OUT TOT'S EYE"). And then there was the *Sun*, of London, with bare breasts on page three. A buy-out option went into effect when the sale became final. This meant a small fortune for people who'd worked there twenty years, but not even bus fare for those of us who were new. Senior reporters and editors left in droves. The rest of us hunkered down against the winds of change.

I was soon receiving calls from papers all over the country. Black reporters were rare. The scarcity was partly the fault of the papers themselves. For decades they'd worked under a shingle that said: Blacks Need Not Apply. Newsrooms had remained as white as snow, while cities grew blacker and blacker around them. The papers competed keenly for the best talent. The wooing included airline tickets, good hotels, and nights on the town.

My first interview out was with the Austin *American-Statesman* in Austin, Texas. The editor was blond and slender and young—only thirty-five years old. His cowboy boots were black, as was the high-performance sports car that sped us through the streets. The offer was flattering: I'd become a senior editor within five years. If things went well, I'd be editor of my own paper by the time I was forty.

These were heady possibilities. But the call from the *Washington Post* was headier still. The call came from the editor of the *Washington Post* magazine. Would I send along samples of my work? Could I schedule a trip to Washington to talk about a job on the magazine? Outwardly I was cool and deliberative. Inwardly I fainted. The paper that had broken Watergate and turned Richard Nixon out of the White House had asked me to apply for a job.

Hanging at the entrance of the *Washington Post* was a facsimile of the plate from which the front page was struck on Nixon's resignation day. "NIXON RESIGNS," it said, in the largest type I'd ever seen. This trophy worked its magic on me. I gawked so long that I was nearly late for my interview.

The magazine editor took me to lunch at a fancy restaurant. He was effusive throughout the meal. "I'd love to turn you loose in this city," he said, "to see what you would bring back." I winced at the word "city"; in journalism "city" meant ghetto. My writing samples had included pieces about race, but not so many that race would define me. Reporters who let that happen were condemned to a writing ghetto that they would never escape. White reporters traveled all over the world, writing about everything. Black reporters were chained to the city desk writing the ghetto story: The pimp buried in a coffin facsimile of a Cadillac. The honor student killed in the crossfire. The youngest heroin addict in the world. The remark about turning me "loose in the city" made me wary, but I held my peace. As I saw it, the job was mine; we could hammer out the details later on.

This was not the case. The power to hire me rested with a senior editor whom I was yet to meet. I found him in a tiny glass box along the wall, in the same room that housed the magazine. The glass box was claustrophobically small. As I sat on the couch, my knees nearly touched the desk. The editor's eyes were greenish gray and dead calm. His broad, lineless forehead did not participate when he smiled. The smile, such as it was, emanated faintly from the corners of his mouth, which made it seem ominously insincere. His khaki pants and button-down Oxford shirt were conspicuously wrinkled. He was the first man at the newspaper I'd seen who wasn't wearing a tie.

What stories would I write? Jazz. Genetic engineering. Books. Nazis. Tanker trucks exploding on the Beltway. I could write about anything.

He asked about my family, just as I'd known he would. A Ph.D. from the University of Chicago; a job as a science writer for the tenth largest newspaper in America: These were a white man's credentials. I was accustomed to being probed about how I'd gotten them.

Were my parents alive? What did they do?

My mother is a housewife. My father is a truck driver, like his father before him. My great-grandfather was a farmer conceived during the last days of slavery in Virginia.

What about my brothers and sisters?

There are nine of us. My eldest sister is a bus driver. The rest of my brothers and sisters are like her, working people. I'm the only one who went to college.

These were what I'd come to call The Real Negro questions. He wanted to know if I was a Faux, Chevy Chase, Maryland, Negro or an authentic nigger who grew up poor in the ghetto besieged by crime and violence. White people preferred the latter, on the theory that blacks from the ghetto were the real thing. Newspaper editors preferred them on the theory that they made better emissaries to the ghetto. My inquisitor was asking me to explain my existence. Why was I successful, law-abiding, and literate, when others of my kind filled the jails and the morgues and the homeless shelters? A question that asks a lifetime of questions has no easy answer. The only honest answer is the life itself.

Usually I answered by talking about my encounter with Sparrow during my final days of high school. How I'd met him at a place where I'd never seen him before and would never see him again. How Sparrow had wedged me into college, even though I'd been a mediocre student and hadn't taken the college boards. How Chance had worked mightily in my favor.

Chance wasn't popular as explanation. People preferred a story about an individual who triumphs over all through force of character. The least charitable of these people cited me as proof that the American dream was alive and well—if only those shiftless bastards in the slums would reach for it. Once I'd kept a wry distance on this process and accepted the halo when it was given. Blake's murder changed this. Now I could see that my "escape" from the ghetto was being marshaled as evidence against him. This role I no longer wished to play.

The editor persisted. Perhaps I spoke of Sparrow, perhaps I didn't. I don't remember because I was blind with rage. Here was this motherfucking son of privilege rummaging my life for racial bona fides. I hated him. I'd have spat blood in his face if I could.

I decided to mangle his sensibilities and started slowly toward that end. Yes, I said, I finished my Ph.D. from the University of Chicago, my thesis in the mathematics of decision making. I'm a science writer right now, but I have a wide range of interests. I review a good many books. "And oh, my family, yes. One of my brothers was a drug dealer. He was murdered not long ago; a guy wearing a ski mask shot him six times with a .44 Magnum. Blew him to pieces." Yes, I am linked to the ghetto by pain and despair. Here's a freshly murdered brother to prove it. Is that real enough for you?

My brother's murder registered as a spike in the vast eventless brow, a seismic disturbance that surfaced and then was gone. The job that had been mine at lunch had slipped away. I can only guess why because the rejection letter never arrived. Perhaps I wasn't experienced enough. Perhaps my tastes were too esoteric for the magazine's needs. Both were possible, but I doubted them as explanations. The explanation, I think, was that I'd broken the rules of engagement.

Several months later I found myself in similar waters during an interview at the *New York Times*. When my anger began to rise, I opened my pocket watch, noted that I was late for my next interview, and left the room. The interviewer was stunned, but better to have fled than not. This time I got the job.

Three years passed before I visited Roanoke again. From the airport I drove to the office of the Commonwealth Attorney, with whom I'd made an appointment to discuss Blake's case. Mine was not an honorable mission. I had abandoned my family during a crisis, and now I sought to atone by finding fault with the prosecution.

The Commonwealth Attorney had seen it all before. He was Don Caldwell, a pale, graying man in his thirties with a muscular thickness that suggested a former football player. Caldwell was polite but impatient. He sat fully erect, hands folded on his desk, ready to rise and show me out at any second. I scribbled down everything he said, which wasn't much. He sensed my motive and kept his answers brief.

"The trouble is that for boys like Staples and McGeorge, there is no amusement, nothing at all to do," he said. This was true enough. Blake and his friends had socialized in windowless cinderblock clubs that reeked of danger. The nastiest of these were in the district called The Yard, named for the Norfolk & Southern freight yards at the center of the city. The clubs had begun ages earlier as places where spike drivers drank on weekends. Now, if you wanted drugs or a fight or a place to be shot, you went "down on The Yard."

Why so light a sentence? Seven years for murder?

"Here in the Commonwealth of Virginia the jury sets the sentence. The judge cannot increase it."

For Caldwell everything about the murder had been said. I ran out of questions in fifteen minutes. Then I asked to see the files on Blake's case.

The secretary brought in a manila pouch. Caldwell handed the pouch to me and excused himself from the room. I rounded the desk and sat in his chair. The folder contained a summary of the trial, an autopsy report, and a separate, inner pouch with twine that clearly, from its shape, contained photographs. I knew what the photographs would show but could not stop myself. I unwound the twine in faster and faster circles. There was Blake dead on the dissection table, that horrendous wound running the length of his abdomen. The floor gave way and I fell for miles. I dug my fingers into the chair, and dug and dug until the falling slowed, then finally stopped.

At the trial, the Commonwealth had cast the case as first-degree murder, with revenge as the motive. Blake had ambushed and shot an unarmed Mark in the disco; Mark had ambushed and murdered an unarmed Blake outside the Playpen. The case for first-degree murder seemed clear enough. Blake was shot three times in the back. No gun was found on or near his body.

The defense presented a gunfight in which Blake was out-drawn and killed. This case was easy to make, despite the three shots in the back. As one witness said, Blake was known as a shooter. "It was known that he'd do somethin' . . . that he would shoot the pistol or whatever." The same witness said that someone in the crowd removed Blake's gun after he'd fallen.

Blake's gunbearer said that my brother's arsenal—a shotgun and two .38 caliber pistols—was inside the nightclub when Blake was gunned down in the parking lot.

But the gunbearer was an implausible witness. He'd borne a drug dealer's weapons through the streets of the city. He'd been brought into court under arrest and forced to testify. He'd given two conflicting accounts of what happened on the night in question. In an interview with the police, he said that Mark had leaped from a car and ambushed an unarmed man. In a sworn statement submitted by the defense, he denied witnessing anything at all.

Several months later I listened to the trial on tape. Mark need not have said a word in his defense, but he took the stand anyway. He spoke in a deep, breathy whisper that was sometimes blunt and defiant, at other times pliant and lyrical. The voice was that tough-guy whisper, Clint Eastwood's, straight out of the movies.

Q: Did you know Blake Staples?

A: I'd been knowin' him all my life . . . well really not all my life. We went through junior high school and high school together.

Q: Did you have any problem gettin' along with him?

A: Not until 1982. In 1982 I was a junior junkie for three years . . . I was shootin' cocaine. I was hooked on cocaine, and Blake Staples was sellin' heroin, was sellin' cocaine. . . . He sold me some bad cocaine so I took the cocaine back to get my money. And he ain't wanna give me my money. We got to fightin', and he tried to draw a pistol on me then, and I took it from him.

Q: Did anything happen in later '82, in July 1982? And later.

A: I was in a disco at Eric's Lounge on the dance floor, discoin', and Blake Staples approached and shot me twice in both of my hips.

Q: What happened after that?

A: Every time I saw him he stuck his hand in his coat on his pistols . . . to let me know he was packed, to let me know he was carryin' pistols and to don't try nothin'. . . .

. . . .

I asked him why every time he see me he be reachin' in his coats on me. I told him, don't be doin' it, because I wasn't goin' to do nothin' to him.

Q: Why weren't you going to be doing anything to him, since he had shot you?

A: I figured since the courts ain't take my warrant under advisement, I figured they wasn't gon' do nothin' regardless. And I ain't wanna get involved in no type of incident because I have a three-year-old son, you know. That right there changed my mind completely. I just said "forget it all."

Q: After you made this comment to Blake Staples, what if any reaction did he have?

A: Only reaction that he had, he put a saw-off shotgun in my face.

Q: Where did he get it from?

A: He got it from [the gunbearer] Chris McCoy. Chris McCoy had it in a bag and he [Blake] reached over the bag, pulled it out bad like that and stuck it in my face.

Q: You say stuck in your face—how far away from your face was the gun?

A: I say 'bout fourteen to fifteen inches.

Q: What were you lookin' at?

A: I was lookin' at the barrels.

Q: You were afraid?

A: Yes, sir.

Q: Why?

A: I was afraid he was goin' to shoot me, kill me.

Q: When was the next time you saw Blake?

A: I seen him the followin' night at a disco, the Playpen on Melrose.

Q: Where were you coming from that night?

A: I was comin' from the Room, another nightclub on First Street.

Q: How'd you get up there?

A: I hitch-hiked a ride.

....

Q: Did you know Blake Staples was at the Playpen that night?

A: No, sir.

Q: Were you looking for him?

A: No, sir.

Q: Did you have any weapons on you or with you?

A: Yes, sir.

Q: Why?

A: 'Cause I was scared.

....

Q: Where was Blake Staples?

A: He was in front of the Playpen on the sidewalk.

Q: About how far?

A: Approximately about, I say about fifteen to seventeen feet away.

Q: What happened after that?

A: He drew down on me. . . . He went for his pistols on me again.

Q: How far apart were you?

A: About six or seven feet.

Q: Did either of you say anything to the other?

A: Yes, sir.

Q: What was said?

A: I told him don't do it.

Q: Don't do what?

A: Don't go for his pistol on me.

Q: When you say going for his pistol, what was he doing?

A: He was reachin' under his shirt like this. . . . He pulled his shirt up like this and reached down in his pants and was pullin' his pistol out like this. By the time he stuck his hands on his pistol, and I seen it, I asked him not to do it.

Q: What, if any, reaction to that statement did he have?

A: He pulled it out on me.

Q: Then what did you do?

A: I pulled mines out.

Q: And did you fire?

A: Yes, sir.

Q: How many times?

A: I don't remember.

Q: Do you remember seeing him while you were shooting?

A: Oh, yes, sir.

Q: After you shot him what happened?

A: I ran.

Q: Why?

A: I was scared.

The Prosecution cross-examines:

Q: If you were afraid that someone was going to kill you, why didn't you just stay at home that night?

A: Excuse me?

Q: If you were afraid that someone was going to kill you that night you killed Mr. Staples, why didn't you just stay at home?

A: I . . . I have no rationale for that.

Q: Whose gun was it?

A: A friend of mine.

Q: Who's your friend?

A: I'd rather not say.

Q: You don't want to tell these people the truth?

A: I am tellin' the truth.

Q: You don't want to tell them the truth about whose gun it was?

A: No, sir.

Q: Where is the gun now?

A: I'm unaware.

Q: Don't have any idea?

A: No, sir.

Q: What did you do with it?

A: I dropped it.

Q: Where'd you drop it?

A: I dropped it in my distance of leavin'.

....

Q: You saw him reach underneath his shirt and take out his gun?

A: Yes, sir.

Q: But he didn't fire? You shot first? To protect yourself?

A: Yes, sir.

Q: And you shot a second time and a third time. You shot six times.

A: I don't remember.

Q: Do you recall at what point Mr. Staples put the gun back into his belt?

A: No, sir.

Q: Don't recall whether that was after the second shot or the fourth or whatever?

A: I don't remember.

What the prosecution might have asked but didn't: Why did

you shoot Mr. Staples three times in the back? Why did you continue shooting when Mr. Staples was lying on the ground?

The jury turned back the request for a conviction of murder in the first degree. They found Mark guilty of second-degree murder: Two years for the gun; five years for Blake's life. The verdict was understandable. The defense in its summation underscored this point: "One thing that hits you right in the forehead is that [these people] do not live, they do not function, they do not carry out their business in the way you do."

These people are not like you; they shoot each other for sport.

I drove from the courthouse to my mother's latest address. She'd moved again and come full circle to the first block she'd lived on when she returned to Roanoke a dozen years earlier. The sense of déjá vu was overpowering. As always she was standing in the kitchen when I walked through the door. The white in her hair startled me; it seemed sudden, as though she'd gone gray overnight.

Blake was buried in a graveyard in Hollins, not far from where my mother was born. The graveyard takes you by surprise. You round a curve in the road and there it is: a herd of ancient tombstones, tilted this way and that, spilling down the hill. Some stones lean so precariously that they seem about to fall. Many have been worn as smooth as glass by the weather; the names and dates washed away.

One of my great-uncles used to stay the night in the graveyard rather than go home drunk. The next morning people on the way to church would see him sleeping upright against a tombstone. Sitting among these stones in the late nineteenth century, you might have seen my paternal great-grandfather passing by. He was the Reverend Frank Patterson, a tall, fair-skinned man on a big black horse, with the reins in one hand and the Bible in the other. John Wesley Staples would have passed here too, first by wagon, and later in his Model T Ford.

My great-grandmother Luella Holmes Patterson, who died at nearly one hundred, is buried here, as is my grandmother Mae Patterson, who was in her eighties but who lied about her age. Across the road is my grandmother's church, First Baptist of Hollins, a red brick building with a modest white steeple. The yellow church bus sits alone in the gravel parking lot.

Level ground is precious here. The geography of the nearby mountains repeats itself endlessly: slope, breach, plateau, hills, mountains. The folds in the earth are like time. To cross over the road to the church or one of my great-aunt's houses, you go down in a bit of a wash and then up again. Even on sunny days dampness in the faults and washes seizes you straight to the bone.

I first saw this graveyard in the late 1950s, from the front seat of Bunny's car. I remember the suddenness of the stones spilling down the hill toward me. Three decades later, I stand at the base of the hill, imagining the funeral I missed. The pastor in vestments, with an open Bible. My mother, stoic, my father in a shambles. The coffin lowered into the ground. The fists of dirt dropped in behind it. The funeral party dispersing down the slope to its cars.

There was a second burial as well. Blake's grave diggers had struck shale before they reached the requisite six feet. When the rains came, water accumulated on the shale and floated the coffin upward. First there was a gentle rounding over the grave, like the rising of dough. Then the skin of the coffin was visible.

Brian, Bruce, Brad, and Yvette dug up the body and moved it to a grave farther down the slope. It's easy to envision the four of them around the grave, to see their faces and assign them feeling.

Yvette stands reverentially by as my brothers have at the work. For her, the act of moving the body is as sacred as was the funeral. She and Blake were world mates who spoke a language all their own. At the funeral Yvette took a picture of Blake lying in the coffin. Back then, people had told me by telephone that Blake had looked "wonderful in the coffin, just like he was asleep." Yvette's picture told a different story. Blake looked beaten up, his eyelids, lips, and hands puffy and discolored by the formaldehyde. He looked like every embalmed person I'd ever seen. This picture of Blake was pinned to the wall in Yvette's living room, among innocuous photographs of friends and family on summer outings, near one of Yvette astride a motorcycle, preening for the camera.

Not long before the murder, Blake was arrested for the theft of a car that he had confiscated in lieu of a drug debt. Yvette bailed him out. Now she wonders often if leaving him in jail would have saved his life. Now she grieves as though she'd led him by the hand to his death.

This is grim drudgery for Brian, Bruce, and Brad, a backbreaking struggle to pull the coffin out of the shale-bottomed grave into a better one just down the slope. It is more difficult to exhume the body than to bury it. Gravity is one factor in this. The absence of a funeral party and of the close-knit grieving is another.

Brian looks small next to the other two, both of whom tower over him and weigh more than two hundred pounds. Brian will make all the noise this day, the one-man riot, as ever. Stalking among the stones, he rails at the grave diggers, rails at the preacher who conducted the funeral. Later he said to me: "You shoulda seen it! My brother's body was coming up out of the ground."

Bruce digs with a quiet determination. He knows about digging. The slate could have been broken with a jackhammer, but where in these hills would a jackhammer come from? The new plot was donated by a friend. For this Bruce is grateful. He hurls one shovelful after another.

Brad, the youngest, will not know which to feel: Yvette's reverence, Brian's rage, or Bruce's methodical patience.

The family portrait taken at the time of Blake's death is the most complete portrait we have, and the only picture I know that contains the likenesses of both of my parents.

My mother sits among my brothers and sisters, chin forward, a portrait of forbearance. I think of her not as a distinct and separate self but as an intersection of traumatic events, like this one.

My father's eyes are gaunt and livery from drink. His jaw is crumpled and sunken from lack of teeth. His body is alarmingly thin, all wind and bone in its clothes. This stuns me because I absorb it all at once. I hadn't laid eyes on him in nine years, not since the time I found him asleep with the rifle across his lap. Even surrounded by family, he is utterly alone and contained within his skin. How like him I have become.

My parents' features have blended to make each of us. The short torsos, the long arms (my father's), the high hips and behinds, the knocking knees and wide feet (my mother's). The faces tend from slender and rakish (Brian's) to wide and with high cheekbones (Bruce's, Sherri's). The same face can change from my father's (vertical and narrow) to my mother's (wide and expansive), depending on the weight of its owner. Yvonne is closest to my father in build, and in temperament. Her eyes are indecipherable. They tell you only that they will never tell you anything.

I stand apart from this portrait, studying my family from a distance. This is the way it has always been.